A Color Guide to iPhone 14 and iPhone 14 Pro for Seniors

A GUIDE TO THE 2022 IPHONE (WITH IOS 16) WITH FULL COLOR GRAPHICS AND ILLUSTRATIONS

SCOTT LA COUNTE

RIDICULOUSLY SIMPLE BOOKS

ANAHEIM, CALIFORNIA

www.RidiculouslySimpleBooks.com

Table of Contents

Disclaimer: Please note, while every effort has been made to ensure accuracy, this book is not endorsed by Apple, Inc. and should be considered unofficial.

INTRODUCTION

A Full Color Guide to the iPhone 14 and iPhone 14 Pro (and iOS 16) with sections just for seniors.

This **full color** guide will explore the things about iPhone that every user (new and old) should know about.

The goal is to get you up and running as quickly as possible so you can take full advantage of all of the phones most powerful features. The guide will help you learn about all the tips and tricks that will make your life easier. It's helpful for new and old users alike.

Seeing images in B&W is helpful, but over the years, I've discovered that many readers prefer to see them in full color as they appear in real life; this manual was created from a B&W version that I am also selling.

Inside, you are going to learn about:

- What's new to iOS 16
- The differences between the iPhone 14 and iPhone 14 Pro
- Using an iPhone that doesn't have a Home button
- Using Face ID
- Cinematic Mode
- Using Dynamic Island (iPhone 14 Pro Only)
- Using a Focus
- How to use Picture-in-Picture for movies and TV shows
- How to add widgets to your Home screen
- Organizing apps with the App Library

- Buying, removing, rearranging, updating apps
- MagSafe
- Unsending and editing text messages
- Using Crash Detection
- Taking, editing, organizing, and sharing photos
- Apple Services (Apple Music, Apple TV+, Apple Card, iCloud, and Fitness+)
- Using Siri
- Using pre-installed apps like Calendar, Reminders, and more
- Making phone calls and sending messages
- And much, much more!

Are you ready to start enjoying your new iPhone? Then let's get started!

Note: This book is not endorsed by Apple, Inc and should be considered unofficial.

Chapter 1: What's New To the iPhone

What's the Big Difference Between Phones?

So with all these new phones, the question a lot of people want to know is what's the difference. Let's take a look.

Price

Pricing for the phones starts as follows: **iPhone 14: $799; iPhone 14 Pro: $999; iPhone 14 Pro Max: $1099.** The price increases depending on the size of the internal hard drive. But it should be noted that many wireless carriers offer discounts on the new model. Apple also offers installment plan payments.

Phone Comparison

September is here. That means two things: it's pumpkin spice latte time; and it's time to wonder if you should upgrade your iPhone. So let's not waste any time here and get into it: what on earth is the big difference between all the phones, and is it time to upgrade?

This year's line-up is a little different than the previous year. For starters, the iPhone Mini is gone. The iPhone now comes in only two sizes, not three.

The Pro Max also got a lot of performance and feature updates that do not come with the normal iPhone. The iPhone 14 has the same 12MP that's been on iPhones for several years; the Pro Max got a big bump, however, it now has a 48MP camera. One of the other big enhancements that's exclusive to the Pro Max is Dynamic Island. I'll write more about that later in the book, but it's a great new way to interact with your phone.

Finally, the Pro Max now has an Always On display.

That's not to say the iPhone 14 doesn't have improvements over the iPhone 13; on the camera, there are improvements to the autofocus on the front facing camera. There's also what Apple calls a Photonic Engine that helps capture even more stunning shots.

Both model phones get the new Crash Detection feature that tells first responders if it detects you've been in a car accident and need help.

On the video side, both phones have an action mode that gives you better stabilization when there's a lot of movement.

All the phones are also getting about an hour of additional battery life (up to 29 hours on the Pro Max and 20 on the iPhone).

Compatibility

For those of you who are still considering if they should upgrade, remember that most iPhone's will get a free software update that adds many of the features that the newest iPhones are getting.

iOS 16 is the latest operating system available for Apple iPhone (and the latest iPod Touch). While iOS is free, it is not available to all devices; if you have an older iPhone, then it may be time to upgrade to get all the best new features. The following devices are compatible, as of this writing:

- iPhone 14
- iPhone 14 Plus
- iPhone 14 Pro
- iPhone 14 Pro Max
- iPhone 13
- iPhone 13 mini
- iPhone 13 Pro
- iPhone 13 Pro Max
- iPhone 12
- iPhone 12 mini
- iPhone 12 Pro

- iPhone 12 Pro Max
- iPhone 11
- iPhone 11 Pro
- iPhone 11 Pro Max
- iPhone Xs
- iPhone Xs Max
- iPhone Xr
- iPhone X
- iPhone 8
- iPhone 8 Plus
- iPhone SE (2nd generation)

It should also be noted that not all features are available on older models. So, if you hear someone talking about a great new feature on their phone and you don't see it, then it's probably because you have an older iPhone.

If you aren't sure what model number you have, go to the Settings app, then tap the General option, and tap About. This will tell you your model's name (i.e. iPhone 14 Pro Max) and the model number and serial number. The model number will indicate things like how large the hard drive is; the serial number is likely only something you would need if you are getting your phone repaired.

How to Update Your Phone?

If you have auto updates on, then there's nothing you need to do. It will download on its own (usually while you sleep). If you want to do it manually, or see if auto updates are on,

go to Settings > General > Software Updates.

The update is quite large, so make sure you download it over Wi-Fi and not data. Once it's downloaded, it will take several minutes to install and you won't be able to use your phone for some of this time, so make sure you aren't expecting any calls.

What's New in iOS 15

There are dozens of new features with each update. Below are some of the biggest ones this year. I'll go over each one of these—and other new features—in forthcoming chapters.

Apple has added a lot of features to iOS 15 to help you stay connected. One of the biggest is changes to FaceTime that let you call someone who doesn't have an iPhone, and watch movies and listen to music together—a feature called SharePlay. Through SharePlay, you can also share your display, which makes it easier to help with troubleshooting.

There's also a new Grid View in FaceTime, which is great for calls with more than three people.

When you message (or people message you) links and photos, they are now automatically saved on your device, so you can see them later. Photos are also grouped together, so you don't see 25 photos show up all at once, one after the other.

Maps continues to evolve. This year, even more detail has been added, to help you recognize landmarks, and know what lanes you should be in.

Safari has been completely redesigned. It largely works the same way, but many of the icons and menus have been changed. The biggest update is a feature called Group Tabs, which lets you save your tabs in a way that's similar to bookmarks.

Focus is a new feature that helps you be more productive; it's a little like Do Not Disturb mode, but much more customizable. The idea is certain features will be turned off, so you aren't distracted and you get done what is needed.

Photos can now read text inside a photo—so if there's a phone number in a photo, for example, you can copy it and don't have to write it down.

Apple Wallet now lets you store your state ID in states that accept it—at this writing many states have not opted into digital IDs.

The biggest update to iOS, as always, comes to the new lineup of phones. The iPhone 13 comes with some game changing features that will make your life easier.

The biggest feature is called Cinematic mode. It's available on all new phones—from Pro models and entry iPhone 13s. With Cinematic mode, you can shoot a video that feels like something you'd see on the big screen! It will focus on the person talking, and switch focus to any new person who speaks—it's really something you have to see! I'll show you how it works in this book.

The Pro model iPhones got camera updates that let you take stunning Macro photos, add photographic styles, and an ultra-resolution ProRes video feature.

CHAPTER 2: CONTROLLING THE IPHONE

So, the real elephant in the room with the iPhone X and up is the Home button, or lack thereof.

By now, many people are probably starting to get used to having no Home button; but there's still lots of people out there who have never used a Home-less iPhone.

In the next chapter, I'll talk about getting set up, so I know this all sounds a little backwards, but because a lot of people are upgrading to the new iPhone from an earlier model, it's worth talking about the main things that will be different.

If you have used the iPhone before, then I bet you'll spend a good day continuously putting your thumb where the button used to be! Don't worry! You're going to get through it. In fact, after you get used to it not being there, you'll actually start seeing it's more effective without it.

Before diving into the gestures, let's cover some other things that look different about this phone.

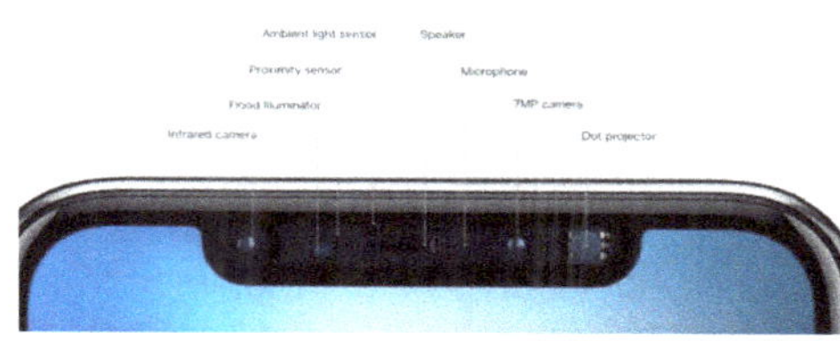

The top portion of the phone (it's known as the top notch) is a black strip. All of it helps your phone work better. To the far right (looking at the phone) is a Dot Projector. It sounds like something that will project your iPhone onto the wall, doesn't it? I wish! That's actually the camera that scans your face for Face ID (I'll cover that in just a second). Next to that is the camera; it's 12MP. There are a few other sensors and cameras to the far left. They all sound fancy, don't they? Proximity sensor. Flood illuminator. Fancy is...well fancy! But what on Earth does that mean in simple terms? It means that the front-facing camera can take pretty impressive selfies! If you've used the iPhone 8 or 8 Plus then you're probably familiar with Portrait mode? If not, in a nutshell, it gives a blurred, professional look to your photo. To do that, you need some extra sensors; beginning with the iPhone X (and any iPhone after), those features are on both the front and back of the phone. That means you can get the same type of photos no matter which camera you use (front or back).

Okay, so all that's interesting, right? But you don't actually do anything with the notch. What about the buttons on the phone itself? Good question! Thanks for asking!

The button placement isn't too far off from previous iPhones.

On the right side of the phone, you have your volume up and down, which does what? You guessed it! Turns your volume up and down! There's also a switch above it that will silence sound.

On the left side you have your "Side Button." Legend has it, they named it the Side Button because it's on the side of the phone! That button is on other phones—albeit a tad shorter—but it functions a little bit differently here.

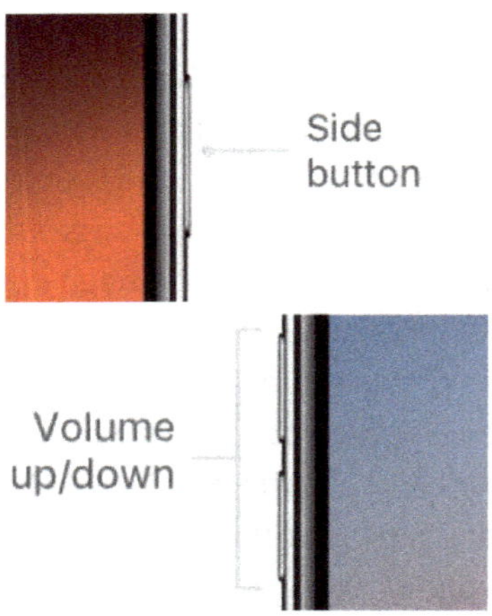

The Side Button is and isn't the Home button replacement. That sounds vague, huh? Here's what I mean: you won't use this button to get back to the Home screen, but you can use it to activate Siri (or you can just say "Hey Siri"). You also use this button to power the phone on and off—or to put it in standby (which is the mode you put it in after you finish playing Angry Birds in the bathroom and need to set the phone down for a minute to wash your hands).

The most common use for the Side Button is to wake up your phone. Picking up your phone and staring at it with an annoyed or confused expression will also do this. But if you ever find yourself stuck and picking up the phone isn't waking it up, then just push down on the Side Button and you should be just fine.

That Side Button is also going to come in handy when you want to use Apple Pay—double push the button and then stare at your phone sadly as money is magically taken away.

Let's Talk About Your Face

Things were going okay with you and the Home button. You could rub your thumb over it and like a genie in a bottle, it would magically read your DNA and turn on. Why'd Apple have to go and ruin a good thing?

Sure, getting rid of the button gives you more screen real estate, but plenty of other phones have added a button to the back of the phone so you can have the best of both worlds. It's like Apple is trying to force you to love it, isn't it? I don't know why Apple does everything, but if past history teaches us anything, we have learned that Apple makes us adapt to better things by taking away the things we love. We loved our CD drives...and Apple took them out and put USB drives in their place; we got through it, though didn't we?! They did it again with the headphone jack. And on new MacBook's, USB is gone and in its place, the faster USB-C.

Change is never fun, but it's not necessarily a bad thing. If you like numbers, you'll love this one. That little finger scanner on your old phone has a ratio of 50,000:1—that's the ratio of how hard it would be for someone to break into your phone. The iPhone with Face ID? 1,000,000:1. So if you're a fan of security, then Face ID is a no-brainer.

If you're that person who is always throwing "What if" into the equation (you're the same person who morbidly asked, "What if someone stole my phone and cut off my finger to unlock it? Would the fingerprint scanner still work?"), then I'm sure you have a few questions. Like:

What if I wear glasses and then take them off or put in contacts?

- **What if I have a beard and shave it?**
- **What if I think I look like Brad Pitt, but the phone says I'm more of a Lyle Lovett?**

Sorry, Lyle, not everyone can be a Brad—but you don't have to worry about those first two points. Face ID has adaptive recognition, so you'll be just fine if you decide to grow it out for Movember.

If you're in a dark room, Face ID will also still work—albeit with a little bit of help from the light sensor—which is a little annoying if you're lying in bed and the only way to unlock your phone is to have a light turn on to scan your face. If you're in a dark room, you can also just press that Side Button to open it manually and skip Face ID.

Reach for the Sky

Several years ago, Apple made a big change to the iPhone by making things...well big! They introduced what would be known as the "plus" model. It was wonderful...and big! If you had Shaq hands, then you'd have no problem getting around the device. If you had normal human hands, then the apps on the top row of the phone were a bit of a stretch.

This wasn't a huge problem on the iPhone X because it was a little smaller than the plus. The next generation phones, however, introduced a "max" model. On the old phones, this was a snap—just double tap (not press, tap) the Home button. New phones? Sorry, but we're back to learning new things...I'm all out of bones for this chapter.

To reach the top, swipe down on the bottom edge of the screen.

Force Restarting

Ideally you should never have to force reset your phone (that means your phone is frozen and you can't do anything). If it ever happens, then what do you do with no Home button?! Not to fret! It's pretty simple:

- **Quickly press and release the Volume Up button.**
- **Quickly press and release the Volume Down button.**
- **Press and hold the Side button until you see the apple Logo.**

Those are the options for forcing your phone to shut off. What if it's not frozen and you just want to turn it off? Press and hold the Side button and Volume Up at the same time. This brings up several options—Slide to power off, Medical ID, and Emergency SOS. The one you want is obviously the first. SOS will call local emergency services, so don't slide that by mistake!

The Ridiculously Simple Chapter One Recap

Okay, so you only got a minute to get up and running, and you need the 1-minute summary of everything important?

Let's cover gestures. The left side will be the way the gesture used to work, and right side will be the way it works on new iPhones.

iPhone 8 and Down	iPhone X and Up
Go to the Home screen - Press the Home button.	Go to the Home screen - Swipe up from the bottom of your screen.
Multitask - Double press Home button.	Multitask - Swipe up from the bottom of your screen, but don't lift your finger until it reaches the middle of the screen.
Control Center - Swipe up from the bottom of the screen.	Control Center - Swipe down from the upper right corner of the screen.
Notifications - Swipe down from the top of the screen.	Notifications - Swipe down from the middle top of the screen.
Search - From the Home screen, swipe down from the middle of your screen.	Search - From the Home screen, swipe down from the middle of your screen.
Access Widgets - From the Home or Lock screen, swipe right.	Access Widgets - From the Home or Lock screen, swipe right.
Reach the Top - Double tap (not press) the Home button.	Reach the Top - Swipe down on the bottom edge of the screen.

Chapter 3: The iPhone Crash Course

Now that you know about the main differences between the physical nature of the phone, let's take a step back and talk about setting it up. If you're already at the Home screen, you can obviously skip this section.

Unboxing the iPhone shouldn't throw you any surprises. It doesn't have a manual, but that's normal for Apple. You can find the manual on Apple's website (https://support.apple.com/manuals/iphone) if that's something you'd like to see. What is worth pointing out is the headphones. A few years back, Apple decided for us that we no longer needed a normal headphone jack. How sweet, right? But to be nice, they always threw in a 3.5m Lightning Adapter—so you could use any headphones when it was plugged in. New models ditch that. If you're keen on using it, then you can buy one for under $10.

Once you turn the phone on with the Side Button, it will load to a setup screen. Setup can be intimating to a lot of people, but Apple's setup is probably the easiest one you'll ever do—even my mom, who hates all electronics, had no problem doing it on her own.

It's pretty straightforward. I suppose I could just write everything that you'll see on the screen, but it seems a little redundant since you are seeing it on the screen. In a nutshell, it's going to ask you your preferred language and country, your wireless network (make sure you connect to your wireless network here, or it's going to start downloading a lot of apps over your LTE, which will eat up your data), and you'll need to activate your device with your wireless carrier.

So that's the basics. There are a few options after here that might be a little less straightforward. The first is a question that asks if you want Location Services turned on. I recommend saying yes. This is how the Map will automatically know where you are. Or when you take a photo at Boring Town, USA, and several years later you say "Where on Earth was this photo taken?" you'll know exactly where it was taken if Location Services is turned on. Remember: anything you don't turn on here (or that you do turn on) can be changed later. So, if you change your mind, it's fine.

You Should Know: Anytime Location Services is being used in an app, you will see a small arrow icon in the upper right corner of your screen.

Face ID

Face ID is probably one of the features you hear about the most. It lets your phone scan your face to unlock it—it's more secure than your fingerprint. To get started, just tap the Get Started button.

Next, you'll be directed to put your face in the center of the camera; then you basically move your head around, so the camera can see all of your features. It's kind of like rolling your neck around. It takes about 20 seconds to complete.

Once it's done, you'll get a message. That's it. Your phone is now ready to unlock at the sight of your gorgeous face!

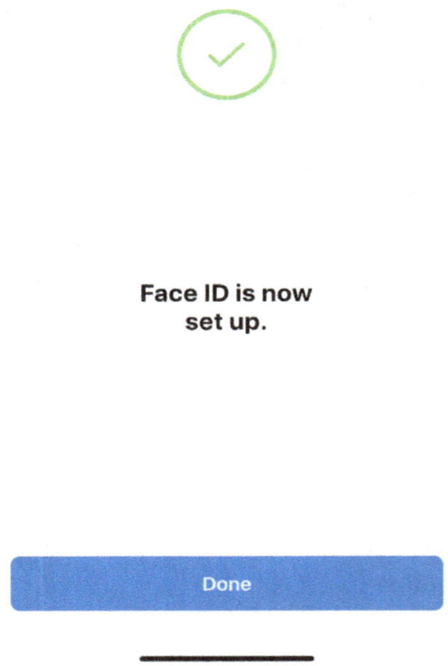

After you set up Face ID, you'll be prompted to enter a passcode. Why do you need a passcode when you have a Face ID? The biggest reason is there may be times when you don't want to use Face ID: like if it's dark and you don't want a bunch of light illuminated from your phone, or you have a friend who needs to get into your phone.

By default, the passcode is six digits. If you don't want to add one, tap "Don't Add Passcode"; in this same area, you can also change it to a four-digit passcode. My only advice here is to be creative: don't use the same four digits as your bank pin, or the last four of your social. And remember: you can change it later.

Once security options are set up, you'll have the option to restore from a backup. If you have a previous iPhone, I would recommend doing this—it will save you time adjusting some of the settings later.

If you have decided to restore from a backup, then make sure your backup is up-to-date. On your old iPhone, go to Settings, then tap your name on the top (it will probably have a picture of you), next tap "iCloud," and finally go to "iCloud Backup." It might be set to automatic. However, just to make sure you get everything, I would tap "Back Up Now." Below the Back Up Now option, you can see when the last backup was performed.

You're almost done! But first Apple needs to understand how to take your money! The next screen is creating an Apple ID. If you already have one, then sign in; if you don't have one, then create a free one. Don't want to give Apple your hard-earned money? I don't blame you! They did, after all, just take $1,000+ from you for your phone! But you still need an Apple ID. Don't worry—you don't have to give them any more money if you really don't want to, but I'm sure you'll want to download free apps (like Facebook), and you'll need an Apple ID for that as well.

Once your phone is all done thinking about how it will take your money, it will be time to set up iCloud. Again, this is something I recommend setting up. iCloud backs everything up remotely; so, if you want to share things across multiple devices (your Apple Watch, iPad, MacBook, Apple TV, for example) it's a breeze.

After iCloud is Apple Pay. "Wait," you say! "I thought Apple already asked how they were going to get more money?!" They did! This is all about how others will take your money! Once you have an expensive phone, everyone wants a piece of you! Apple Pay will basically create a virtual credit card so when you're at the grocery store you can pay by tapping your phone instead of whipping out your wallet.

Apple also has a card of its own (Apple Card) that I'll cover later.

Is Apple Pay really safe? In a word: yes. It's safer than the card you carry around in your wallet. Unlike that card, no one can see the numbers on it. And if someone were to steal your phone, they wouldn't be able to use Apple Pay unless they knew your password. The encryption on Apple Pay is also much more sophisticated—you are much more likely to get your number hacked online than on your phone.

Most banks are on Apple Pay, but unfortunately some are not. If you don't see yours, you will have to wait. You can't add it manually.

Next up is iCloud Keychain. Like most things in the setup, it's all about what you are comfortable with. Keychain stores all your passwords in one place. So, if you are shopping online, you don't have to add it in or remember it. It's all secure—no one can see it but you. And, of course, you can turn it on or off later.

Only a few more steps! Painless so far, right?

Up next is Siri. Siri is your personal assistant. You can say things like, "Hey, Siri: what's the weather?" and like magic, she'll tell you. I'll cover it later in the book, but for now I would turn it on.

After enabling Siri, decide whether or not to report diagnostic and usage data to Apple. If you're worried about privacy, tap "About Diagnostics and Privacy" to learn what information Apple will receive and how it will be used.

Finally, decide whether or not you'd like to use a zoomed-in display or not. If you prefer larger icons, you can choose Zoomed View for a magnified display. It's entirely up to you, and this setting can be changed later.

And finally, setup is done! The last screen says "Welcome to iPhone - Get Started." Tapping on that will bring you to the Home screen, and that's where the fun really starts.

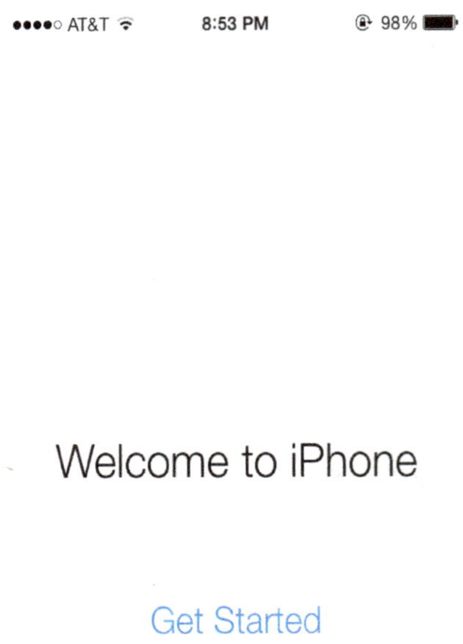

I Feel Charged!

Before digging into using your phone deeper, I want to talk really quickly about charging. You probably know how to plug the charger into your phone. If you can't figure out how to stick an out-y into an in-y, then call that nephew who never returns your phone call and ask him. He's going to love hearing from you, I'm sure.

What might not be so obvious is the iPhone doesn't need to be plugged into anything to be charged. New iPhones can be charged wirelessly. To do this you need what's called a "Qi charger." They're not terribly expensive ($20 range). Qi chargers are compatible with other phones, so a lot of cafes and hotels have them ready to use. To use it, you just set your phone on top of the wireless charging mat and make sure the charging light (⚡) comes on. It's really simple.

In 2020, Apple introduced MagSafe and their own wireless charger. The bad news…it's going to cost you extra. Apple does not include a wireless charger in the box. A MagSafe wireless charger cost $39. But there's more! You also need an adaptor: a 20W USB-C Power Adapter, to be precise. That's another $19. The reason you need a special adaptor is to make sure you get the fastest charge. Use less, and the phone will charge slower.

And speaking of MagSafe, if you want to take advantage of it, then you'll need a MagSafe case. These cases have a special magnet on the inside. These magnetic rings help snap the charger to the iPhone and make sure it is appropriately placed for wireless charging.

The MagSafe charger can also charge older iPhone's, and even Android devices. While you can charge AirPods with it, you cannot charge the Apple Watch. There are, however, accessories, to wirelessly charge the iPhone and Apple Watch at the same time.

Enough About Setup! How Do I Use This Thing, Already?!

The iPhone is a touchscreen device, so to use it you'd think you'd have to worry about only one thing: touching it!

That's true. But there are different ways you can touch it. Fortunately, unlike gestures, nothing has really changed; so, if you know how to use gestures, you'll be just fine. Below is a quick summary:

GESTURES

Tap

This is the "click" of the iPhone world. A tap is just a brief touch. It doesn't have to be hard or last very long. You'll tap icons, hyperlinks, form choices, and more. You'll also tap numbers on a touch keypad in order to make calls. It's not exactly rocket science, is it?

Tap and Hold

This simply means touching the screen and leaving your finger in contact with the glass. It's useful for bringing up context menus or other options in some apps.

Double Tap

This refers to two rapid taps, like double clicking with your finger. Double tapping will perform different functions in different apps. It will also zoom in on pictures or webpages.

Hidden Gesture!

The microphone is sort of a gesture on your phone. You can set up your phone to recognize tapping. So if you tap the back of your phone twice (or three times) it triggers something—like it pulls up your notifications. It kind of sounds problematic —like it would mistake typing for taps or something, but it works surprisingly well.

To add back tapping, go to the Settings app, then select Accessibility > Touch > Back Tap. Next, select from the list of available options.

Swipe

Swiping means putting your finger on the surface of your screen and dragging it to a certain point and then removing your finger from the surface. You'll use this motion to navigate through menu levels in your apps, through pages in Safari, and more. It'll become second nature overnight, I promise.

Drag

This is mechanically the same as swiping, but with a different purpose. You'll touch an object to select it, and then drag it to wherever it needs to go and release it. It's just like dragging and dropping with a mouse, but it skips the middleman.

Pinch

Take two fingers, place them on the iPhone screen, and move them either toward each other or away from each other in a pinching or reverse pinching motion. Moving your fingers together will zoom in inside many apps, including web browsers and photo viewers; moving them apart will zoom out.

Rotate and Tilt

Many apps on iPhone take advantage of rotating and tilting the device itself. For instance, in the paid app Star Walk, you can tilt the screen so that it's pointed at whatever section of the night sky you're interested in—Star Walk will reveal the constellations based on the direction the iPhone is pointed.

How Do You Send Cute Emojis to Everyone?

The reason you got an iPhone is to send adorable emojis with your text messages, obviously! So how do you do it? It's all in the keyboard, so I'll cover that next!

Anytime you type a message, the keyboard pops up automatically. There are no extra steps. But there are a few things you can do with the keyboard to make it more personal.

There are a few things to notice on the keyboard—the delete key is marked with a little 'x' (it's right next to the letter M), and the shift key is the key with the upward arrow (next to the letter Z).

By default, the first letter you type will be capitalized. You can tell what case the letters are in though at a quick glance.

To use the shift key, just tap it and then tap the letter you want to capitalize or the alternate punctuation you'd like to use. Alternatively, you can touch the shift key and drag your finger to the letter you want to capitalize. Double tap the shift key to enter caps lock (i.e. everything is capitalized) and tap once to exit caps lock.

Special Characters

To type special characters, just press and hold the key of the associated letter until options pop up. Drag your finger to the character you want to use and be on your way. What exactly would you use this for? Let's say you're are writing something in Spanish and need the accent on the "e"; tapping and holding on the "e" will bring that option up.

Using Dictation

Let's face it: typing on the keyboard stinks sometimes! Wouldn't it be easier to just say what you want to write? If that sounds like you, then Dictation can help! Just tap the microphone next to the spacebar and start talking. It works pretty well.

Number and Symbol Keyboards

Of course, there's more to life than letters and exclamation points. If you need to use numbers, tap the 123 key in the bottom left corner. This will bring up a different keyboard with numbers and punctuation.

From this keyboard, you can get back to the alphabet by tapping the ABC key in the bottom left corner. You can also access an additional keyboard which includes the remaining standard symbols by tapping the #+- key, just above the ABC key.

Emoji Keyboard

And finally, the moment you've waited for! Emojis!

The emoji keyboard is accessible using the smiley face key between the 123 key and the dictation key. Emojis are tiny cartoon images that you can use to liven up your text messages or other written output. This goes far beyond the colon-based emoticons of yesteryear—there are enough emojis on your iPhone to create an entire visual vocabulary.

To use the emoji keyboard, note that there are categories along the bottom (and that the globe icon on the far left will return you to the world of language). Within those categories, there are several screens of pictographs to choose from. Many of the human emojis include multicultural variations. Just press and hold them to reveal other options.

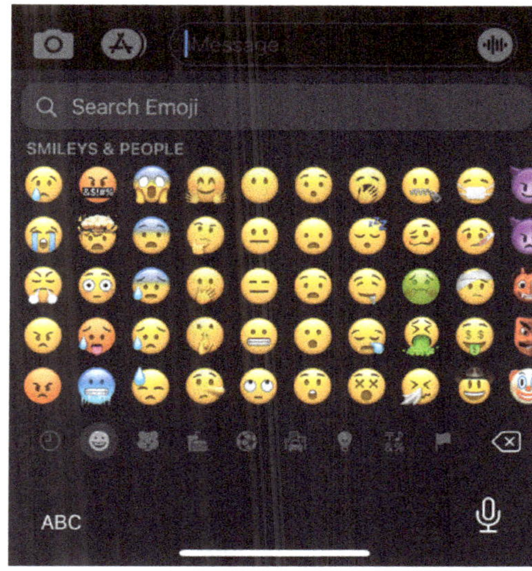

Emoji Search

If you love emoji's, you probably hate searching for emoji's. The days of one or two emoji's are over—emoji keyboards now have dozens and dozens and dozens of expressions to pick from! That's great for options! But lousy for discovery!

You can search your emoji keyboard by typing in an expression in the search bar.

I'll search for "Happy" for example. It brings back emoji expressions that match that term.

You can return to the normal keyboard by tapping on the several emoji's next to the space bar.

Multilingual Typing

Most people are probably all set. They know all they need to know about typing on the iPhone and they're ready to blast emojis at their friends. There are a few other features that apply to some (not all people).

One such feature is Multilingual Typing. This is for people who type multiple languages at the same time. So, if you type between Spanish and English, you won't keep seeing a message saying your spelling is wrong.

If that sounds like you, then you just need to enable another dictionary, which is simple. Go to Settings > General > Dictionary.

Configuring International Keyboards

If you find yourself typing in a different language fairly often, you may want to set up international keyboards. To set up international keyboards, visit Settings > General > Keyboard > Keyboards. You can then add an appropriate international keyboard by tapping "Add New Keyboard." As an example, iPhone has great support for Chinese text entry—choose from pinyin, stroke, zhuyin, and handwriting, where you actually sketch out the character yourself.

When you enable another keyboard, the smiley face key will change to a globe icon. To use international keyboards, tap the globe key to cycle through your keyboard choices.

Your iPhone is loaded with features to help prevent slip-ups, including Apple's battle-tested autocorrect feature which guards against common typos. In iOS 8, Apple introduced a predictive text feature that predicts what words you're most likely to type, and its accuracy is even better in the new iOS.

Three choices appear just above the keyboard—the entry as typed, plus two best guesses. Predictive text is somewhat context-specific, too. It learns your speech patterns as you email your boss or text your best friend, and it will serve up appropriate suggestions based on who you're messaging or emailing. Of course if it bothers you, you can visit Settings > General > Keyboards and turn off predictive text by sliding the green slider to the left.

Third Party Keyboards

Lastly, you can add third-party keyboards to your phone. So, if you hate the iPhone keyboard and want something similar to what's on Android, then you can go to the App Store and get it (more on that later).

Chapter 4: iPhone 101 – The Basics

Welcome Home

There's one thing that has pretty much stayed the same since the very first iPhone was released: the Home screen. The look has evolved, but the layout has not. All you need to know about it is it's the main screen. So, when you read "go to the Home screen," this is the screen I'm talking about. Make sense?

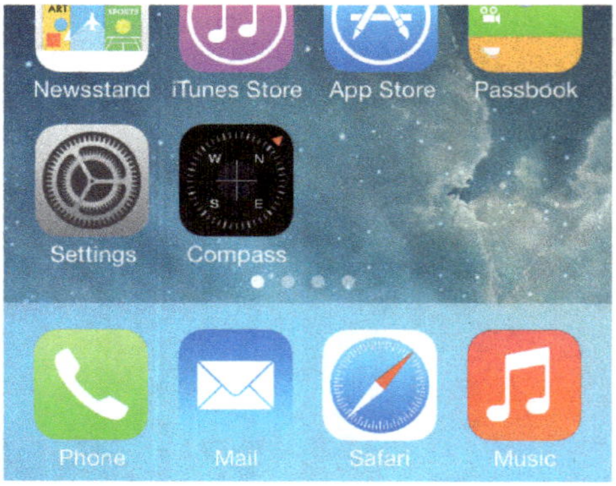

Control Center

Even if you don't know the term for it, you probably have used Control Center; it's where you'll find shortcuts that control commonly used features on your phone, like volume and the camera.

Control Center is more powerful than it used to be. iOS 13 introduced two new features to the Control Center: Night Mode and joining Wi-Fi network (covered below). However, there are older features you might not be aware of.

Swipe in the upper right corner to bring down your Control Center.

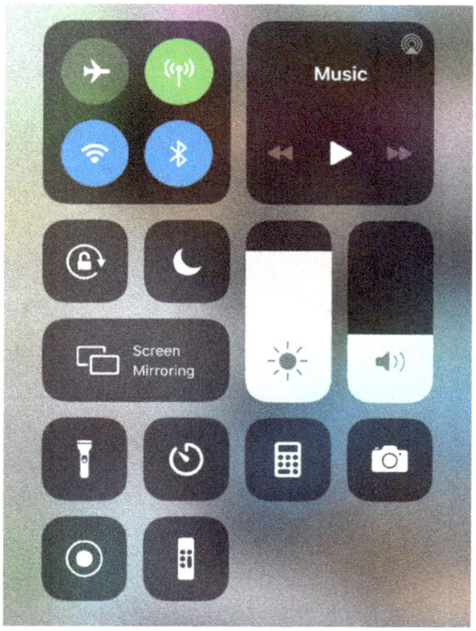

Using Control Center

Let's take a look around each section of Control Center. The first group is what controls the wireless activity on your phone. Starting in the upper left corner, the airplane icon is Airplane Mode, which quickly turns off all cellular, Wi-Fi, and Bluetooth; next to that is the Cellular Data; under the airplane is the Wi-Fi toggle; and finally, the Bluetooth toggle.

If you long-press any of these buttons, then you'll get an expanded list of options.

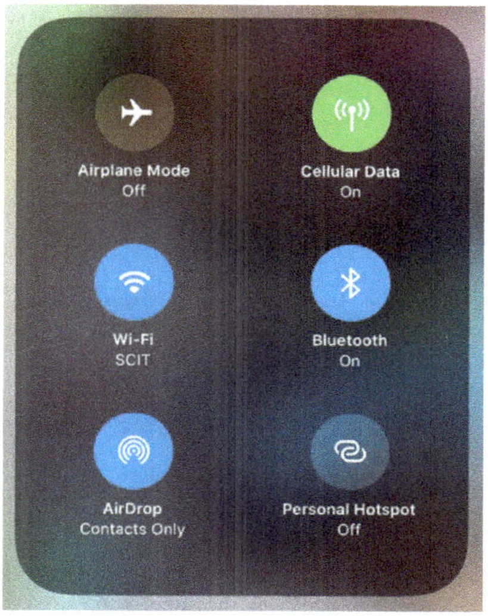

If you long-press the Wi-Fi button on the above screen, then you get all the Wi-Fi networks within range, and you can join one—you no longer have to go into your Settings app to join a Wi-Fi network.

Under the wireless settings is: screen rotation lock (press it and your screen won't autorotate when you tilt your phone sideways), Do Not Disturb mode, and Screen Mirroring (if you have an Apple TV, you use this button to mirror your phone to your TV).

Over on the right side is the Music control (tap in the upper right corner of that and you can select where you want to listen to music if you have an AirPlay device—such as AirPods or HomePod). Below that is the phone brightness and volume.

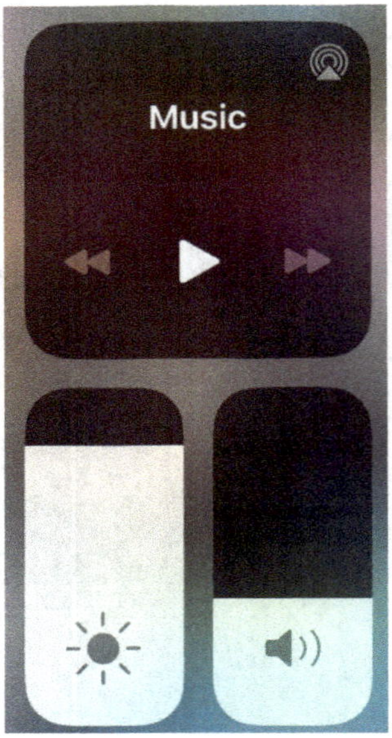

Long-press the brightness button and you can select if you want night mode turned on. Night mode turns areas of your phone that are white to black—for example when you are reading a book in iBooks, the pages are dark. You can also use Night Shift here, which lessens the amount of blue light that emits from your phone—exposure to this kind of light at night can affect your sleeping habits.

At the bottom of Control Center is the Flashlight, Timer, Calculator, Camera

Shortcut, Screen Record (I'll cover why you may not have this below), and Apple TV remote (again, you may or may not have this).

Long-pressing most of these will bring up shortcuts to options for the app. Long-pressing the camera button, for example, will bring up shortcuts to different kinds of photos you can take.

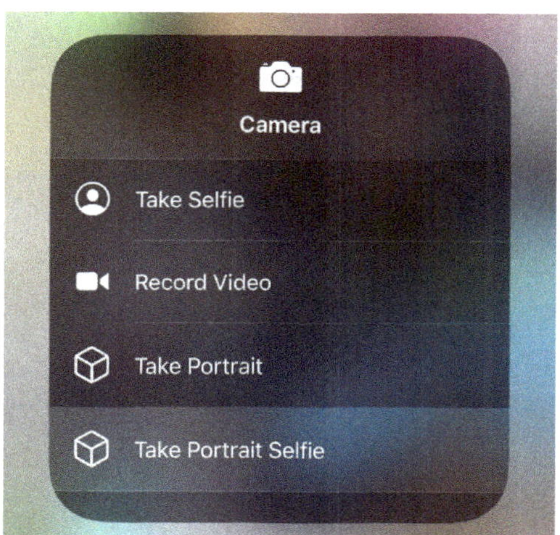

Customizing Control Center

You can add and remove some of the options on the Control Panel by going to Settings > Control Center, then selecting Customize Controls.

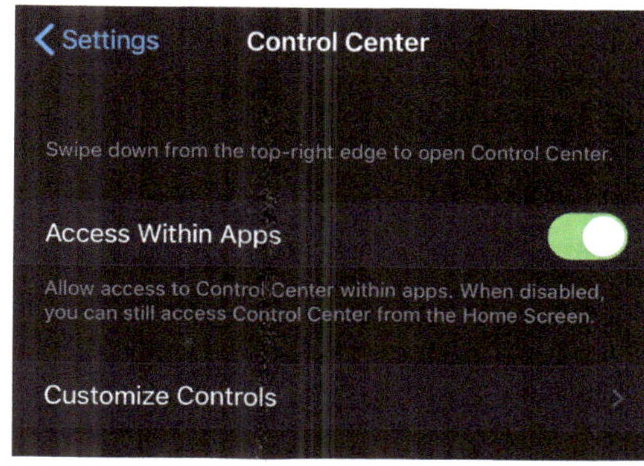

The top has the controls currently included (the ones you can remove, that is). Hit the red minus to remove them.

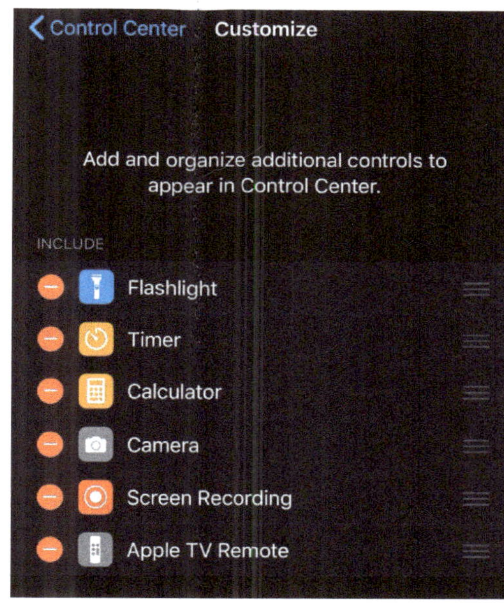

Remember I said there were some controls I had that you may not? Here's where you can add them in. Below this are the ones that you can add to Control Center. Tap the plus sign to add them.

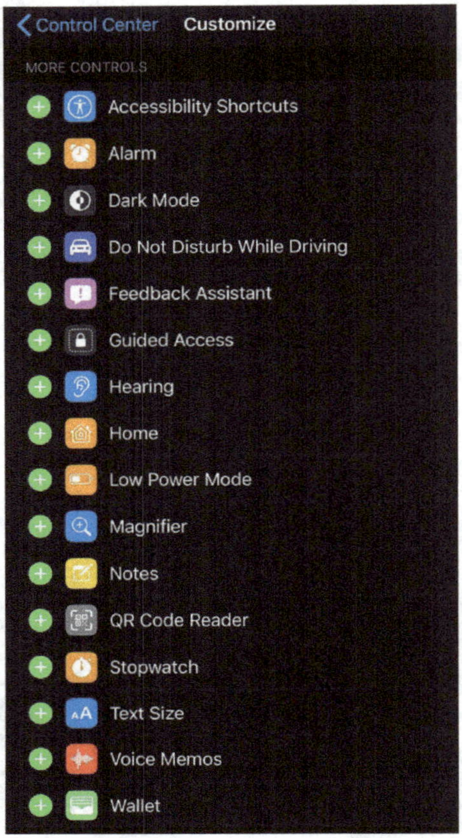

The Lockscreen

The lockscreen got a fresh new look in iOS 16. Gone are the days when the lockscreen was for a single photo and notifications. It's now much more customizable. Let's see how. First, long press your finger on the lockscreen.

This brings up a swipeable list of different lockscreens. Now, you can have a whole collection of lockscreens for different occasions—sleep, work, school, etc.

Keep swiping to the left and there's an Add New screen.

There are all kinds of dynamic wallpapers to pick from. You can even do a rotating photo album. If you just want a plain old picture, then pick "Photos."

You can also add widgets to your lock screen. Just tap that area that says Add Widgets.

Next, select the widget that you want to appear—you can do two big widgets or four small ones.

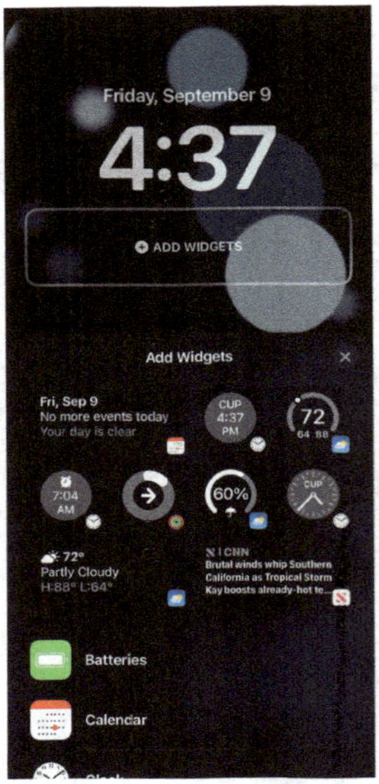

If you want to delete one, just swipe up, then tap delete.

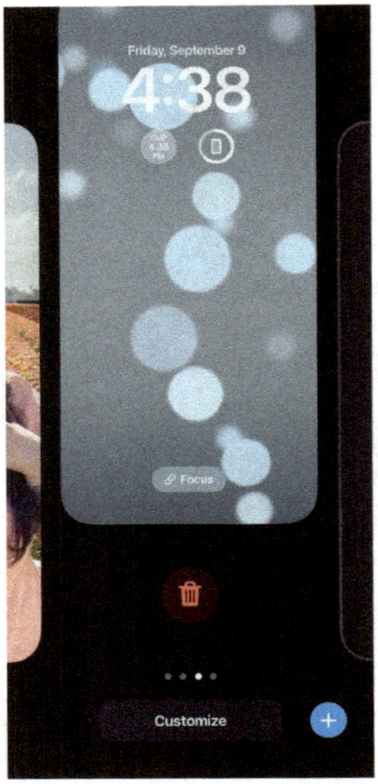

Something you might not catch right away is how photos can have a 3D-type effect. You won't see it on all of them, but if there's an object or person that's just slightly above the time, it will give the impression that it's in front of the numbers. See the example below—notice how the dog's face pops out a little because it's in front of the time? That's the position you want your person or object if you want to give it that effect—just slightly over the number; if you position it too high, then it won't work.

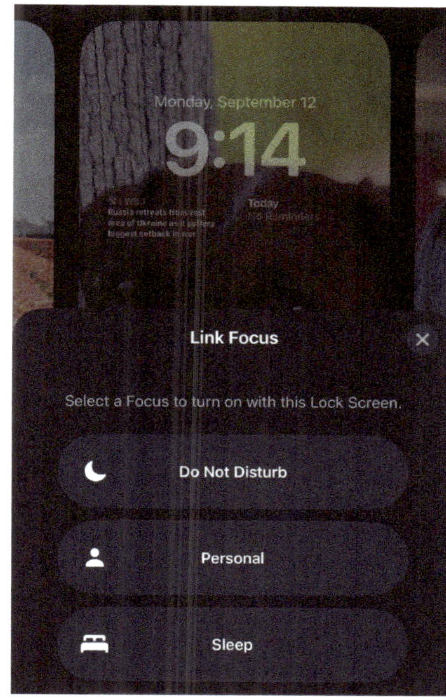

Changing Focus

If you want to change the focus of a lockscreen, long press the screen, then select the Focus option on the bottom of the screen that you want to change.

Making Calls

You know what always amazes me when I see commercials for the iPhone? It's a phone, but people never seem to be talking on it! But it actually can make phone calls!

If you actually need to call someone, then tap the green Phone icon in the lower left corner of your Home screen. This will bring up the iPhone's keypad. Tap in your number and hit the green Call button. To hang up, just tap the red End button at the bottom of the screen. You'll see other options on the call screen, too. If you needed to use the keypad while on a call, just tap the Keypad circle to bring it up. Similarly, you can mute a call or put it on speaker here.

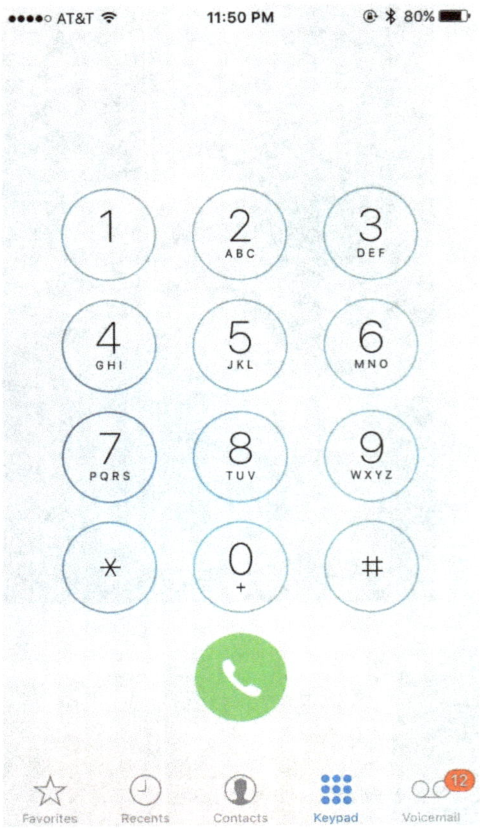

Receiving a call is fairly intuitive. When your phone rings, your iPhone will tell you who's calling. If their name is stored in your contacts (more on this later), it'll be displayed. All you have to do is swipe to answer the call. There are some additional options as well—you can ask iPhone to remind you of the call later by tapping "Remind Me," or you can respond with a text message. iOS includes some handy canned responses, including "Can't talk right now…", "I'll call you later," "I'm on my way," and "What's up?" You can also send a custom message if you need to. If you miss a call, iPhone will let you know the next time you wake up your phone. By default, you can respond to a missed call directly from the Lock screen.

When a call from an unknown number comes in, iPhone will check other apps like Mail where phone numbers might be found. Using that information, it will make a guess for you and let you know who might be calling. Kind of creepy, right? But also really useful.

If you want to feel extra special, you can have Siri announce your call. To turn this feature on, go to Settings > Phone > Announce Calls. Select Always, Headphones & Car, Headphones Only or Never to choose your preferred way to announce calls.

Messaging

More and more smartphone users are staying connected through text messages instead of phone calls, and the iPhone makes it easy to keep in touch with everyone. In addition to sending regular SMS text messages and multimedia messages (pictures, links, video clips and voice notes), you can also use iMessage to interact with other Apple users. This feature allows you to send instant messages to anyone signed into a Mac running OS X Mountain Lion or higher, or any iOS device running iOS 5 or greater.

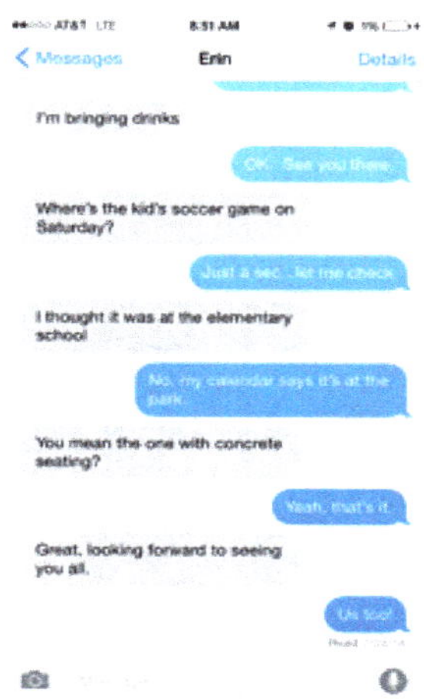

On the main Messages screen, you will be able to see the many different conversations you have going on. You can also delete conversations by swiping from right to left on the conversation you'd like and tapping the red Delete button. New conversations or existing conversations with new messages will be highlighted with a big blue dot next to it, and the Messages icon will have a badge displaying the number of unread messages you have, similar to the Mail and Phone icons.

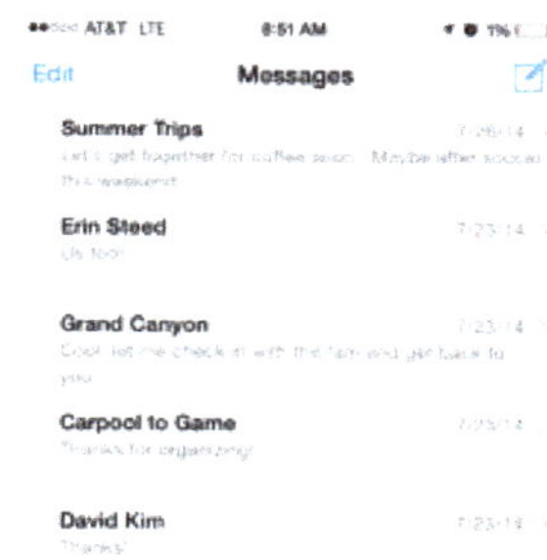

To create a message, click on the Messages icon, then the Compose button in the top right corner.

Once the new message dialog box pops up, click on the plus button (+) to choose from your contacts list, or just type in the phone number of the person you wish to text. For group messages, just keep adding as many people as you'd like. Finally, click on the bottom field to begin typing your message.

iMessage has added in a lot of new features over the past few years. If all you want to do is send a message, then just tap the blue up arrow.

But you can do so much more than just send a message! (Please note, if you are sending a message with newer features to someone with an older OS or a non-Apple device, then it won't look as it appears on your screen).

To start with, go ahead and push (but don't release that blue button—or if you are using a phone with 3D Touch or Haptic touch, press down a little firmer). This will bring up several different animations for the message.

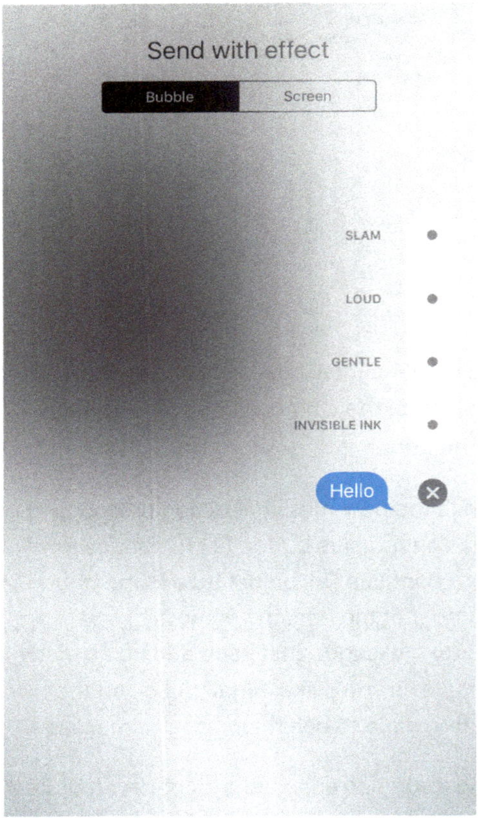

On the top of this screen, you'll also notice two tabs; one says "Bubble" and the other says "Screen"; if you tap "Screen" you can add animations to the entire screen. Swipe right and left to see each new animation.

When you get a message that you like and you want to respond to it, you can tap and hold your finger over the message or image; this will bring up different ways you can react.

Once you make your choice, the person on the receiving end will see how you responded.

If you'd like to add animation, a photo, a video, or lots of other things, then let's look at the options next to the message.

You have three choices—which bring up even more choices! The first is the camera, which lets you send photos with your message (or take new photos—note, these photos won't be saved on your phone), the next lets you use iMessage apps (more on that in a second), and the last lets you record a message with your voice.

Let's look at the camera option first.

If you just want to attach a photo to your message, then after you tap the camera, go to the upper left corner and tap the Photo icon; this brings up all the photos you can attach.

If you want to take an original photo, then tap the round button on the bottom. To add effects, tap the star in the lower left corner.

Tapping effects brings up all the different effects available to you. I'll talk more about Animoji soon, but as an example, this app lets you put an Animoji over your face (see the example below—not bad for an author photo, eh?!)

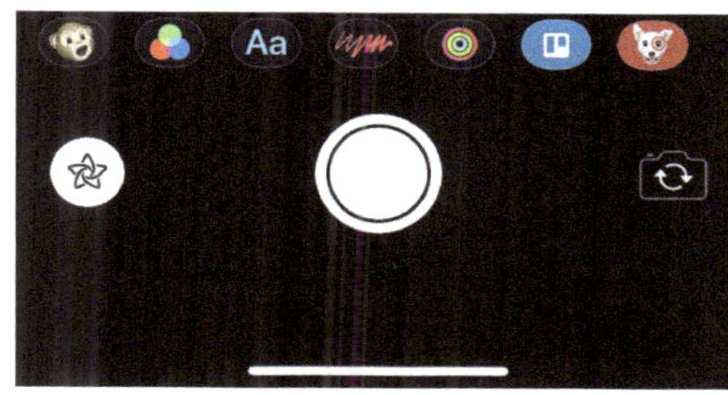

Finally, the last option is apps. You should know all about phone apps by now, but now there's a new set of apps called iMessage apps. These apps let you be both silly (send digital stickers) and serious (send cash to someone via text). To get started, tap the '+' button to open the iMessage App Store.

You can browse all the apps just like you would the regular App Store. Installing them is the same as well.

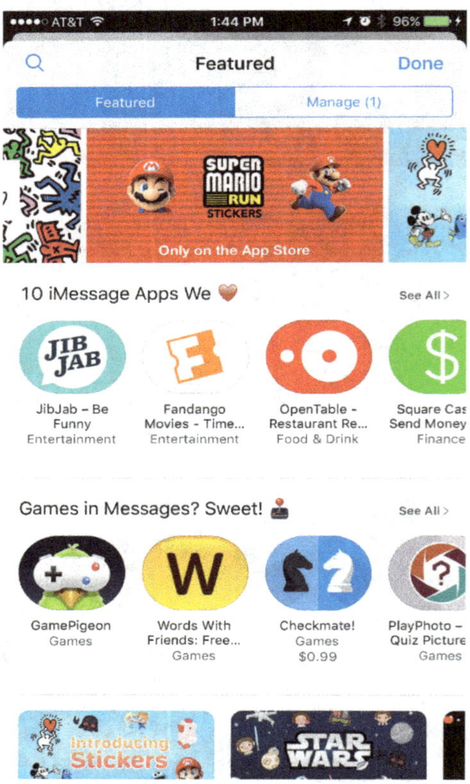

When you're ready to use the app, just tap apps, tap the app you want to load, and tap what you want to send. You can also drag stickers on top of messages. Just tap, hold and drag.

Also in the app section is a button called "#images."

If you tap on this button you can search for thousands of humorous memes and animated GIFs. Just tap it and search a term you want to find—such as "Money" or "Fight".

One final iMessage feature worth trying out is the personal handwritten note. Tap on a new message like you are going to start typing a new message; now rotate your phone horizontally. This brings up an option to use your finger to create a handwritten note. Sign away, and then hit done when you're finished.

Message Tagging

If you have used messaging programs like Slack, then you are probably all too familiar with tagging someone in a conversation. Tagging gets the person's attention and starts a new thread within the conversation.

So if you are in a large text message exchange, then when you tag someone, everyone can read it, but everyone is not notified. So it's a little less unobtrusive.

To tag someone in a conversation, just put an @ in front of their name when you reply.

If you want to reply in-line to a message, then long-press the message. By in-line, I mean this: let's say there's a message several texts up—you can long-press to reply to it, so they know what message you are referring to.

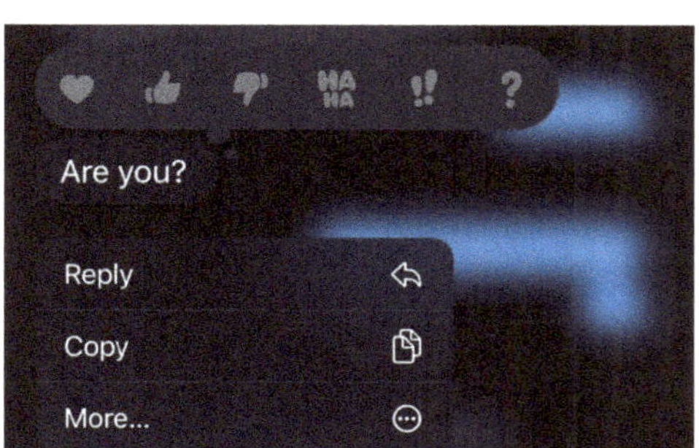

Once you tap Reply, you just reply as you normally would.

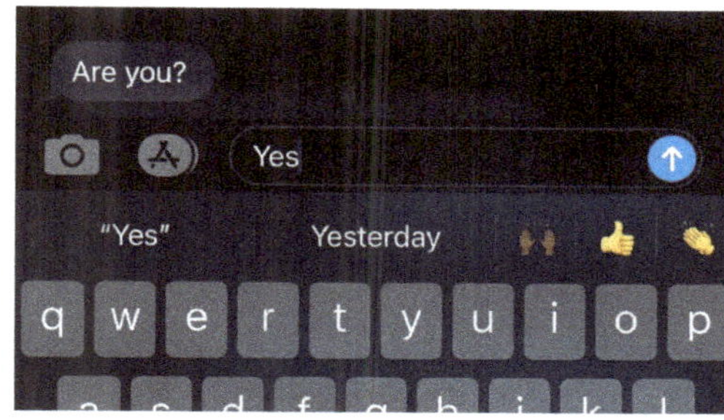

This is going to alert the person and they'll see the message with a reply notification under the message.

If it's several texts above, they'll also see it like the below message.

Pinning Messages

If you text a lot, then it might get a little cumbersome replying. The way Messages works is the most recent conversations go to the top. This mostly works well, but you can also pin favorites to the top.

In the example below, my wife is pinned to the top of the conversations. Even though other people have written me more recently, she will always be up there (unless I remove her). That makes it easy to reply.

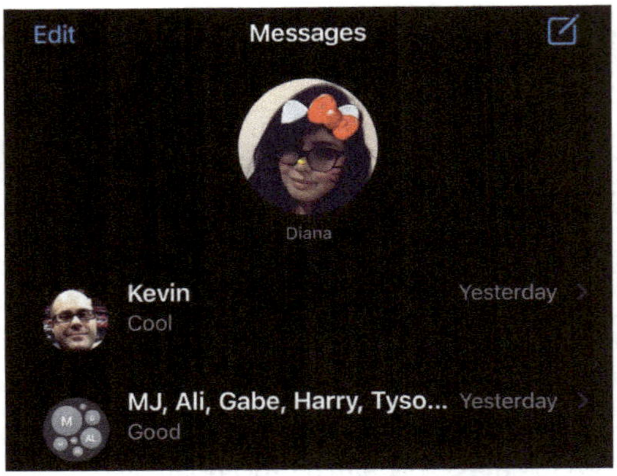

To add or remove someone from the top, tap the Edit button in the upper left corner, then select Edit Pins.

If you want to remove them, tap the minus icon above their photo (in the upper left corner); if you want to add them, tap the yellow pin icon.

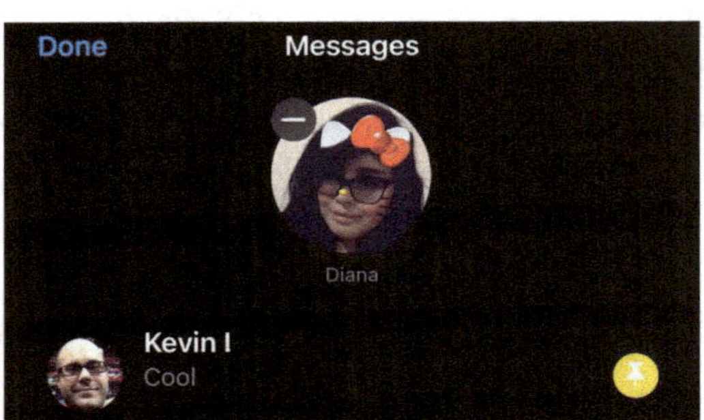

You can have several people pinned to the top. Personally, I find three is good, but you can add even more.

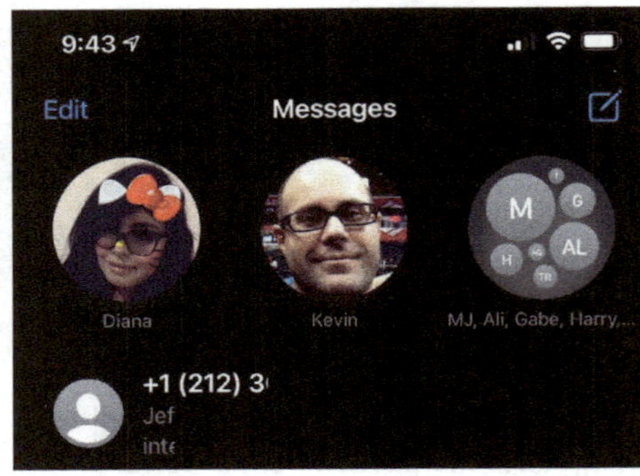

Sending Photos In Messages

When you send groups of photos, Messages will lay out photos of less than three vertically. Tap them to make them bigger.

If you send more than three photos, then they'll stack on top of each other, and you swipe through them.

Unsend Messages

Let's be honest here: we've all sent text we've regretted. You can unsend or edit those text. Just tap and hold the message (you have to do this relatively quickly—if too much time passes, the option disappears), then select either Undo Send or Edit.

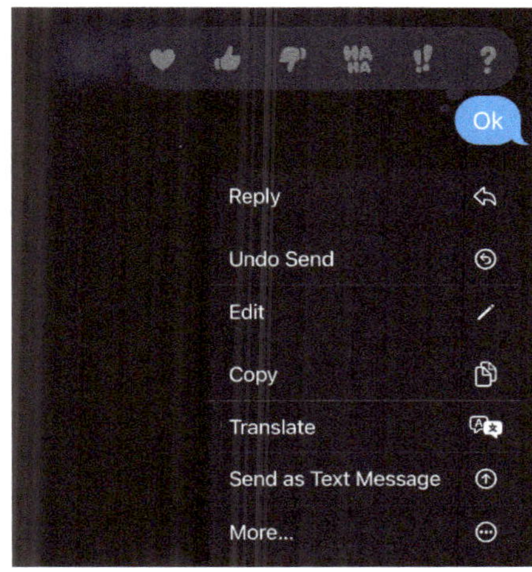

If you think this will get you out of the doghouse and you can say "I never said that!" Think again! The person on the other end of the text will see that the message has been unsent or edited.

There's An App for That

App is short for application. So, when you hear the term "There's an app for that," it just means there's a program that does what you want to do. If you're a Windows user, all those things you always open (like Word and Excel) are apps. Apple has literally millions of apps. Opening an app is as simple as touching it.

Unlike apps on a computer, you don't have to close apps on your phone. It's all automatic. For most apps, it will even remember where you were, so when you open it again it's saved.

Organizing Apps

If you're like me—and pretty much most people are—you love your apps and you have a lot of them! So, you'll need to know how to move them around, put them in folders, and delete them. It's all easy to do.

The Home screen may be the first screen you see, but if you swipe to the right, you'll see there are more; you can have 11. Personally, I keep the most used apps on the first screen, and not-so-used apps in folders on the second. The bottom dock is where I put the apps that I use all the time (like Mail and Safari).

To rearrange apps, take your finger and touch one of your apps. Instead of tapping, hold your finger down for a few seconds; you'll see an app option pop up but keep holding until the apps jiggle. When the apps are jiggling like that, you can touch them without opening them and drag them around your screen. Try it out! Just touch an app and drag your finger to move it. When you've found the perfect spot, lift your finger and the app drops into place. After you've downloaded more apps, you can also drag apps across Home screens.

You can delete an app using the same method for moving them. The only difference is instead of moving them, you tap the 'x' in the upper left corner of the icon. Don't worry about deleting something on accident. Apps are stored in the cloud. You can delete and install them as many times as you want; you don't have to pay again—you just have to download them again.

Putting apps on different screens is helpful, but to be really organized you want to use folders. You can, for example, have a folder for all your game apps, finance apps, social apps, whatever you want. You pick what to name it. If you want an "Apps I use on the toilet" folder, then you can absolutely have it!

To create a folder, just drag one app over another app you'd like to add into that folder.

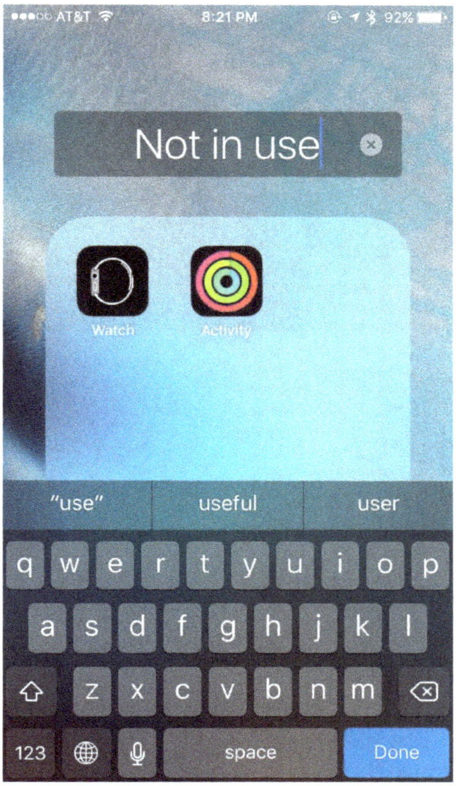

Once they are together, you can name the folder. To delete the folder, just put the folder apps in "jiggle mode" and drag them out of the folder. iPhone doesn't allow empty folders—when a folder is empty, iPhone deletes it automatically.

When you are finished organizing apps, tap the Done button in the upper right corner.

Goodbye Clutter, Hello App Library

Apple's App Store is huge! Thousands and thousands of apps! So many choices that there really does seem to be an app for everything. It's wonderful! It's terrific! It's amazing! It...takes up so much space on your Home screen!

The problem with all those apps is after using your phone for a while, they start building up. Your phone becomes cluttered with apps. Some you use all the time, but you spend several minutes trying to find them.

That's where App Library is going to help you. You can still have your most important apps on the Home screen where they are easy to find, but then you can have the rest organized in the app library, where they are organized in one list.

Send to Library

Have you ever downloaded an app and it starts installing it on your Home screen? Personally, I find this annoying! The Home screen is a privilege on my phone! It's reserved for only apps that have proven themselves to me to be life-changing—like Candy Crush and Words With Friends! How dare they install an unproven app on that screen.

You can change that by going to the Settings app, then Home Screen; next select the toggle for App Library Only under Newly Download Apps. Next time you download an app, it will send it right to the App Library.

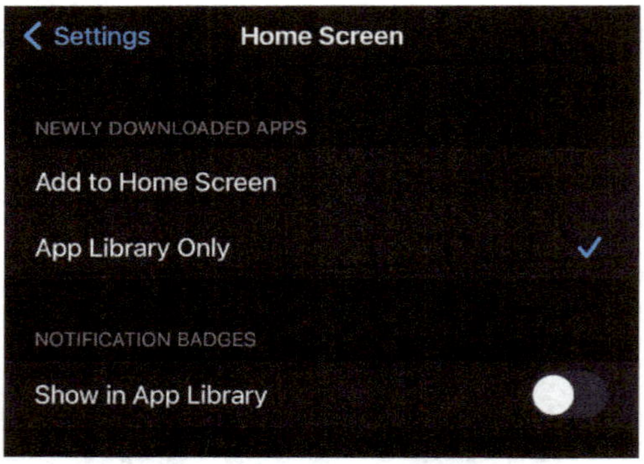

If you find the app is a gamechanger that you are using all the time, you can still move it to another screen—just tap and hold your finger over it, then drag it out (just as you would when rearranging other apps).

You can also move apps from your Home screen to the App Library. Just tap and hold it, then tap the minus button in the upper left corner of the app. It will ask you if you want to delete the app or move it to the App Library.

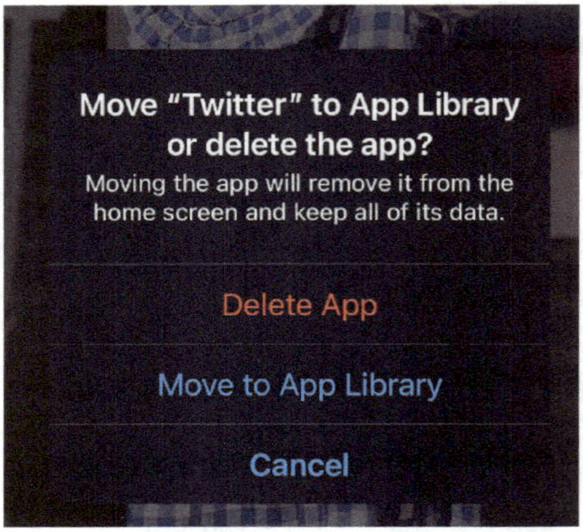

There's a Widget for That!

Android users have probably been showing off widgets to you for years. iPhone has had widgets for a while, but they've never been something you could have on your Home screen. That changes in iOS 15.

It's simple to do. Tap and hold your Home screen. I already have a photo widget on my phone in the example below. To add another, tap the + icon in the upper left corner.

You can either search for widgets or scroll through them.

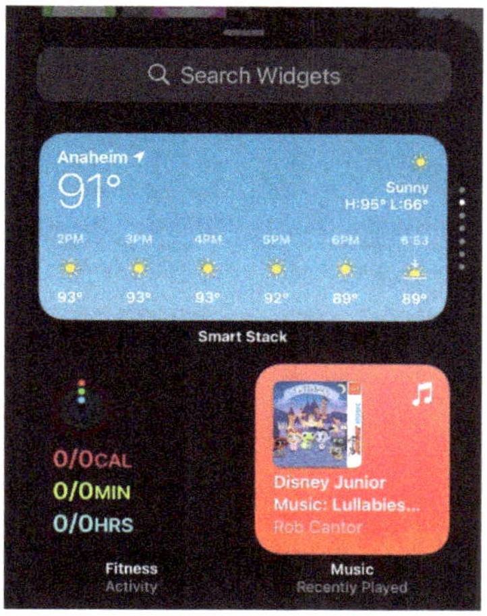

When you find the one you want, tap it; some widgets will have several variations and sizes that you can pick from.

Once you add it, you can drag it around your screen just as you would an app icon shortcut. If you decide you don't want it, just tap the - icon in the upper left corner of the widget.

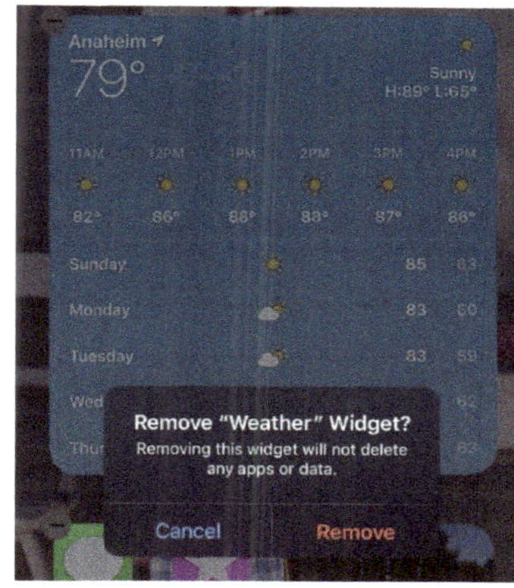

Smart Stacks

You can also add what's known as a Smart Stack—which changes based on what it predicts you will use during one point in the day.

If the widget is the same size, you can drag it into another widget box to create your own Smart Stack.

Once added, you can swipe up and down within that widget to toggle between the app.

If you long-press on it, you are able to edit the stack.

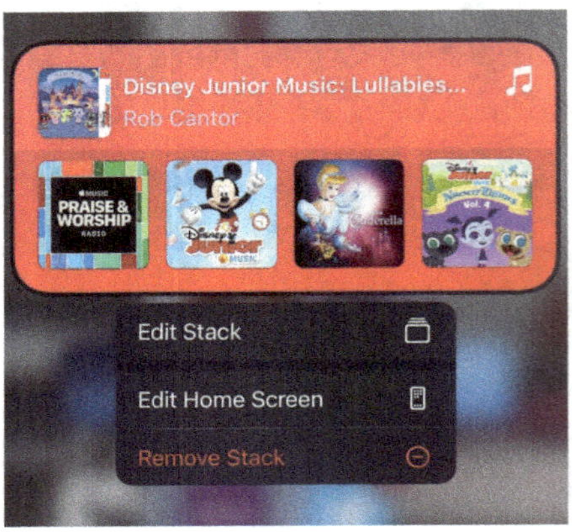

When you edit it, you can move what's in the stack and turn off Smart Rotate, so it doesn't rotate throughout the day.

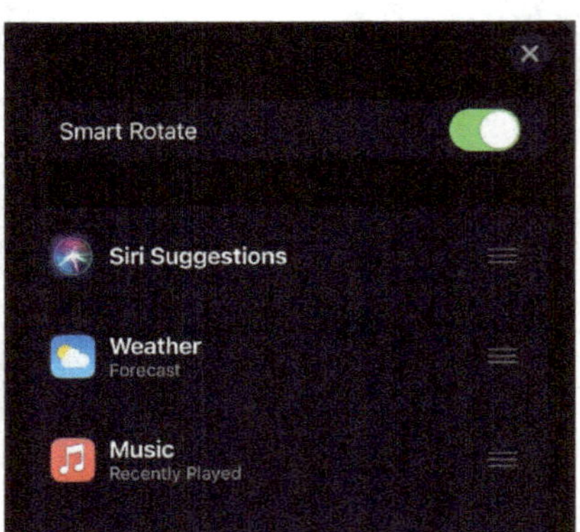

Search Text in App

When you swipe down from the middle of the screen, you can quickly search for apps, which is helpful if you have a lot of them. You can also search for text within apps by scrolling down to the section titled "Search in Apps."

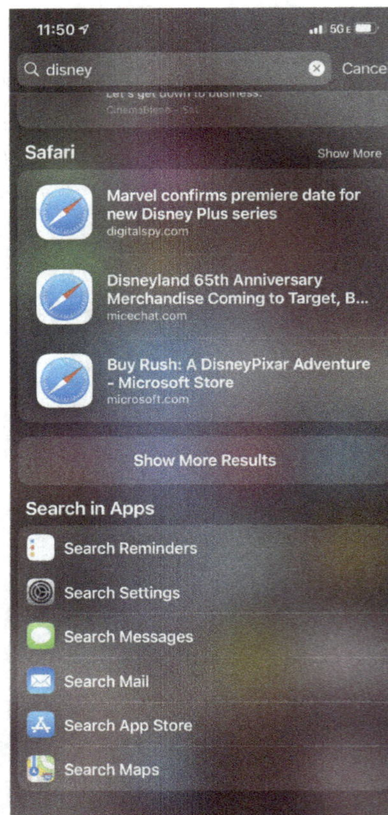

Notifications

When you have your phone locked, you'll start seeing notifications at some point; this tells you things like "You have a new email," "Don't forget to set your alarm," etc.

So, when you see all your notifications on your Lock screen, they'll be organized by what they are. To see all the notifications from any one category, just tap it.

Not a fan of grouping? No problem. You can turn it off for any app. Head to Settings, then Notifications, then tap the app you want to turn grouping off for. Under Notification Groupings, just turn off automatic.

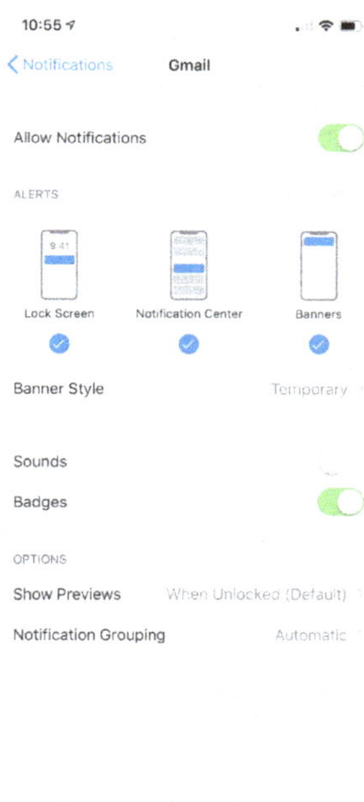

Notification Summary

Notifications can get a bit...much. If you have connected devices like Nest, email, and messages, then your phone will start going off way to often. Notification summary helps you not get overwhelmed by letting you set up a schedule for when different notifications come.

To get started head to the Settings app, then Notifications.

Next go to Scheduled Summary.

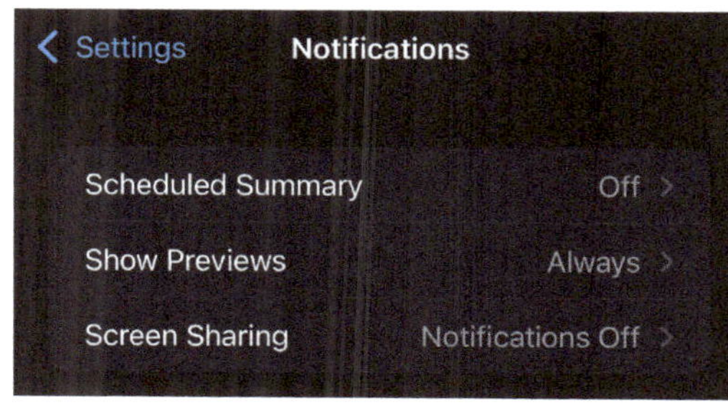

If it's off, toggle it to on, then set up your schedule.

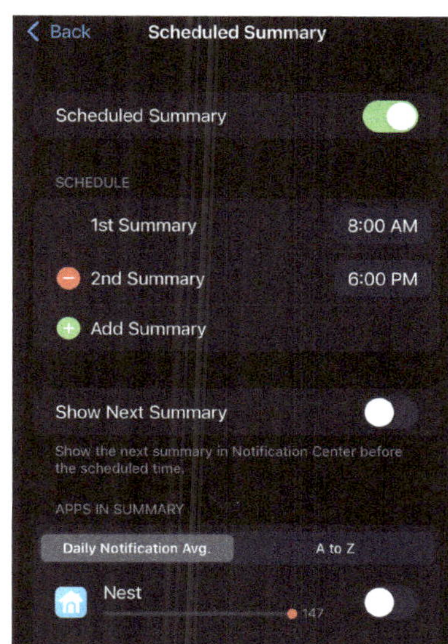

Using AirDrop

AirDrop was introduced in iOS 7, though Apple fans have likely used the Mac OS version on MacBooks and iMacs. In Mac OSX Sierra and Yosemite, you'll finally be able to share between iOS and your Mac using AirDrop.

AirDrop is Apple's file sharing service, and it comes standard on iOS devices. You can activate AirDrop from the Share icon anywhere in iOS. If other AirDrop users are nearby, you'll see anything they're sharing in AirDrop, and they can see anything you share.

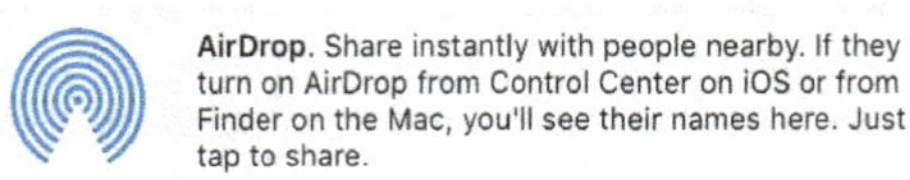

Focus

Phones can distract us from things we need to be doing. Yes, they're great for playing games on the toilet, but you really need to get back to work. To help you, there is a Focus mode. To access it, swipe down from the upper right corner, then tap the Focus button.

There are several different focus modes—each with different settings. Some will send you notifications, but not calls, for example.

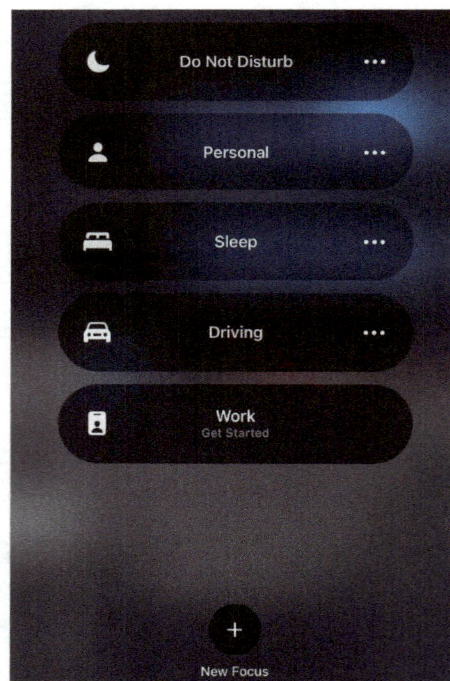

Clicking on the three dots in the corner of the mode lets you select how long it will be on (if you don't do this, it will stay on until you turn it off).

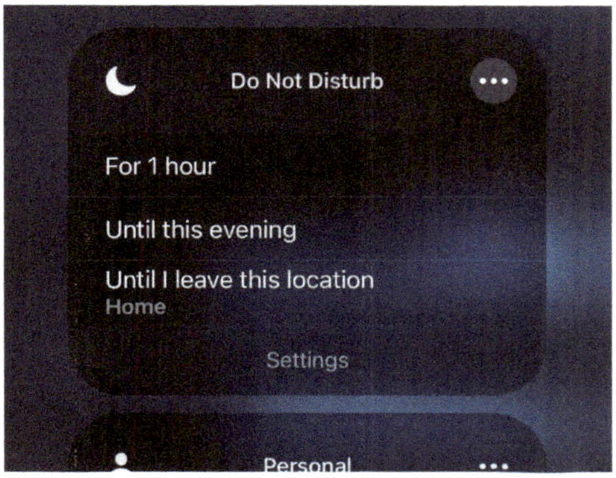

You can also add a mode. There are predefined modes that you can add.

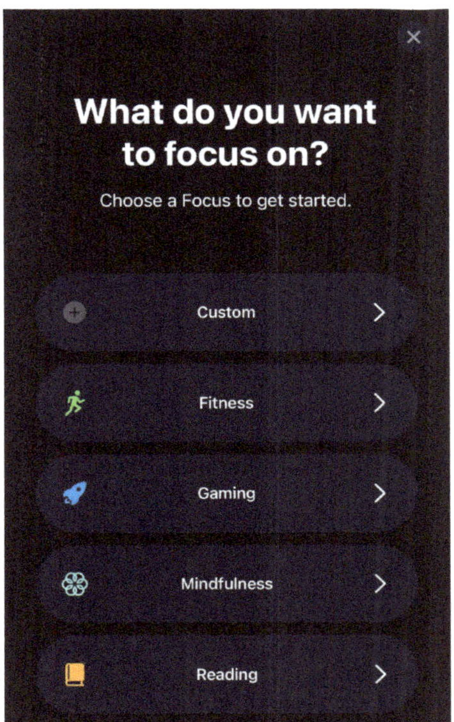

Tapping on each mode tells you what the mode does.

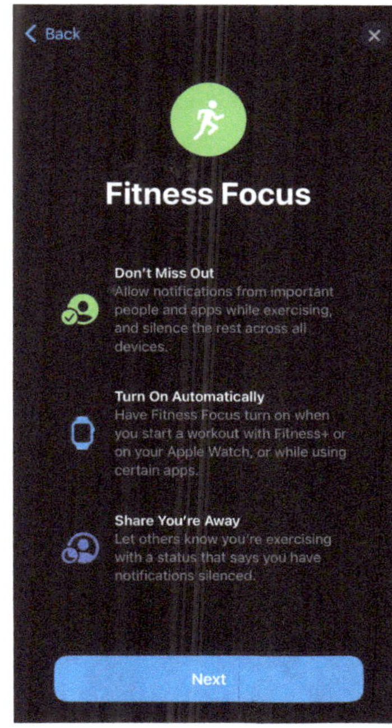

You can also create your own custom mode.

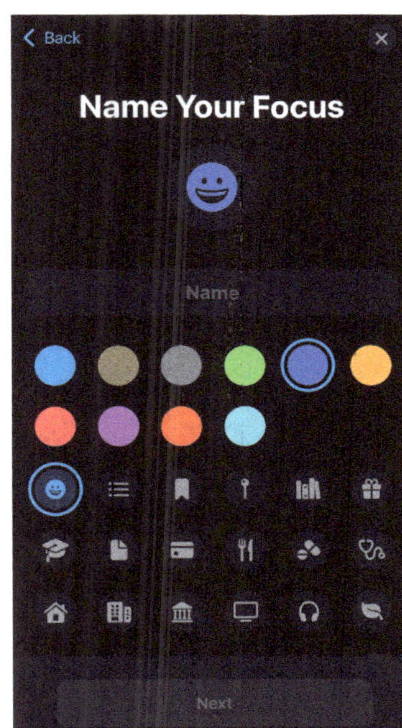

Creating your own mode lets you define the limits.

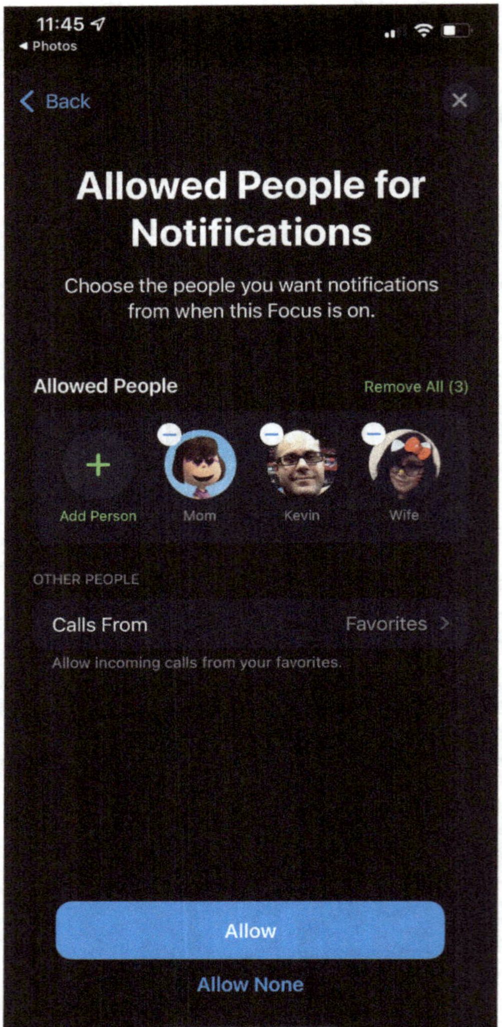

You also can pick and choose the apps that are allowed for notifications. So you can tell it that you can get Tweets, but not Facebook messages.

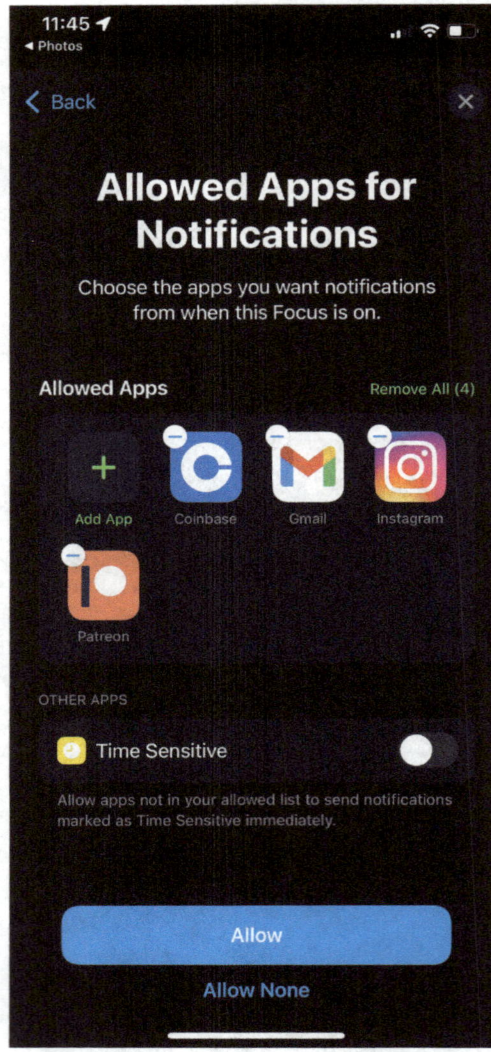

Just hit Done and it will be added.

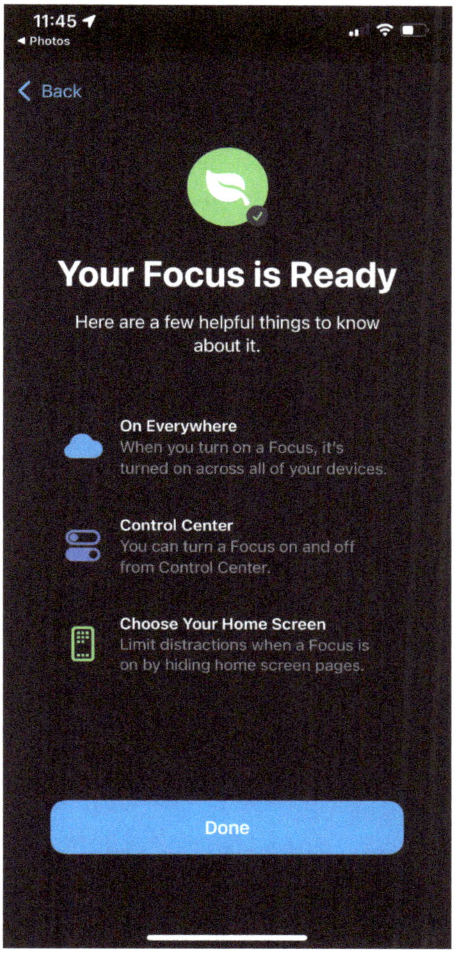

WALLET

Apple Wallet is where you can store digital versions of things like credit cards, insurance cards, and even IDs and keys. It is getting bigger and bigger every year, but, unfortunately, it is up to businesses to add it into Apple's system. So if you don't see your credit card company or can't add something like an ID, it is because it is not yet supported.

The Apple Services section of this guide will talk more extensively about the features.

To add something to your Wallet, open the Wallet app, then tap the + icon in the upper right corner.

Next, select what you want to add. You can also apply for an Apple Card. Apple Card is Apple's credit card.

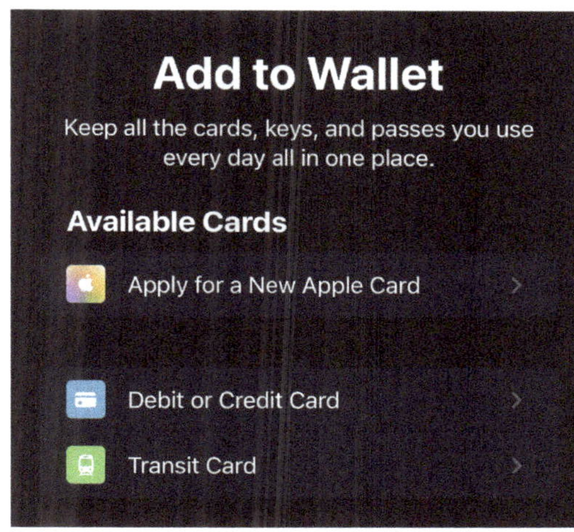

Just because you may be reading this in the U.S. don't assume you won't see things from other countries. If you are travelling somewhere like China, you'll even see transit cards for that country.

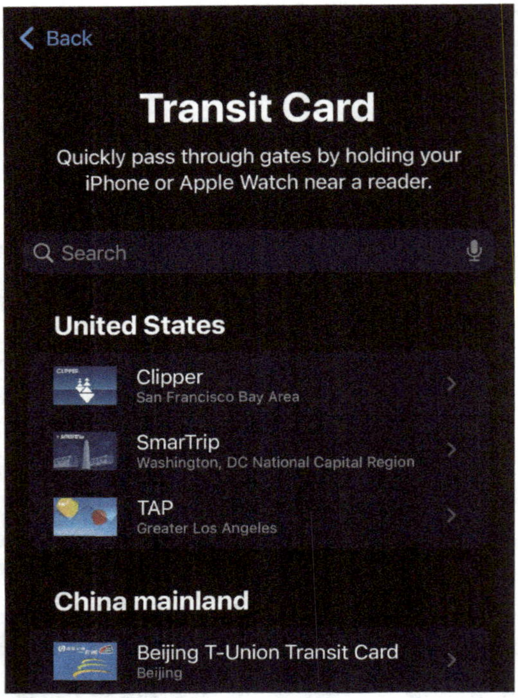

Spotlight

Spotlight is where you go to find things on your phone. There's two ways to get there: swipe up from your Home screen, or swipe left from your main Home screen.

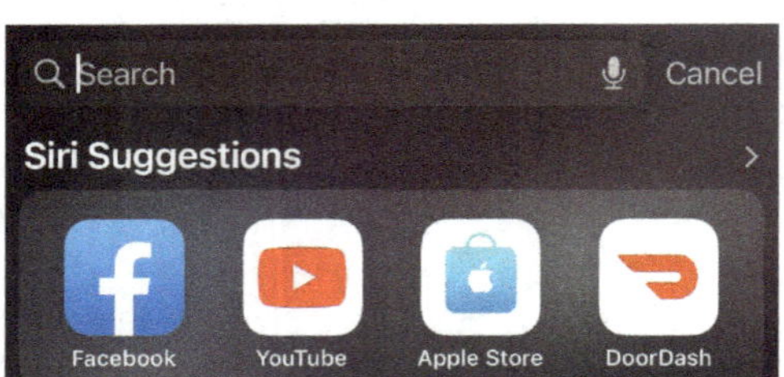

What can you search for? In a word: everything! Well pretty much everything. You can search for TV shows, movies, people, but with recent updates you can search for even more—including Live Text within your photos. It's incredibly smart and it's getting smarter, so if you can't find something on your phone, then try searching for it.

CHAPTER 5: THE MAIN IPHONE APPS

There are millions of apps you can download, but Apple invests a lot of time making sure some of the best apps are their own. When you get a new iPhone, there are dozens of apps already installed. You're free to delete them (and later download them again), but before you do, make sure you know what they are.

PHONE

In previous chapters, you got a very high-level look at making calls. Now let's go a little deeper.

Open your Phone app. Notice the tabs on the bottom of the screen. Let's go over what each one does.

- Favorites: These are the people you call most frequently. They are also in your contacts. It's kind of like your speed dial.
- Recent: Any call (outgoing or incoming) will show up here. Incoming calls are in black, and outgoing calls are in red.
- Contacts: This is where every contact will be. Do you notice the letters on the side? Tap the letter corresponding to the person you want to call to jump to that letter.
- Keypad: This is what you use if you want to call the person using an actual keypad.
- Voicemail: all your voicemail is stored here until you erase it.

Personally, I like to add contacts by going to iCloud.com and signing in with my iTunes

Account. It automatically syncs with the phone and is web-based which means that it doesn't matter whether you are using a Mac or a PC. I prefer this way because I can type with a real keyboard.

For the sake of this book, however, I am going to use the phone method; which is almost identical to the iCloud.

To add a contact, tap on "Contacts," and then tap the '+' button in the upper right corner. Additionally, you can remove contacts by tapping on the Edit button instead and then tapping on the person you want to delete, then hitting "Delete."

To insert information, all you need to do is tap in each field. If you tap on "add photo" you will also have the option of taking someone's photo or using one you already have. If you want to assign a ringtone or a vibration, so that it plays a certain song only when this person is calling, then add that under ringtones. When you are finished, tap "Done." It will now give you the option of adding the person to your favorites if this is someone you will call often.

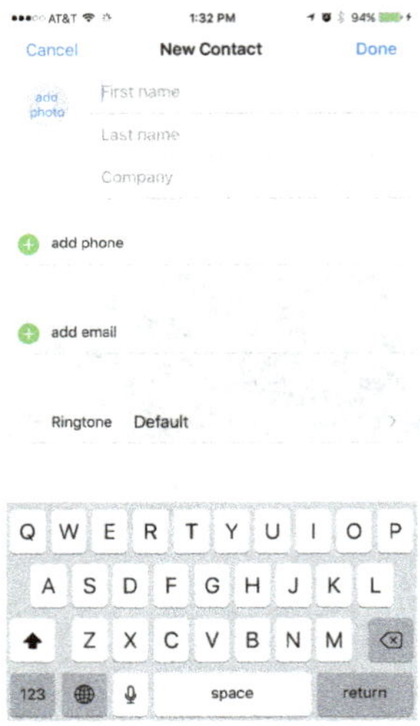

To call any person, simply tap their name. If you want to send them a text message instead, tap the blue arrow to the side of their name. Note that only the blue arrow shows up if in the "Favorites" section. To call someone not in your favorites, tap on their name in contacts and it will ask you if you want to call or text. If you prefer to call the person using Facetime (if they have Facetime) you will also have the option by tapping the blue exclamation button.

One highly advertised feature on the iPhone is Do Not Disturb. When this feature is turned on, no calls get through; you don't even see that your phone is ringing unless it's from someone in your approved list. That way you can have it set to ring only if someone in your family is calling. To use this feature, you need to go to Settings on your Home screen.

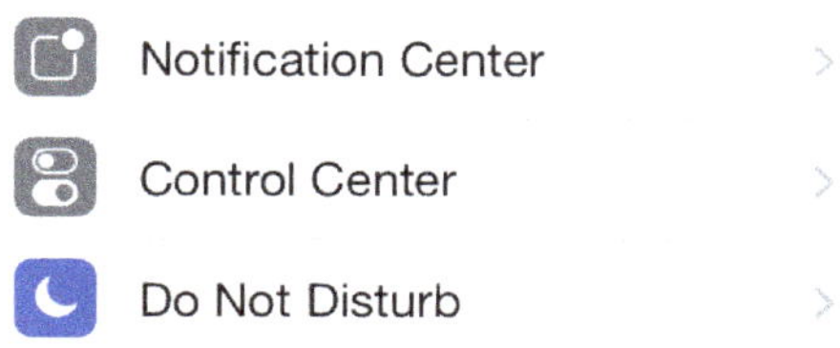

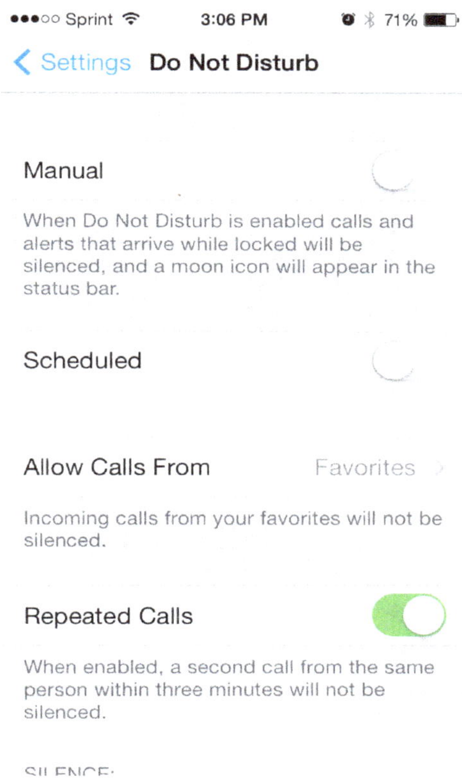

By default, when Do Not Disturb is on, anyone in your favorites can call. Also, notice the Repeated Calls button which is switched on by default. What that means is that if the same person calls twice in three minutes, it will go through.

If you want to set it to let no calls go through, tap on the "Allow Calls From." To get back to the previous menu, just tap the Do Not Disturb button in the upper left corner. Anytime you see a button like that in the upper left corner, it means that it will take you to the previous screen. The information here saves as soon as you tap it, so don't worry about a Save button.

FaceTime

How do you keep people together when they are apart? This is something Apple has thought deeply about. FaceTime on the iPhone looks better than ever. Later in fall 2021, you will be able to watch movies together, listen to music together, and even troubleshoot device problems by sharing your iPad screen. It's called SharePlay. Unfortunately, some of these features are coming later in the fall, so this instructional guide cannot include them at this writing.

To get started open the FaceTime app; you have two options: Create Link or New FaceTime Call.

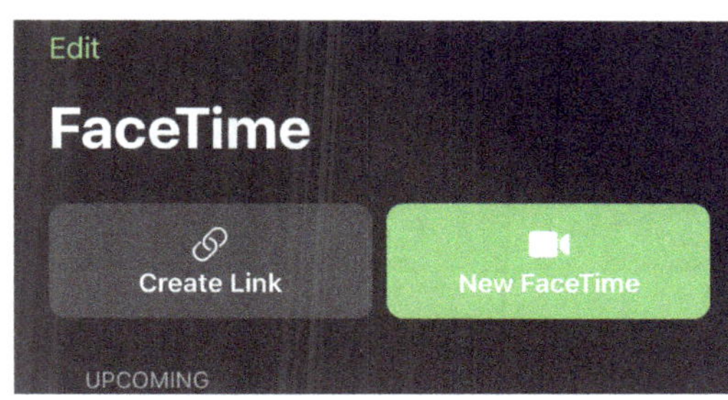

The Create Link button will give you a sharable link that you can give out to people. What's really cool about this is it can be shared with people who don't have iPhones—so they can open it inside Chrome on a Windows computer. Just tap the copy button and paste it wherever you want people to see it. You can also tap Add Name to give it a name.

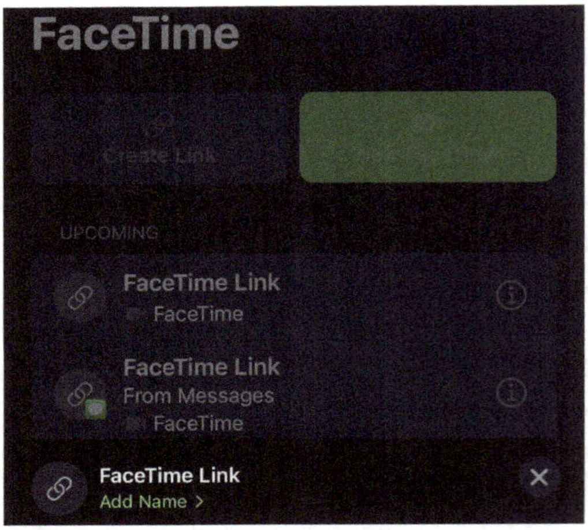

If you prefer to call someone directly, then tap the green New FaceTime button and type in their name.

Your preview box is in the lower corner, but it can be moved anywhere on the screen by tapping and holding it, then dragging.

If you make this preview box larger, there's several options you have. In the upper left corner, you have a little image icon—that makes your background blurred or not blurred. The lower right will flip your camera from the front facing camera to back. The lower left corner will bring up effects you can add in.

Effects can be moved around by tapping and holding, or enlarged by pinching on them.

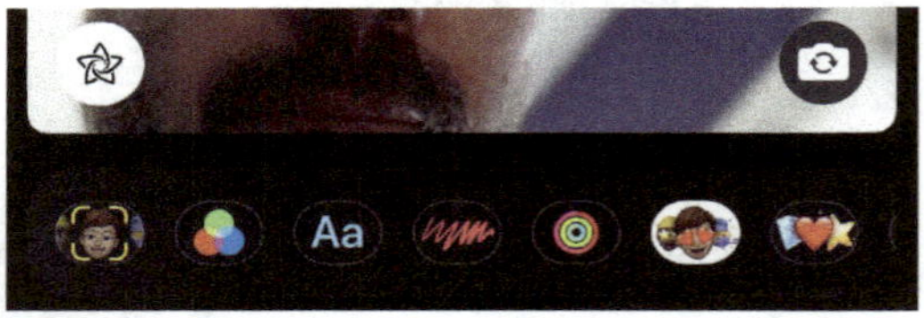

When you tap the screen, you'll also have a floating box with more controls. If you haven't started the call yet, for example if someone calls you on FaceTime, then you have to accept it, then tap the Join button; if you are on the call, then this button turns to a Leave button—tap that to hang up. From left to right, the other buttons are Messages to send everyone on the call a message, Speaker if you want to transfer the sound to something like a HomePod, Microphone if you want to turn off your mic so they can't hear you, and Camera, which is where you go to turn off your video—they can hear you but not see you.

The Monalisa of FaceTime?

Have you ever seen one of those paintings where the eyes follow you? Apple appears to be mimicking this technique with a setting for FaceTime that tries to focus on your eyes to give the viewer constant eye contact. So even if you are staring at your screen playing a game, it will appear that you are looking at the camera!

To turn it on, go to the Settings app, then select FaceTime. Make sure Eye Contact is toggled on.

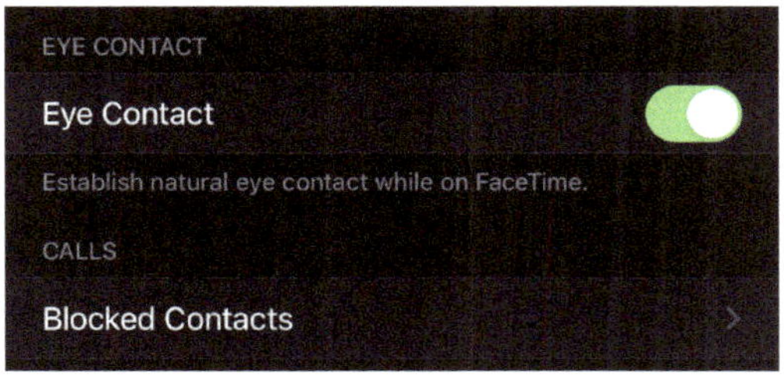

Mail

The iPhone lets you add multiple email addresses from virtually any email client you can think of. Yahoo, Gmail, AOL, Exchange, Hotmail, and many more can be added to your phone so that you will be able to check your email no matter where you are. To add an email address, click on the Settings app icon, then scroll to the middle where you'll see Mail, Contacts & Calendar. You will then see logos for the biggest email providers, but if you have another type of email just click on "Other" and continue.

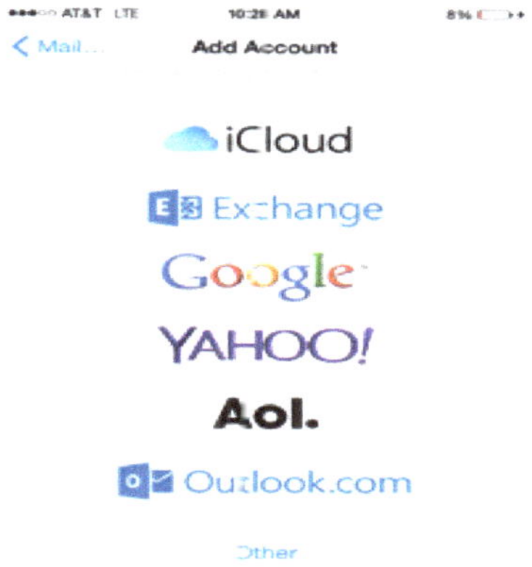

If you don't know your email settings, you will need to visit the Mail Settings Lookup page on the Apple website. There you can type in your entire email address, and the website will show you what information to type and where in order to get your email account working on the phone. The settings change with every one, so what works for one provider may not work with another. Once you are finished adding as many email accounts as you may need, you will be able to click on the Mail app icon on your phone's Home screen, and view each inbox separately, or all at once.

Surfing the Internet with Safari

If you are using the iPhone, you are probably already paying for a data plan, so chances are you want to take full advantage of the Internet.

There's a good chance you are using a carrier that doesn't have unlimited web surfing. This means that if you use the Internet a lot, then you will have to pay extra. What I recommend is using Wi-Fi when you have it (like at home). So, before we go back into Safari, let's look very quickly at how to enable Wi-Fi.

On your Home screen, tap the Settings icon.

The second option in the Settings menu is Wi-Fi; tap anywhere on that line once.

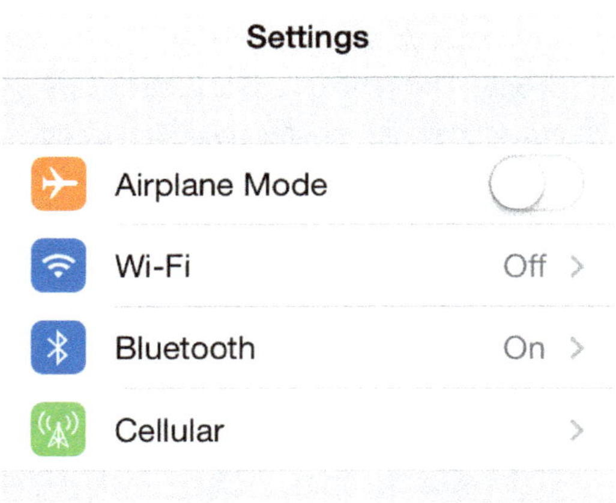

Next, switch the Wi-Fi from off to on by swiping or tapping on the "Off."

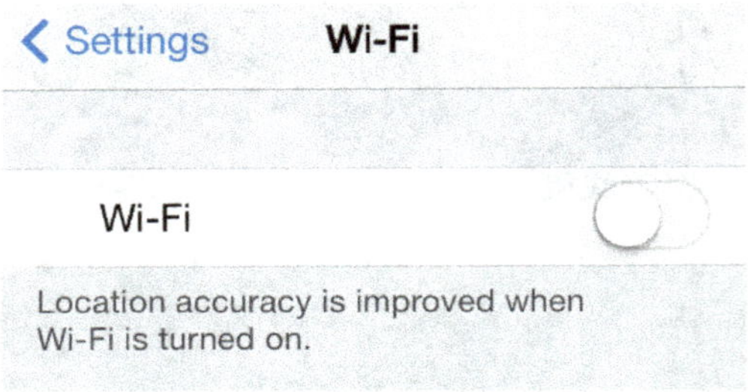

Your Wi-Fi network (if you have one) will now appear. Tap it once.

If there is a lock next to the signal symbol; that means the Wi-Fi access is locked and you need a password to use it. When prompted, type in the password and then tap "Join."

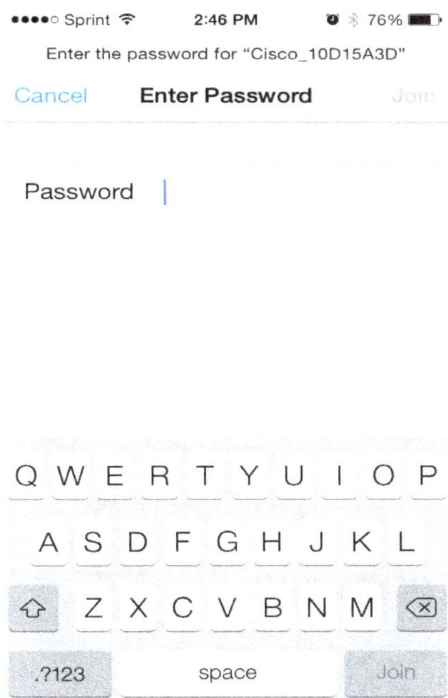

You will now connect to the network. Remember that many places, like Starbucks, McDonald's, Nordstrom, Lowe's, etc., offer free Wi-Fi as a way to entice you into the store and get you to stay. Take advantage of it and save data usage for the times you need it.

Let's see how Safari works.

Safari Interface

For years, the toolbar on Safari was on the top. It's the place you are most likely to search for it because that's where it is everywhere else—desktops, tablets, etc. In iOS 15, the toolbar was moved to the bottom. Annoying, right?! At first, yes. Why mess with something that works?! Because it doesn't work.

Think about how you use your phone. Your fingers are at the bottom of the phone—you don't hold it from the top. So, when you're typing an address, then what do you have to do? Move your hand to the top to tap the address bar, then move it back to the bottom where the keyboard is. It's two steps. This speeds things up. You don't have to adjust your hand.

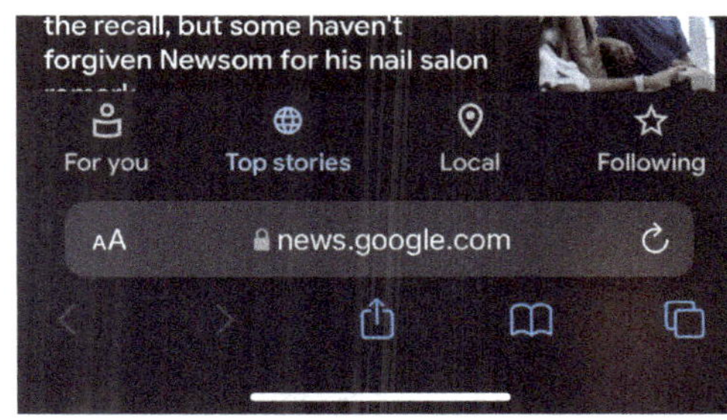

If you have used Safari before, then this will feel odd; just try it for a day or two. If you really can't stand it, there is an easy way to reverse it. Tap the double AAs on the address bar.

At the very top, there's an option that says "Show Top Address Bar"; tap that and you are done.

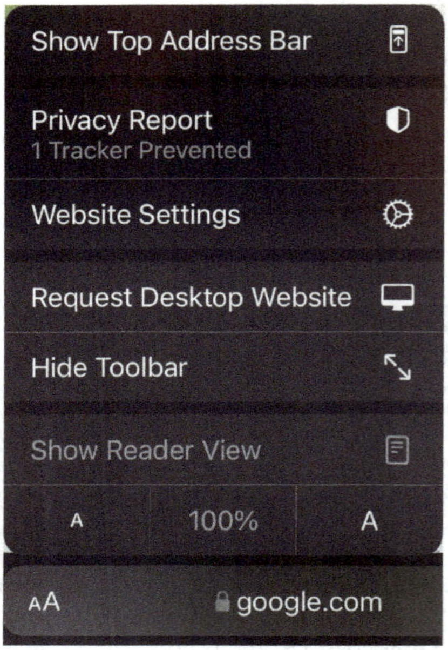

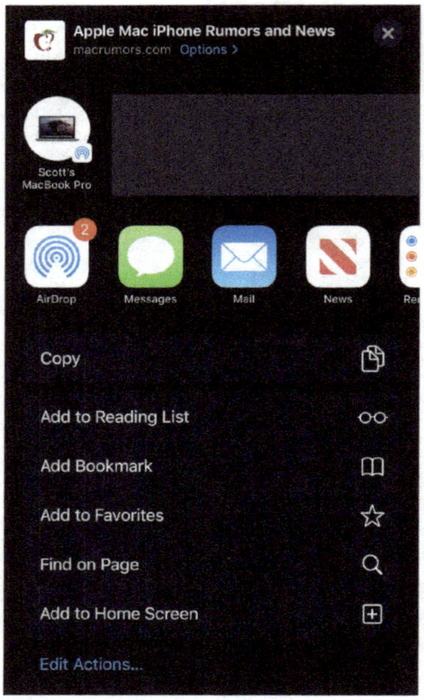

To search for something, you use the same exact box. That's how you can search for anything on the Internet. Think of it like a Google, Bing, or Yahoo! search engine in the corner of your screen. In fact, that's exactly what it is. Because when you search, it will use one of those search engines to find results.

On the bottom of the screen you'll see five buttons; the first two are Back and Forward buttons that make the browser go either backwards or forwards to the website you were previously on.

Next to the forward arrow, right in the middle, is a button that lets you share a website, add it to the Home screen, print it, bookmark it, copy it, or add it to your reading list.

That's great! But what does it all mean? Let's look at each button on the menu:

The first row lets you send the link to your nearby devices or text it to people you often text.

Below that are the apps you can open and send the link to.

Finally, below those are different actions you can take with the link:

Add to Home screen: If you go to a website frequently, this can be very convenient. What this button does is add an icon for that webpage right to your Home screen. That way whenever you want to launch the website, you can do it directly from the Home screen.

Copy: This copies the website address.

Add Bookmark: If you go to a website often but don't want to add it to your Home screen, then you can bookmark it. I will show you this in more detail in just a moment.

Add to Reading List: If you have a bunch of news stories open, you can add them to a reading list to read later (even if you are offline).

The next button over from the share link covered above looks like a book. It is the Bookmark button.

When you add a bookmark (remember you do this from the previous button, the Share one), it will ask you to name it. By default it will put it in the general bookmarks tab, but you can also create new folders by clicking on "Bookmarks."

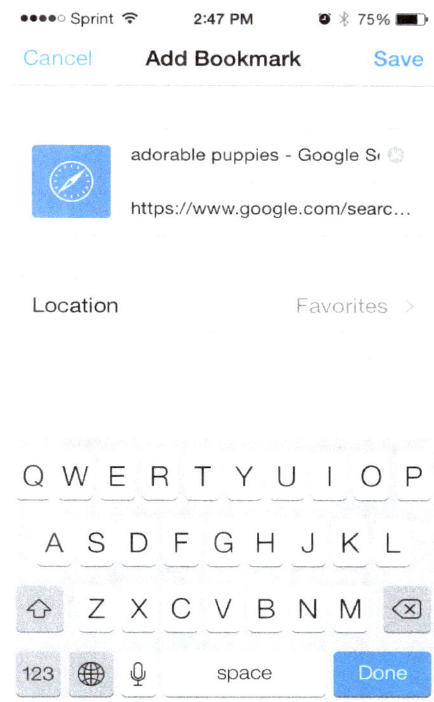

Now you can access the website anytime you want without typing the address by tapping on the Bookmarks button.

Reading List is the middle icon that looks like a pair of glasses where you can view all of the webpages, blog posts, or articles that you've saved for offline reading. To save a piece of internet literature to your reading list, tap on the Share icon and then click on "Add to Reading List." Saved pages can be deleted like a text message by swiping from right to left and tapping on the red Delete button.

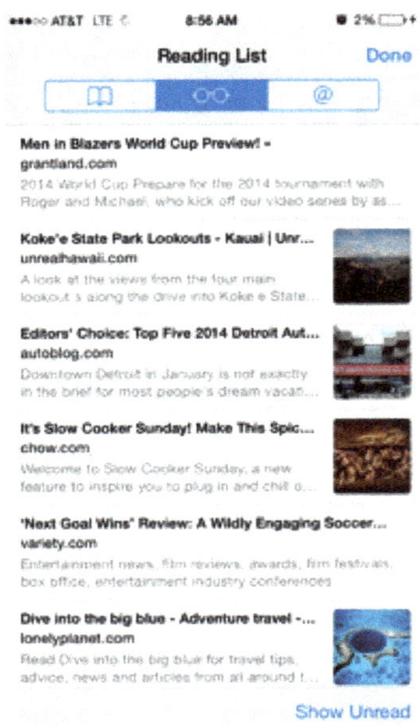

The third tab on the Bookmarks page is where you can view your shared links and subscriptions. Subscriptions can be created from any webpage that provides RSS feeds, and your phone will automatically download the latest articles and posts. To subscribe to a site's RSS, visit the website, tap the Bookmarks icon, and select "Add to Shared Links."

The last button looks like a box on top of a transparent box.

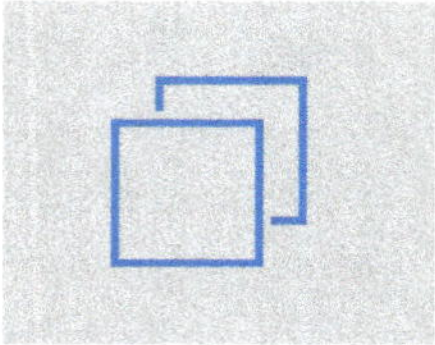

If you use a computer or an iPad; then you probably know all about tabs. Apple decided to not use tabs on Safari. Tabs are there in another way though, that's what this button is; it lets you have several windows open at the same time. When you press it, a new window appears. There's an option to open a new page. Additionally, you can toggle between the pages that you already have opened. Hitting the 'x' will also close a page that you have opened. Hit done to go back to normal browsing.

The iCloud option (the cloud at the bottom) is something you'll want to pay attention to if you use another Apple device (like an iPad, an iPod Touch or a Mac computer). Your Safari browsing is automatically synced; so, if you are browsing a page on your iPad, you can pick up where you left off on your iPhone.

When you put your phone in landscape (i.e. you turn it sideways), the browser also turns, and you will now have the option to use full screen mode. It looks similar, but there's now a '+' button—that lets you open a new Tab.

You can have tabs in both modes, but in full screen you see the tabs on top.

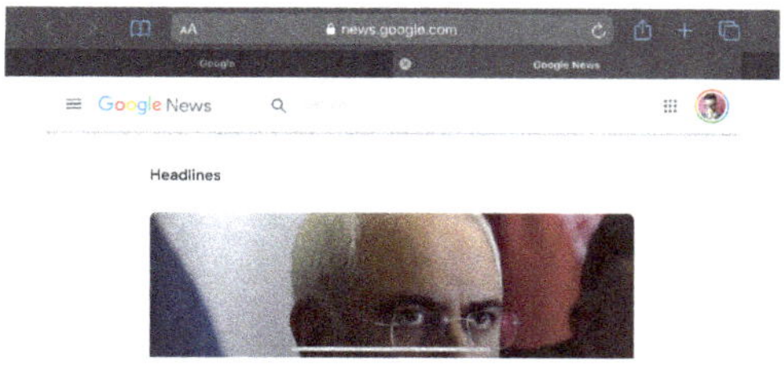

In portrait mode, tabs are seen by tapping the two transparent boxes in the lower right corner.

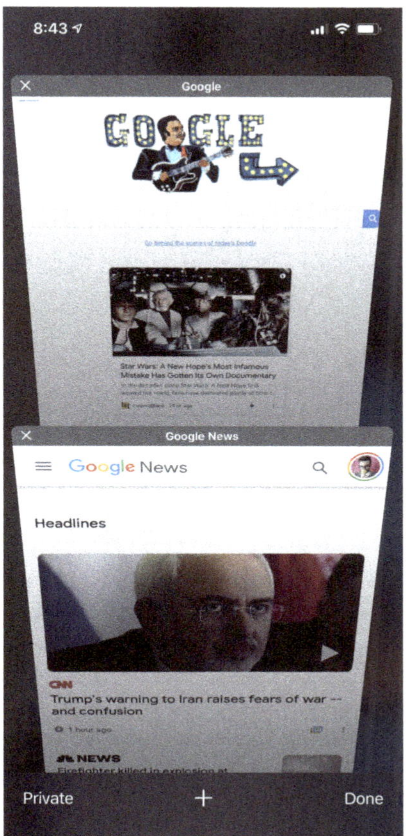

If you hate closing tabs, your life got easier in iOS. You can have all tabs automatically close after a set period of time.

Go to Settings > Safari > Close Tabs and select if you want to do it Manually, After One Day, After One Week, or After One Month.

Tab Group

Tabs can be your best friend. Tab Group is the evolution of this friend. Tab Groups are kind of a combination of bookmarks and tabs. You basically save all your tabs into a group. So, for example, you can have a group called "Shopping" and when you click it, like magic, all your favorite shopping websites open into tabs.

To get started, tap the icon on the bottom right (the two stacked pages), then tap the arrow next to tab.

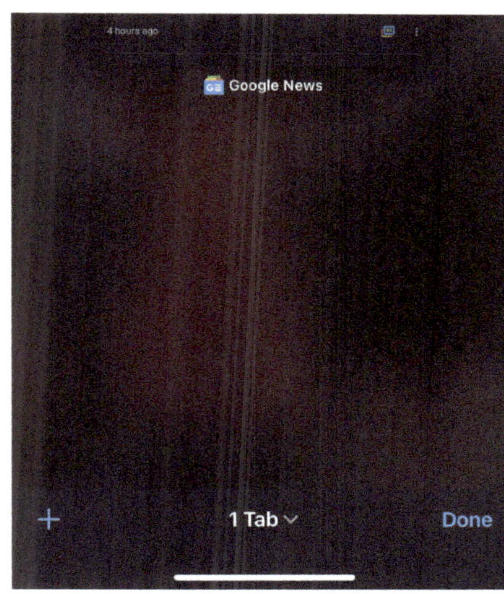

This will show you other tabs you have opened as well as any tab group that can be opened. You'll see I have created a shopping tab group and a news tab group—tapping these immediately opens anything in that group. To put the current page into a group, just tap New Tab Group from 1 Tab—want several pages in that group? Open all the pages now, then save them as a group.

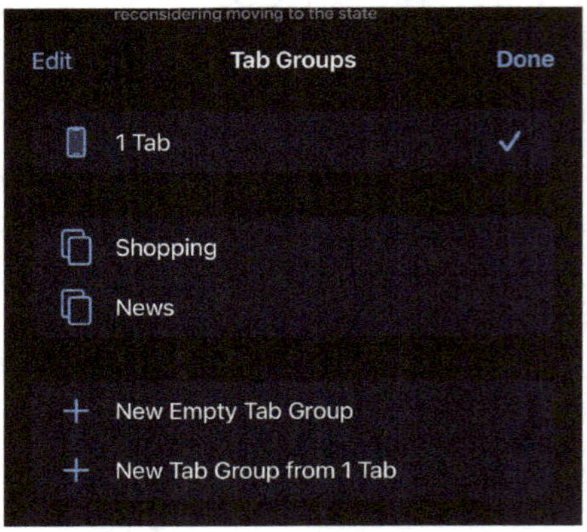

Next, give your group a name.

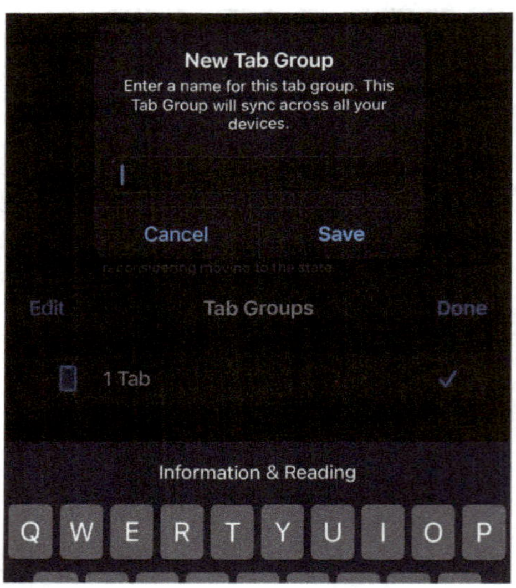

When you open a group, you can see previews of all tabs in that group; just tap the page you want to go into.

Set Your Default Email / Web Browser

For a number of years, you were able to use other Mail and Web browsers in iOS, but you could not set it as a default. This changed in iOS 15...kind of. You can now have alternative default browsers and email clients, but the app has to be updated.

It's the developers (not Apple's) responsibility to update the app to take advantage of this feature; so when you try and change it using the steps below, and you don't see your preferred app, it's probably because either they haven't updated the app yet or you haven't updated the app yet (go to the App Store and make sure there's not an update for the app).

To change your preferred app, go to the Settings app. Next, go to the app you want to make the default (I'm using the Chrome browser in the example below); next, tap Default Browser.

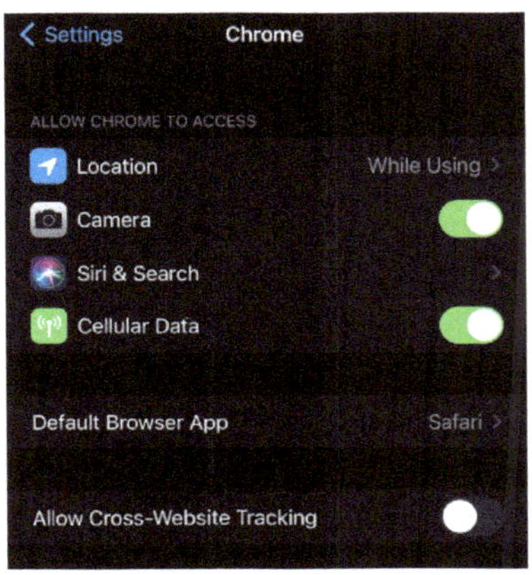

Finally, check off your preferred browser. It saves automatically.

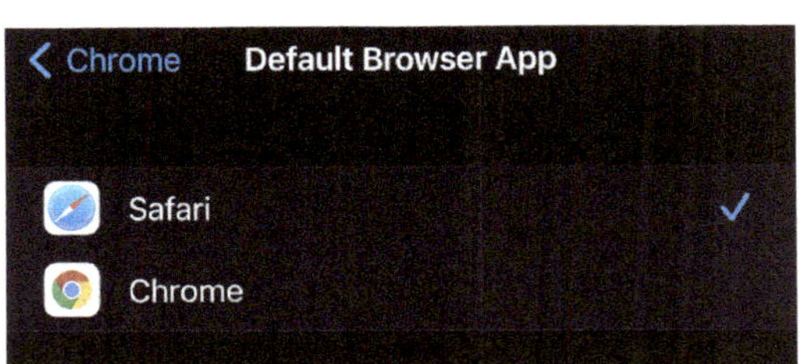

Privacy

Apple has always been proactive on user privacy. When you use Safari it will warn you if there's been a data breach on a website and if you should consider changing your password. It will also give you the option of hiding your email when you are shopping through Safari. When it sees someone is asking for an email, it will ask if you want to hide your email; if you say yes, then it will generate a unique, random, email address; any email you get from the company to that email will be forwarded to you. So you get mail from the company, but they don't know your real address.

The Privacy heading in Settings lets you know what apps are doing with your data. Every app you've allowed to use Location Services will show up under Location Services (and you can toggle Location Services off and on for individual apps or for your whole device here as well). You can also go through your apps to check what information each one is receiving and transmitting.

When you are using any app that is using either the camera or microphone, you will now see a green indicator just above your cellular signal bar.

Compromised Password

Data breaches are pretty common these days; Apple is doing its part to be transparent about when they happen and help you fix it before it's a problem.

Go to the Settings app, then scroll until you get to Passwords.

Within this area (which is password protected) you can see all your stored passwords, but under Security Recommendations, you can also see if your password "may" have been compromised. I say "may" because this does not mean you have been hacked. It just means some data from a company was taken, and you might be on that list because you've had an account there in the past.

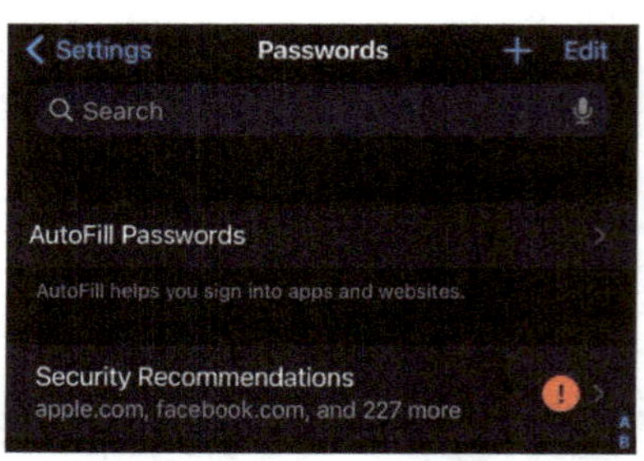

When you click the recommendations, it will take you one by one to each possible breach and show you why it's making the recommendation. In the example below, it says Apple had a breach and they are suggesting I change my password.

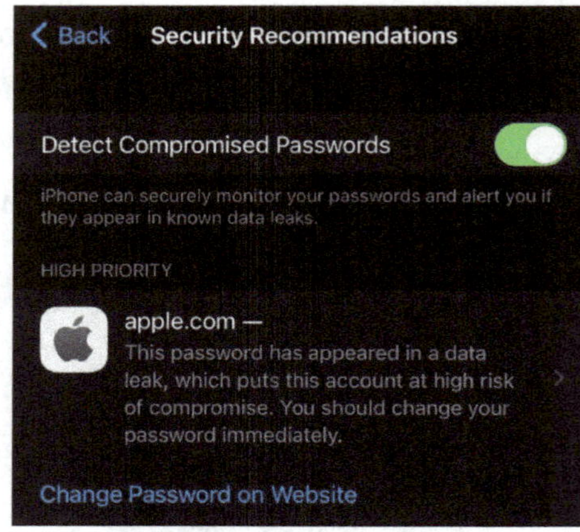

I can tap the Change Password on Website to change the password, or I can click the message to read a little more about it. In the example below, it's saying that it noticed I used the same password on another website, so I should change that one as well.

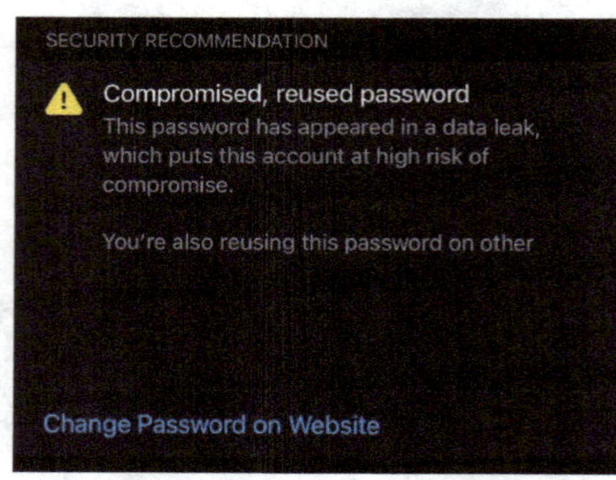

Privacy Report

In Safari, you can tap the AA icon next to the web address to see a Privacy Report.

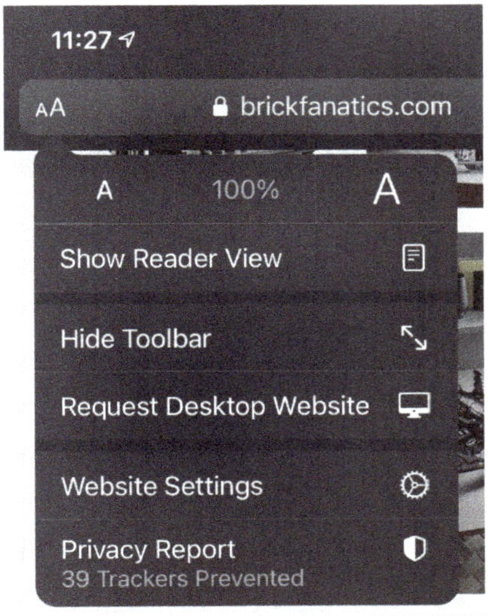

The Privacy Report will tell me more about trackers that have been trying to follow me. A tracker is basically a little code embedded in a website to follow what I do. For example, it tells Facebook that I've visited a website about Legos, so it should start showing me Lego ads. Creepy, right?!

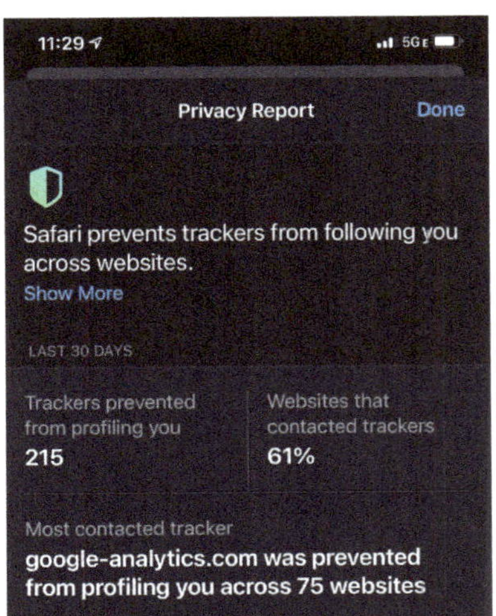

Location Sharing

Within each app is a series of privacy tools about what they can and can't see. One of the most common is your location. In the example below, I have gone to the Settings app, then selected Maps. From here, I tap on Location.

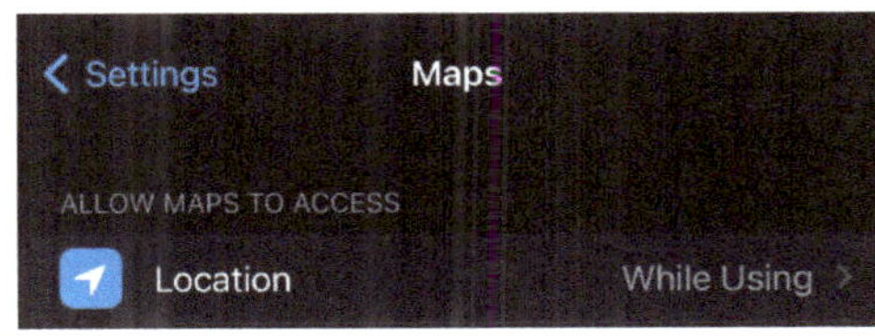

Because it's a map, I want it to know my location, but I have the option to select when it can grab that location. There's also a toggle to let it see your precise location. Turning it off, shows that app approximately where you are.

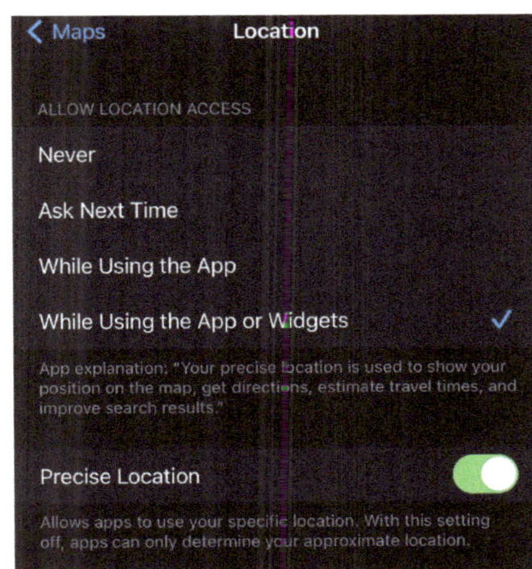

ITUNES

The iTunes app found on your Home screen opens the biggest digital music store in the world. You will be able to purchase and download not just music, but also countless movies, TV shows, audiobooks, and more. On the iTunes home page, you can also find a What's Hot section, collections of music, and new releases.

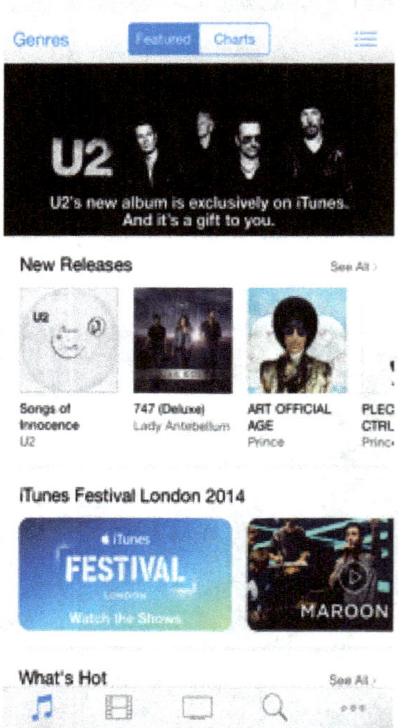

At the top, you will see the option to view either featured media or browse through the top charts. On the upper left corner is the Genres button. Clicking "Genres" will bring up many different types of music to help refine your search.

DYNAMIC ISLAND

If you have the iPhone 14 Pro, then the most noticeable feature is the dynamic island. Unfortunately, regular iPhones do not have this feature. You've probably noticed it even if you aren't sure what it does.

The Dynamic Island is kind of like a shortcut bar. It lets you see apps (like music and timers) that might be running in the background. In the example below, a song is playing on my phone, so the bar shows a very small cover as well as an audio playing icon.

If I press the island, the Music app launches; if I tap and hold on the island, then a preview of the music shows.

But what if you have two apps running in the background? A timer and music, for example? The island won't leave you marooned! It will show both apps—see the example below.

If I were to open the music app, that app would leave the island and it would just show the timer.

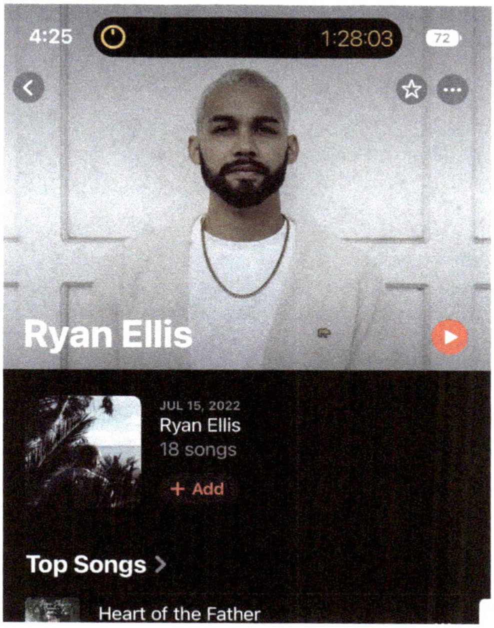

If I stop the music, then only the timer would show when I close the app.

Crash Detection

Should the unthinkable happen and you are in a car accident (a major one—on a "I backed into a trash can one"), your phone can alert first responders to help you.

The way it works is an alert will display on your phone saying that it has detected a car accident; if you don't respond within 20 seconds and cancel it, the iPhone will call emergency services.

By default, Crash Detection should already be on (as long as your phone supports it), but you can double check by going to Settings > Emergency SOS, and then turning on / off Call After Severe Crash.

Buying Apps

So how do you buy, download and finally remove apps? I'll look at that in this section.

To purchase apps (and I don't actually mean paying for them because you can purchase a free app without paying for it):

The first thing you see when you open the App Store is the Today screen.

This is a little different than the App Store you may be familiar with from older OS's. Apple gave it a more magazine look where you discover apps based on editor-curated lists.

The bottom has tabs to discover games, apps, arcade (a new Apple service), and search for apps. If you want to see app categories, then go to Apps and scroll a little. See All will show you all.

To update apps, you used to tap on the last tab, which would say update. That option is gone. The easiest way to update apps is to have the auto update option turned on at setup. To manually update an app, or see if it was recently updated, tap your avatar photo in the upper right corner. This brings up your account information and updates available (if it says "open" that means it was recently updated; if it says "update" that means there's an update available).

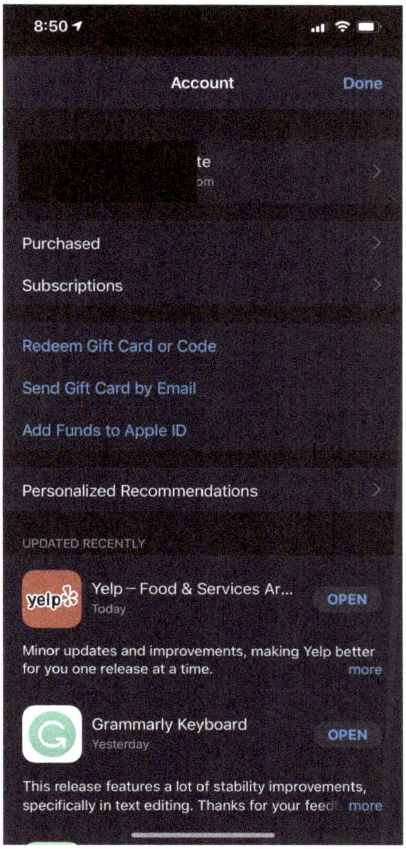

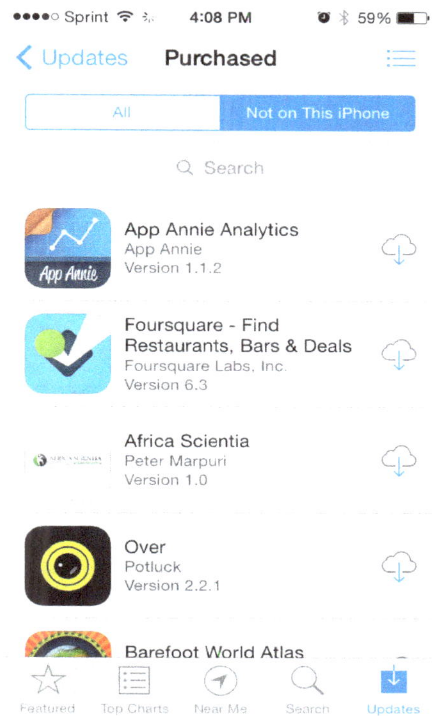

If you bought an app, but accidentally deleted it, or changed your mind about deleting it, don't worry! You can download the app again in the same place that you see the updates. Just tap on "Purchased."

When you tap the Purchased button, you will see two options: one is to see all the apps you have purchased, and one to see just the apps that you have purchased but are not on your phone. Tap the one that says "Not on This iPhone" to re-download anything, at no cost. Just tap the Cloud button to the right of the screen. You can even download it again if you bought it on another iPhone as long as it's under the same account.

Deleting apps is easy; on your Home screen, tap and hold the icon of the app you want to remove, then tap the 'x' on top of the app.

Picture-In-Picture

I was so excited when I heard about Picture-in-Picture on the iPhone; it's been on the iPad for a while, and it's a great feature. Finally, I can watch movies while surfing the Internet! It's like Apple knew I'd want to look up an actor on Wikipedia as I watched the movie, right?

To use it, just have your video running in full screen, and then swipe up from the bottom. That's going to pop it out. This also works when you are using Facetime. So you can search the Internet or play a game while you are using FaceTime to talk to someone. How personal, right?!

The problem with Picture-in-Picture is it's not entirely supported. When it came out, for example, YouTube wasn't compatible. YouTube! It's how most of us watch videos, these days!

There's a workaround, however. While it is not compatible with some video streamers, it is compatible with Safari. See the example below? The video is playing within Safari.

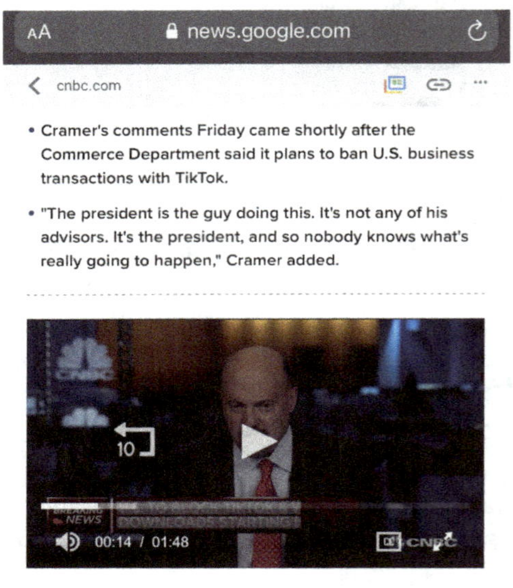

If I make that video play full screen and then swipe up from the bottom, then it goes PiP. If I were to watch that video on a native app (like YouTube), then it may not be supported. It's not the perfect solution, but it is a workaround until more apps support the mode.

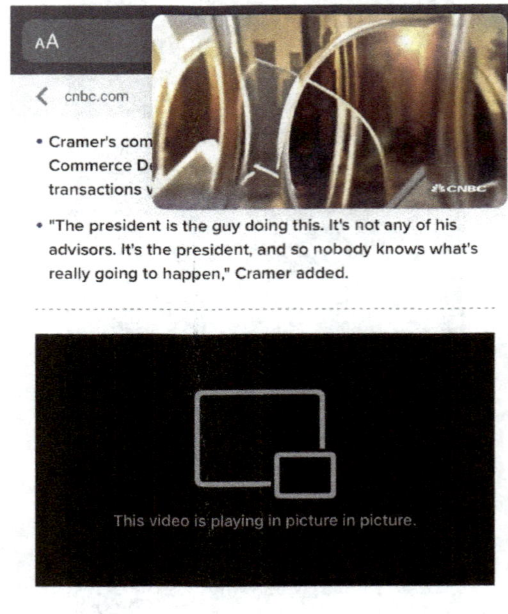

Calendar

Among the other pre-installed apps that came with your new iPhone, perhaps one of the most used apps you'll encounter is the Calendar. You can switch between viewing appointments, tasks, or everything laid out in a one-day, one-week, or one-month view. Turn your phone on its side and you will notice everything switch to landscape mode. A first for the iPhone, many new apps now take advantage of the larger iPhone's 1080p resolution by displaying more information at once, similar to the iPad and iPad mini display. Combine your calendar with email accounts or iCloud to keep your appointments and tasks synced across all of your devices, and never miss another appointment.

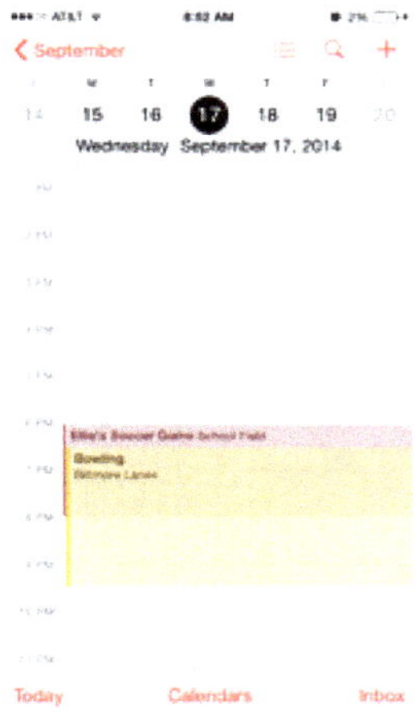

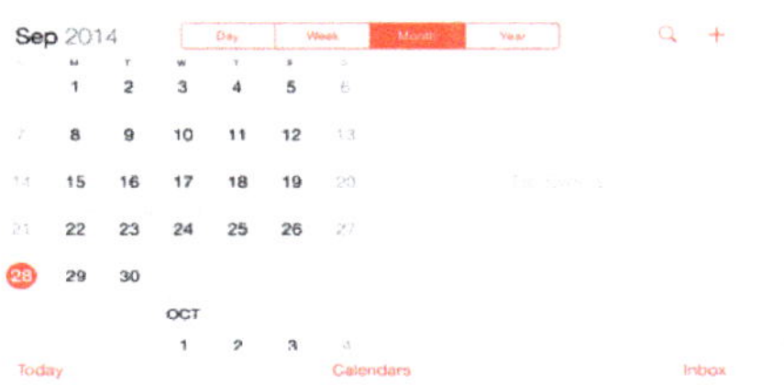

Creating an Appointment

To create an appointment, click on the Calendar icon on your Home screen. Click on whichever day you would like to set the appointment for, and then tap the '+' button in the corner. Here you will be able to name and edit your event, as well as connect it to an email or iCloud account in order to allow for syncing.

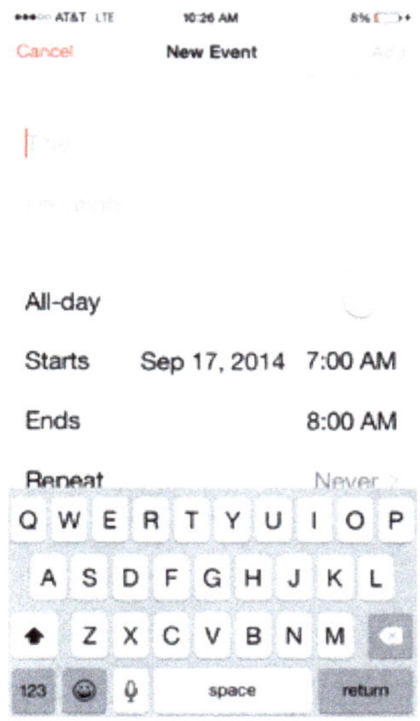

When editing your event, pay special attention to the duration of your event. Select the start and end times, or choose "All Day" if it's an all-day event. You will also have a chance to set it as a recurring event by clicking on "Repeat" and selecting how often you want it to repeat. In the case of a bill or car payment, for example, you could either select Monthly (on this day) or every 30 days, which are two different things. After you select your repetition, you can also choose how long you'd like that event to repeat itself: for just one month, a year, forever, and everything in between.

A recent update to Calendar now let's you include attachments to your appointments; you can add an attachment by selecting "Add Attachment" at the bottom of the New Event screen.

Battery

If you are like a lot of people, that little battery indicator up in the right corner is nice, but it can get a little vague. It's hard to tell by the battery indicator if your battery is at 10% or 5%, for example.

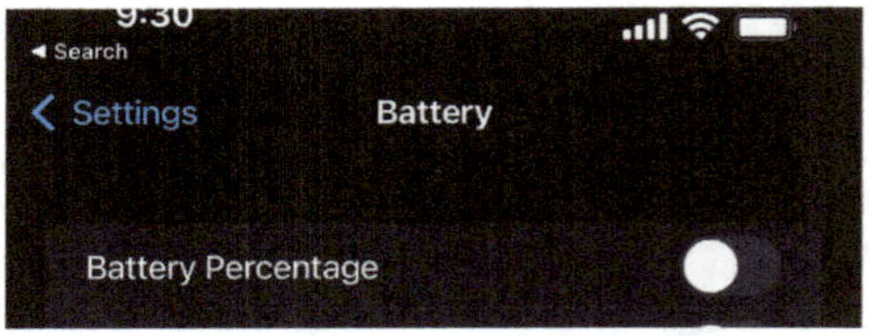

If you prefer to see a visual number that tells you how much battery you have, go to Settings > Battery, and toggle on the Battery Percentage option.

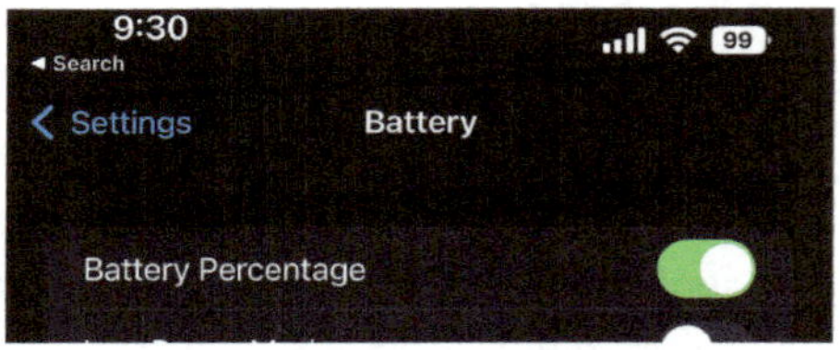

Weather

The weather app has been around for years, but iOS 16 gave it some big enhancements. It's no longer just an app to get the weather. It's an app to get precise details about the weather.

When you click on a specific day, it will give you an hourly forecast, so you can plan your day.

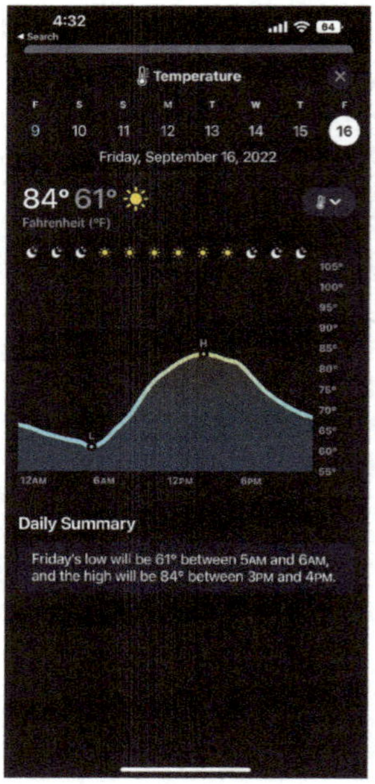

Clicking the dropdown on the right side lets you see not only the temperature, but the UV index, humidity, what the weather feels like, and more.

When you return to the main weather screen, you can also click the map to see where things like rain are occurring.

MAPS

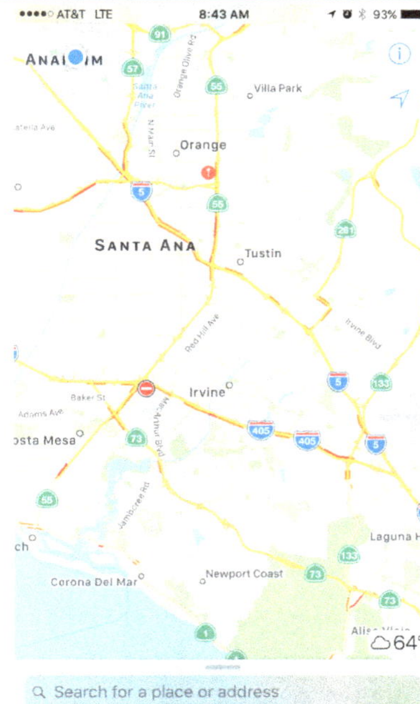

The Maps app is back and better than ever. After Apple parted ways with Google Maps several years ago, Apple decided to develop its own, made-for-iPhone map and navigation system. The result is a beautiful travel guide that takes full advantage of the newest iPhone resolutions. Full screen mode allows every corner of the phone to be filled with the app, and there's an automatic night mode. You'll be able to search for places, restaurants, gas stations, concert halls, and other venues near you at any time, and turn-by-turn navigation is available for walking, biking, driving, or commuting. Traffic is updated in real time, so if an accident occurs ahead of you or there is construction going on, Maps will offer a faster alternative and warn you of the potential traffic jam.

The turn-by-turn navigation is easy to understand without being distracting, and the 3D view makes potentially difficult scenarios (like highway exits that come up abruptly) much more pleasant. Another convenient feature is the ability to avoid highways and toll roads entirely.

To set up navigation, tap on the Maps icon. On the bottom of the screen is a search for place or address; for homes you need an address, but businesses just need a name. Click on it and enter your destination once prompted.

When you find your destination's address, click on "Route," and choose between walking or driving directions. For businesses, you also have the option of reading reviews and calling the company directly.

For hands-free navigation, press and hold the Side button to enable Siri (which will be discussed in the next section) and say, "Navigate to…" or "Take me to…" followed by the address or name of the location that you'd like to go to.

If you'd like to avoid highways or tolls, simply tap the More Options button and select the option that you want.

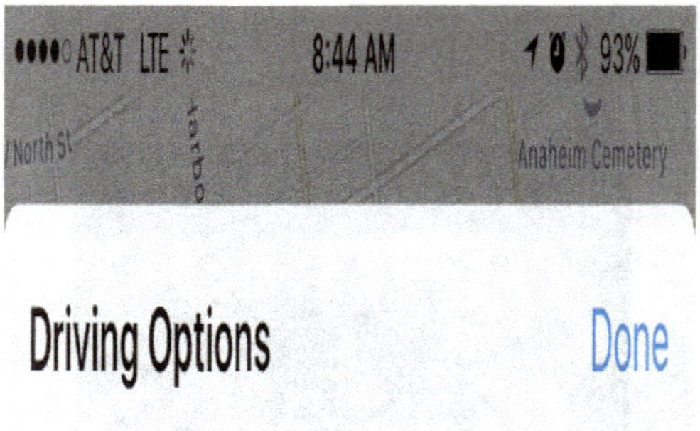

Apple Maps also lets you see a 3D view of thousands of locations. To enable this option, tap the 'i' in the upper right corner. After this, select satellite view.

If 3D view is available you'll notice a change immediately. You can use two fingers to make your map more or less flat. You can also select 2D to remove 3D altogether.

Switch back to the normal map and you will see a little magnifying glass in the upper right corner.

Google has Street View, Apple Map now has a competitor called Look Around (hint, you have to zoom in a little to see it). You won't see this option in every city yet, but you probably will soon. With Look Around on, you can drag the magnifying glass anywhere you want to see a ground view.

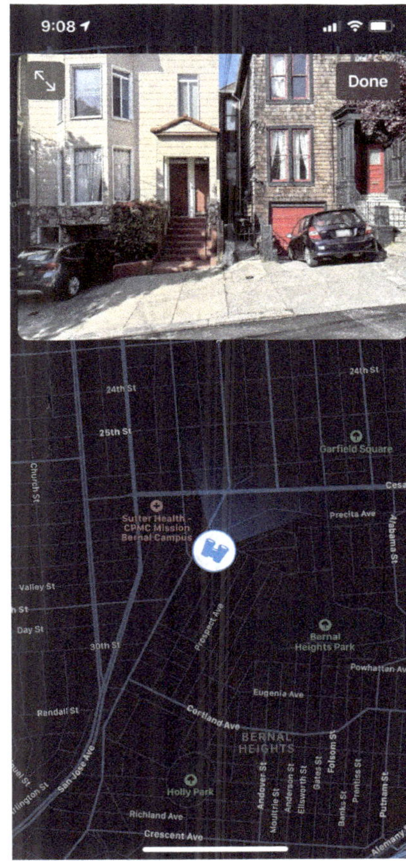

When you tap inside the search bar, you'll also notice two newer areas:

Favorites—which are just places you frequently go.

Collections—this is where you can create several locations and group them together. So, for example, you might be planning a trip to Europe; you could create a list of all the places you want to see in a collection and jump to them when you are in the city.

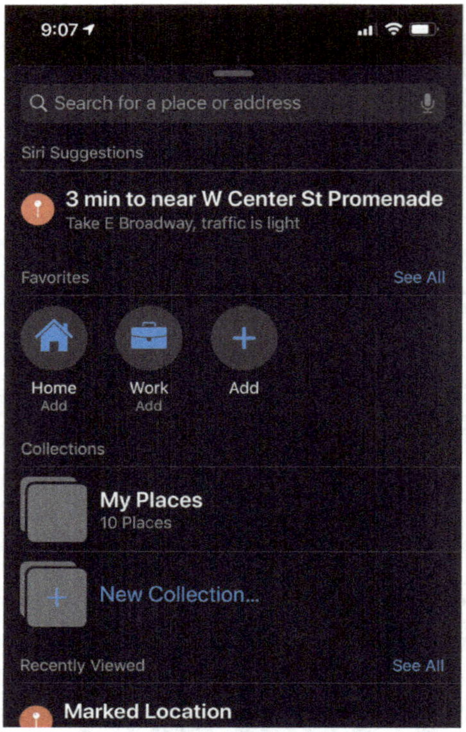

Maps interface has looked pretty similar for several years, but it did get a feature improvement in iOS 15. When you zoom into roads (and this is only in some areas—mostly big metro cities), the lanes will now appear. This doesn't sound like a lot, but if you are like many and drive in places like Los Angeles, freeways can get very complicated—merging on and off a freeway is sometimes on the left and sometimes on the right. The level of detail can help you be better prepared. It will also show you biking lanes (when available). Finally, walking directions have a look around mode, so you can see landmarks as you walk and have a better feel for if you are going the right way—but, again, look around mode is not available everywhere.

Directions

Maps has several choices when you are getting directions: car, walk, public transportation, cycle, or ride share.

The directions will be changed based on what you pick; if you pick cycle, for example, the time will change and it may also give you a path that a car cannot travel on.

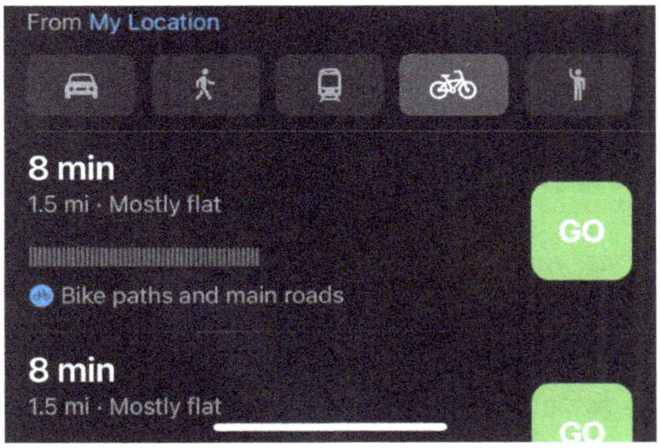

MAPS (MULTIPLE STOPS)

Getting directions is nice, but you probably often like to make a few stops along the way. You can add multiple stops if that's the case.

Let's say I want to figure out how to get my kid to an amusement park from the location I'm staying. I type in the name of the park, then tap directions.

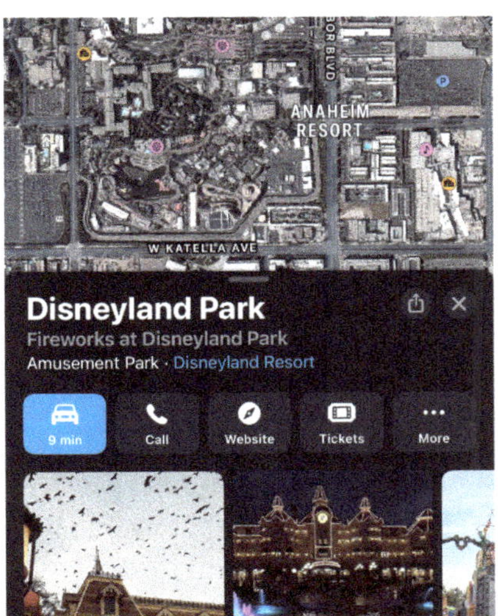

Easy, peasy, right! But, oh, no! I just got in the car and I'm out of gas! That's no problem with maps. I just tap the Add Stop button.

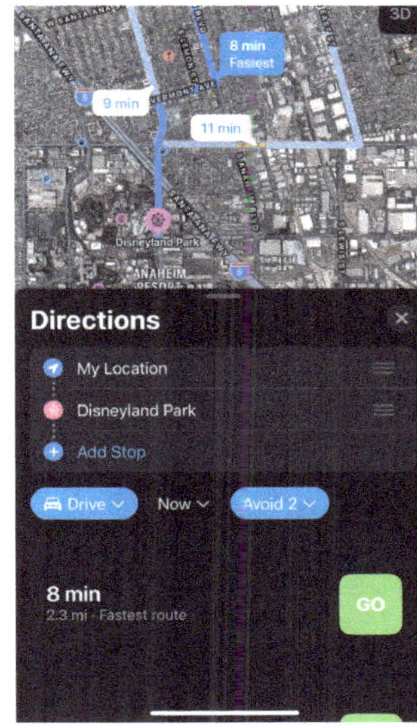

Next, I type in the address, or, in this case, just type in "Gas." That's going to give me all the nearby gas stations. When I see the one I want, I just tap Add.

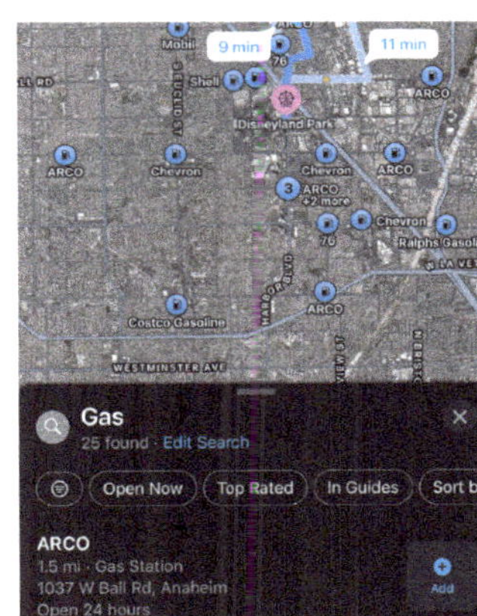

Now the stop has been added into the directions—but with a caveat: it's added to the end. You can easily move the order of stops, however, by tapping and holding on the three lines to the right of the stop, then dragging it up or down to the order you want it.

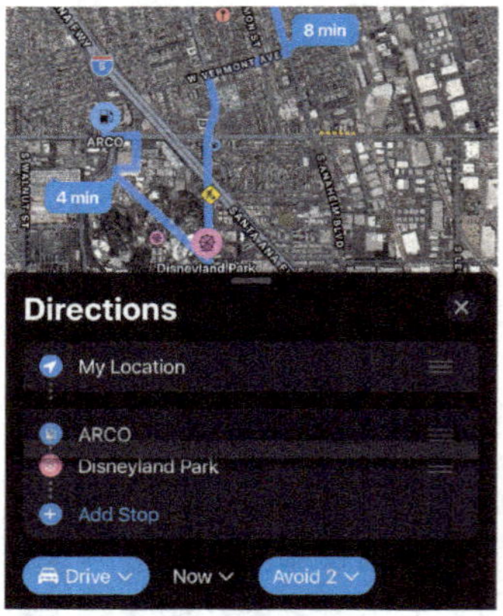

What if the kids are also saying they're hungry?! You don't want to pay amusement park prices for breakfast, do you?! Just tap Add Stop again. Now I have a map to get to the donut place, a gas station, and finally the amusement park.

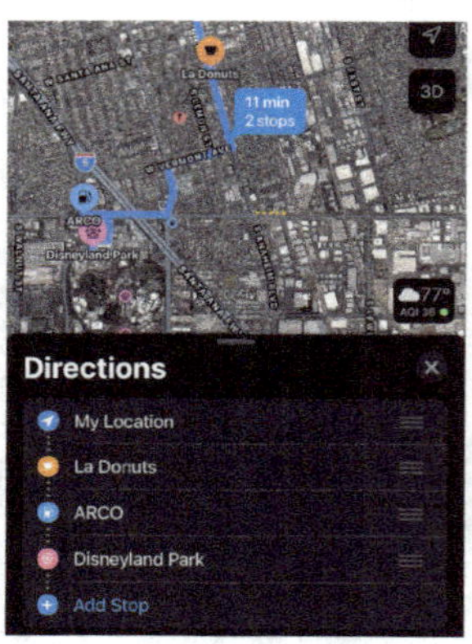

Map Guides

Map Guides are only available in larger cities. When you search for a city in the Map app, you will see the guides right under the directions button. You can also share the guide or save it.

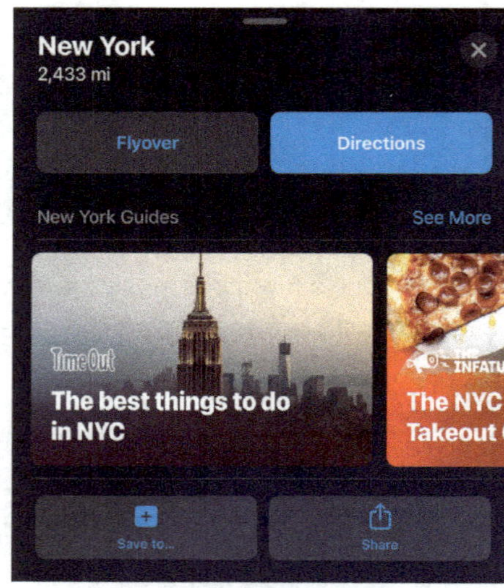

As you look at the guides, it will show you recommendations on the map, and you can save them for later.

HEALTH

The release of the latest iPhone models brought with it a much greater focus on one's health, and as such, the new iPhones come with the Health app. The Health app keeps track of many different things pertaining to your health, including calories burned, your weight, heart rate, body measurements, and even an emergency card that lets you store important health information such as your blood type and allergies in the event of an emergency. iOS 13 also added a cycle tracker.

Health is something that's always been important to Apple; if you have an Apple Watch, the Health app works especially well because they sync together and it keeps track of things like ECG (depending on the watch you have). It's also a great place to go to remind me how much I really need to walk more!

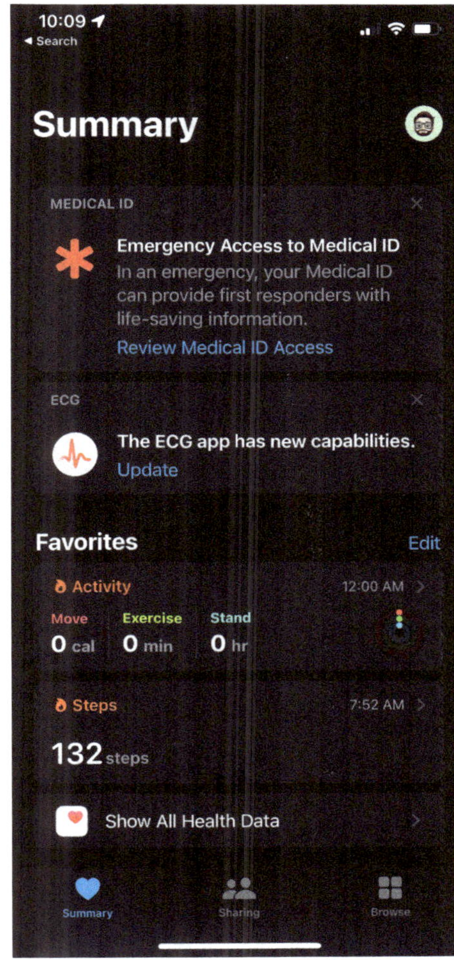

Seeing your health may be encouraging, but where it really is helpful is when you can share it with your loved ones, and even your doctor. You can do this by tapping on the sharing icon on the bottom middle of the app. If you want to share it with loved ones, tap "Share With Someone." If you want to share it with your doctor, tap "Share with your doctor." Not all doctors will support this—it's up to them to do this; also, make sure whoever you are sharing it with has updated their phone to iOS 15 or higher.

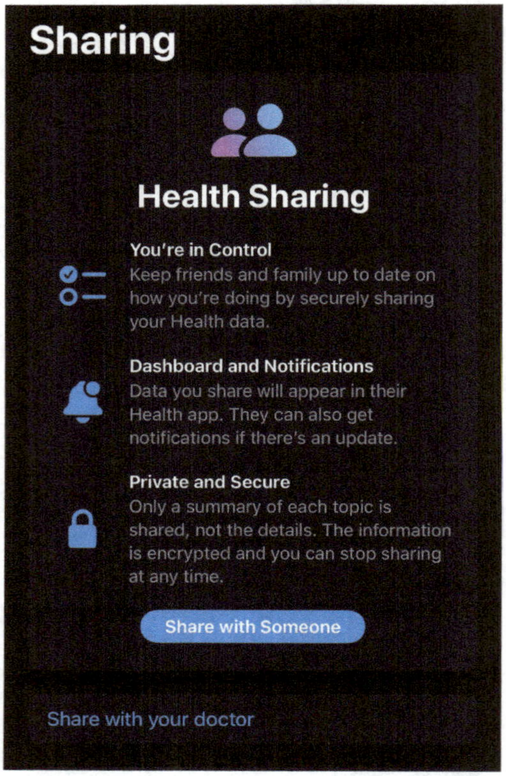

Find My

If you used Find My Phone or Find My Friend on previous OS's, then shocker: they're gone! These two powerful apps let you see where your friends were on a map or where your devices were on a map.

They're essentially the same app with a different purpose; so instead of keeping both, Apple decided to delete them and combine them into one app called Find My.

The app is pretty simple. Three tabs on the bottom. One to find your friends (i.e. People), one to find your devices, and one to change settings (i.e. Me).

If you want to see where your friend is at, ask them to share their location with you in the People section.

It's not very helpful using an app to find your iPhone if you don't have your iPhone. If that's the case, you can also use your computer browser to see it at iCloud.com.

Reminders

The Reminders App has been on iOS for a long time; in iOS 13, however, the app got a facelift. Creating lists is now more visual, intuitive, and it's now easier to share and collaborate.

To get started, tap the Reminders icon.

Creating a list is still very simple. Tap Add List from the lower right corner of your screen.

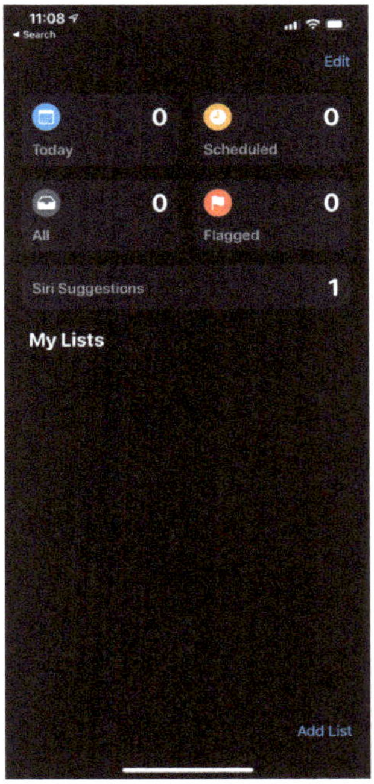

Once you create a list, you can change the color of the icon that represents the list, and rename the list; tap Done to save it.

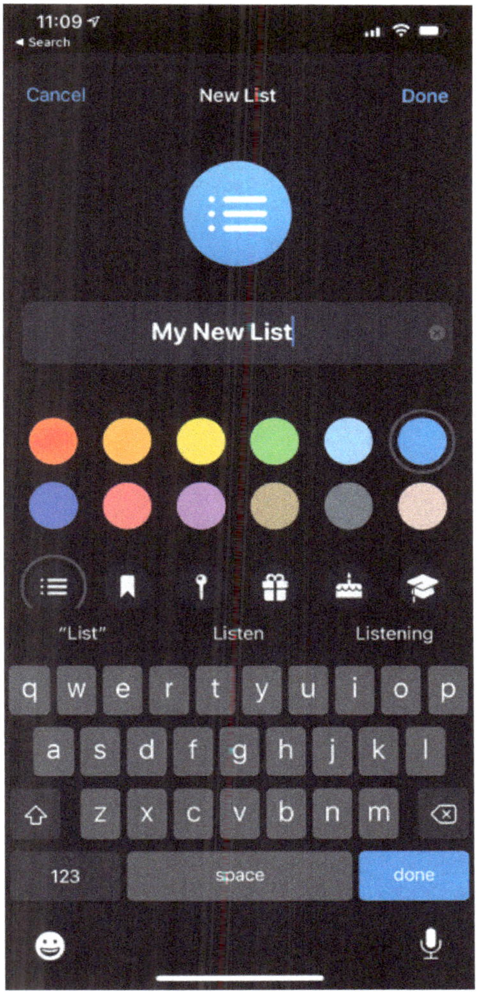

Once you create your first list, you can start adding to it by tapping Add Reminders from the bottom left corner of the screen.

Tap Return on your keyboard to add another item, or Done when you have added everything (you can add more later).

If you tap the i at any point, you'll be able to add more details (such as a due date or even what location to remind you at—you could, for example, have it remind you when you get to the grocery store).

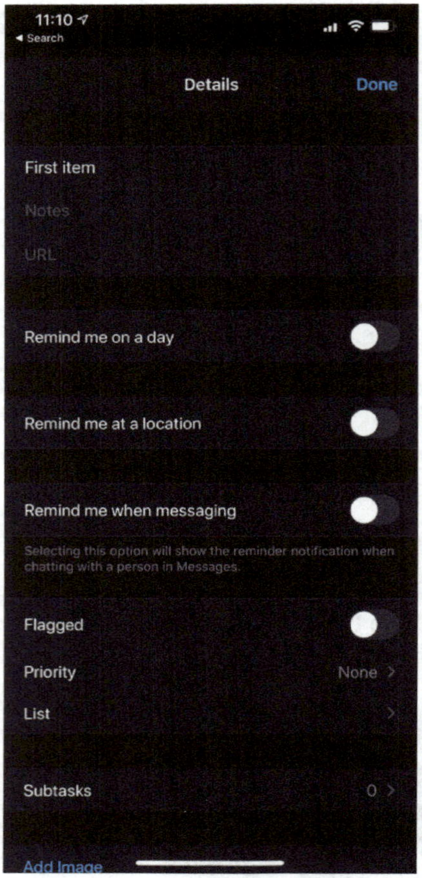

Tapping on the three dots in the upper right corner brings up additional list options. In addition to changing things like the name, you can add people to the list so they can collaborate and add things of their own.

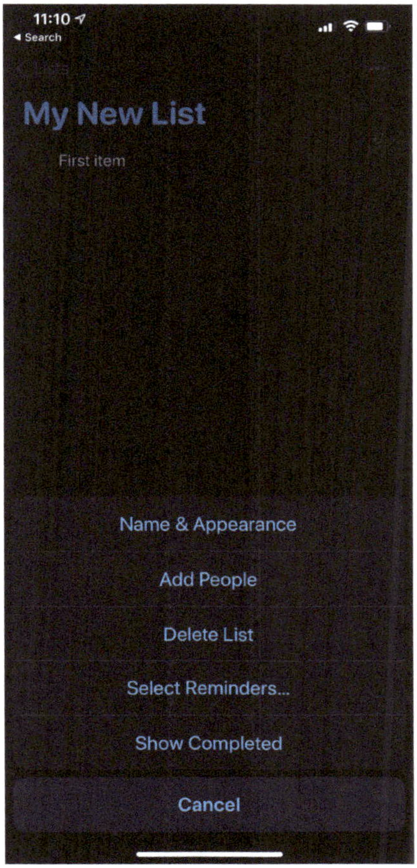

To remove or flag a list item, just swipe over it to the left.

Swiping to the list on the previous screen will also let you delete an entire list.

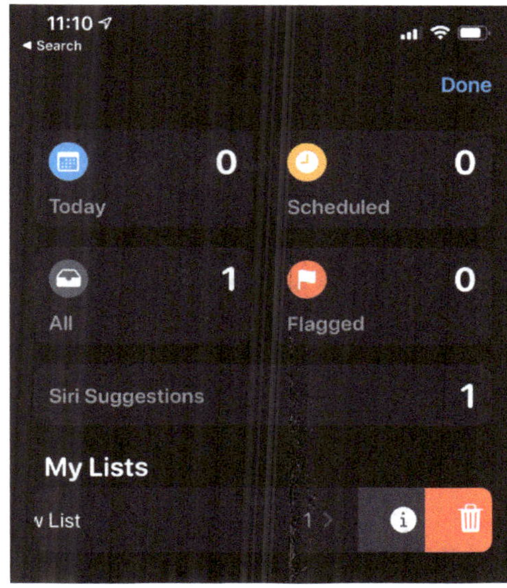

From the main list menu, you can select Edit in the upper right corner and organize the order of your lists.

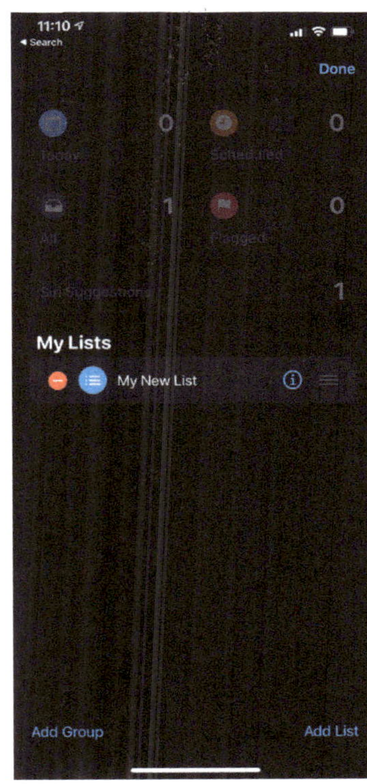

In this edit mode, you can also select Add Group and group different lists together.

Home

The Home app integrates HomeKit with iOS to help you better integrate all your home appliances and utilities, like lights, thermostats, refrigerators, and more. HomeKit uses Siri to control all of your smart home devices, which is a pretty handy tool, and the Home interface allows for a much cleaner and straightforward experience. To add your smart home device to Home, simply stand next to it with its power on and your Home app enabled. You can also use your 4th generation Apple TV to control HomeKit-enabled smart home devices. HomePod is something else that is housed here.

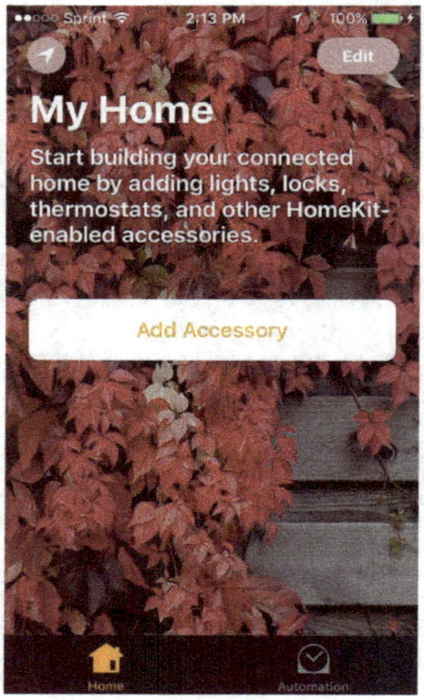

ARKit

iPhone is all about augmented reality; they see this as the future. Many new apps have AR support.

ARKit for iOS 12 introduced a new measurements tool. That's still there in iOS 15.

To use the new measurements tool, open the Measure app. Point your camera at a rectangle option, and watch a box automatically form over it.

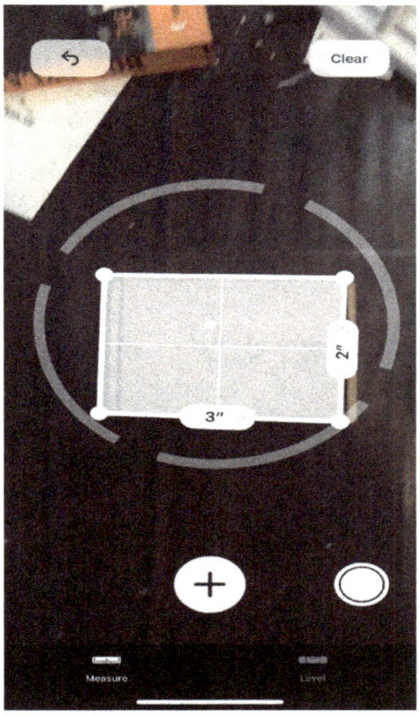

The app will tell you how long something is, and also allow you to add points, so you can measure it as well.

Apple Translate

Google pioneered the idea of translating what someone says in real-time, but Apple is now trying to improve it.

Added in iOS 15 is a translation app made by Apple. There are over a dozen languages and dialects built in. You can even download the dictionaries, so you can translate without Wi-Fi.

If you've used Google Translate, the UI will probably look similar to you. Tap the microphone and start talking. It autodetects the language, so if you are in a store and they speak a different language, then hold it up to them and press the mic. That's it.

If you want to select either the language you want it translated to or the language being spoken, then just tap that language. This will bring up a list of available languages. Tap the one you want—you can also tap the icon with the down arrow that's circled to download the language. If it's not downloaded, then it will translate using Wi-Fi or data. It's kind of like Siri—it sends it to a computer in the cloud that translates it and then sends it back. It only takes a few seconds.

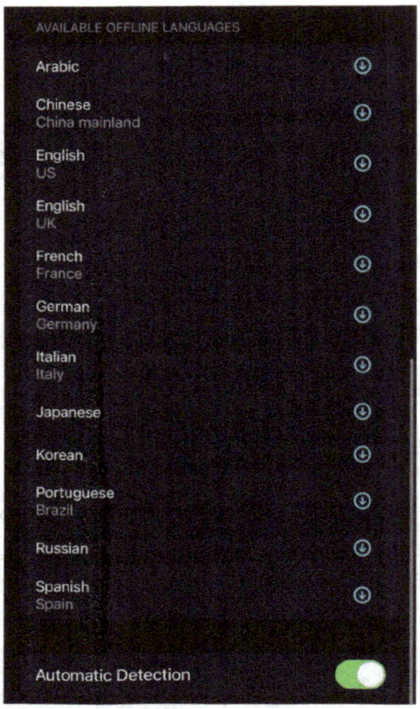

App Clips

App Clips are kind of like mini apps—or lite versions of full apps. The benefit of them is you don't have to download the app to use it. Think of those times when you've been at a restaurant or paying for meter parking, and you need an app to redeem something; you know you'll never use the app again, but you still have to download it. Annoying right? That's where an App Clip helps. The way it works is you can now scan a QR code, and if it's supported, an App Clip will launch. The "if it's supported" should be in bold letters here. It's a great feature, but it's not going to work everywhere you see a QR code.

Magnifier

The Magnifier app can be turned on and off by going to the Settings app, then tapping on Accessibility, and Magnifier.

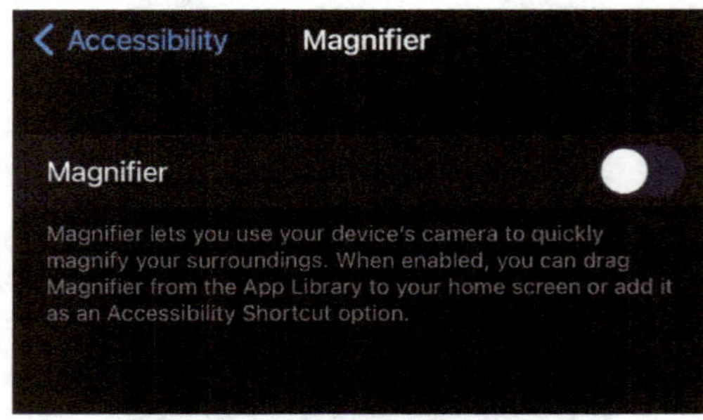

The app goes to your App Library; from there you can drag it out and put it wherever you want on your wallpaper.

When you open the app, it works a little like a camera (in fact, you can use the shutter button to take a picture of what you are looking at); you can adjust the contrast, exposure and more to make it easier to see.

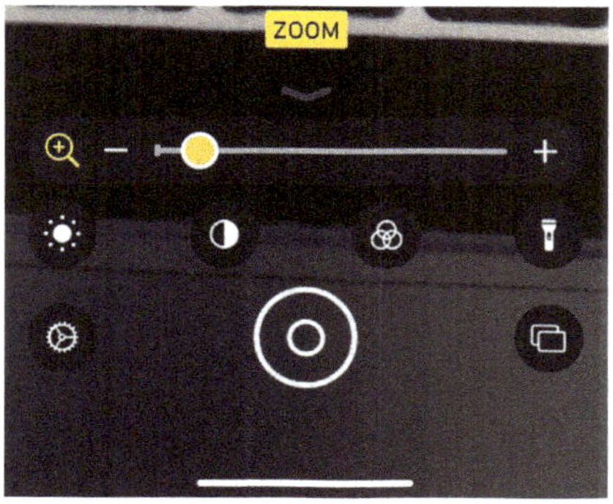

Password Protect Notes

Notes has come a long way since it was first introduced. It's no longer just a place to quickly jot things. It's a place to collaborate, handwrite, and do really complex notetaking. It's understandable that some people might want to password protect what notetaking they're keeping.

If you want to make sure no one gets into your notes, go to Settings > Notes > Password.

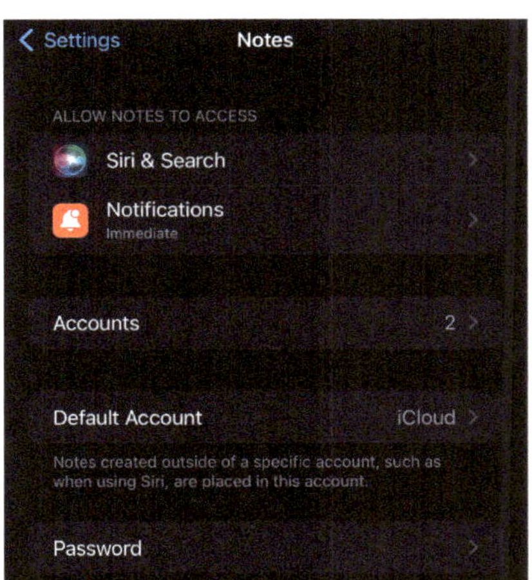

From here select the password option that you want.

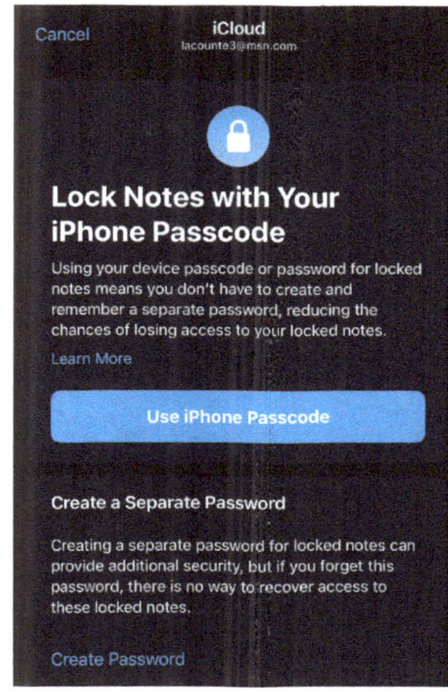

Translate Notes

Notes also lets you translate words, sentences and phrases into different languages. Just type your sentence, then highlight it, and select the translate option.

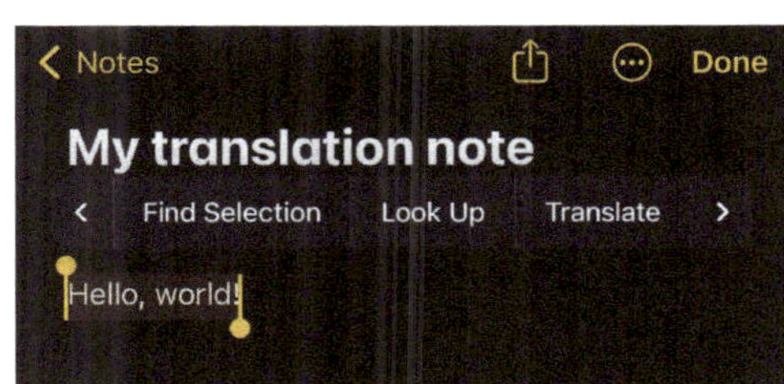

From here it will show you what it looks like translated—and also let you play what it sounds like. Tap the Replace with Translation and it will replace it.

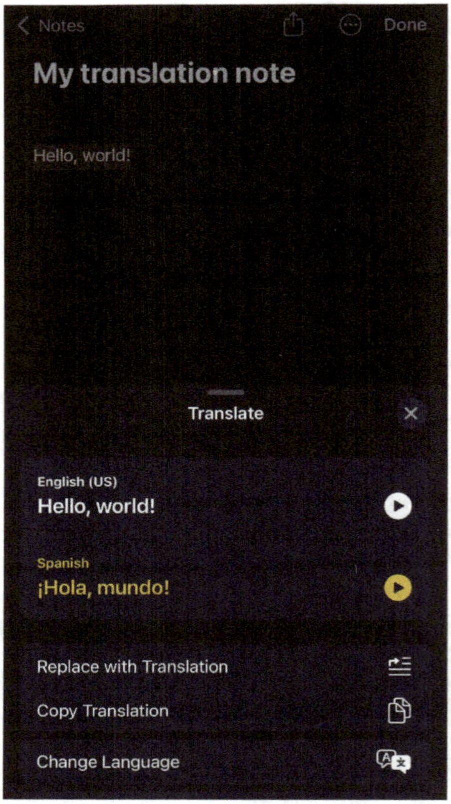

Want a different language? Just tap the Change Language button, then select the language you desire.

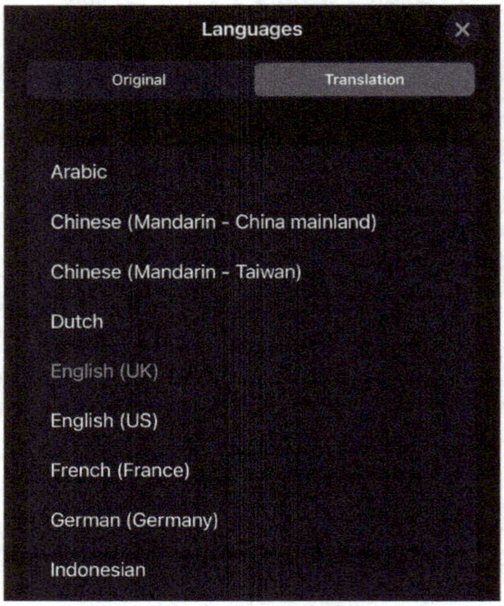

Medications

If you are taking medications, you can use your phone to help you track (and remind you) of when you take it. Just go to the Health app, and select "Browse," then tap on Medications.

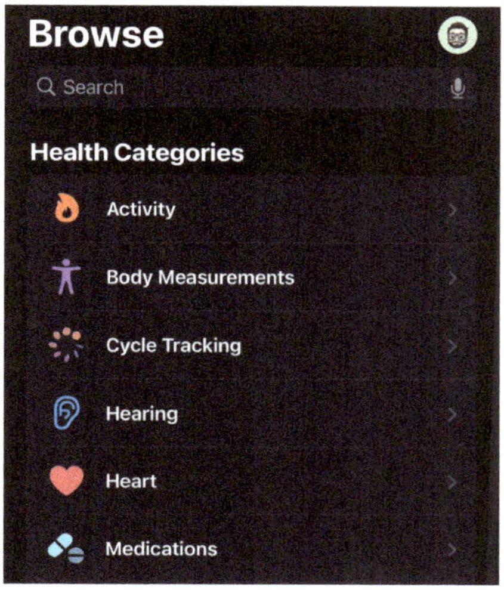

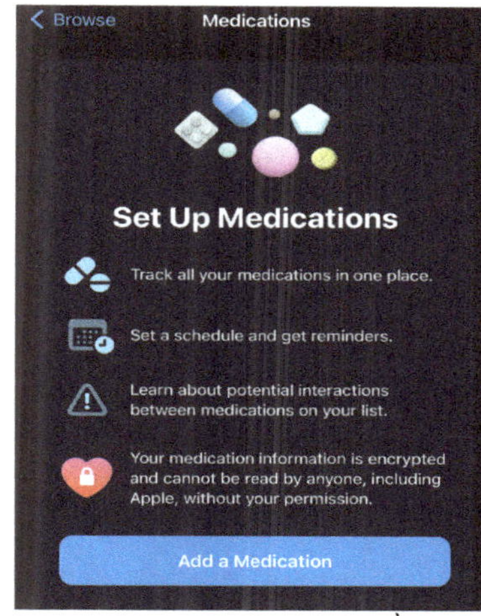

From here, just tap on the blue Add a Medication button.

Chapter 6: Getting Customized

Now that you know your way around, it's time to dig into the settings and make this phone completely custom to you!

For most of this chapter, I'll be hanging out in the Settings area, so if you aren't already there, tap Settings from your Home screen.

Do Not Disturb Mode

Do Not Disturb mode is a handy feature located near the top of your Settings app. When this operational mode is enabled, you won't receive any notifications and all of your calls will be silenced. This is a useful trick for those times when you can't afford to be distracted (and let's face it, your iPhone is as communicative as they come, and sometimes you'll need to have some peace and quiet!). Clock alarms will still sound.

To turn on, schedule and customize Do Not Disturb, just tap on "Do Not Disturb" in Settings. You can schedule automatic times to activate this feature, like your work hours, for example. You can also specify certain callers who should be allowed when your phone is set to Do Not Disturb. This way your mother can still get through, but you won't have to hear every incoming email. To do this, use the Allow Call From command in Do Not Disturb settings.

Do Not Disturb is also accessible through the Control Center (swipe down from the upper right corner of the screen to access it at any time).

Notifications and Widgets

Notifications are one of the most useful features on the iPhone, but chances are you won't need to be informed of every single event that's set as a default in your Notifications Center. To adjust Notifications preferences, go to Settings > Notifications.

By tapping the app, you can turn notifications off or on and finesse the type of notification from each app. It's a good idea to whittle this list down to the apps that you truly want to be notified from—for example, if you're not an investor, turn off Stocks! Reducing the number of sounds your iPhone makes can also reduce phone-related frazzledness. For example, in Mail, you may want your phone to make a sound when you receive email from someone on your VIP list, but to only display badges for other, less important email.

General Settings

The General menu item is a little bit of a catchall. This is where you'll find information about your iPhone, including its current version of iOS and any available software updates. Fortunately, iOS ushers in an era of smaller, more efficient updates, so you won't find yourself scrambling to delete apps in order to make space for the latest improvements.

The Accessibility options are located here as well. You can set your iPhone according to your needs with Zoom, VoiceOver, large text, color adjustment, and more. There are quite a few Accessibility options that can make iOS easy for everyone to use, including Grayscale View and improved Zoom options.

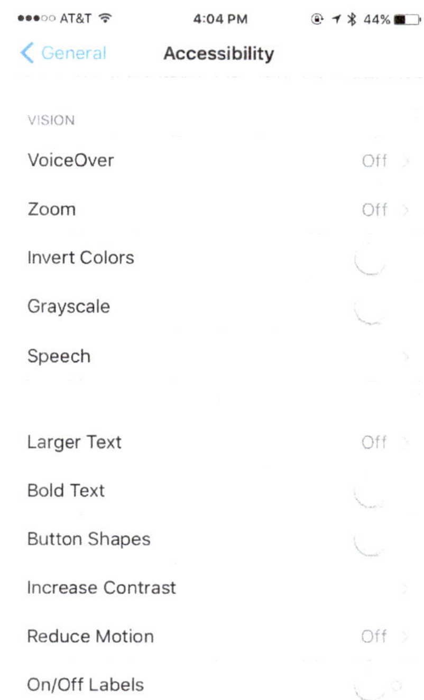

A handy Accessibility option that's a little disguised is the Assistive Touch setting. This gives you a menu that helps you access device-level functions. Enabling it brings up a floating menu designed to help users who have difficulty with screen gestures like swiping, or with manipulating the iPhone's physical buttons. Another feature for those with visual needs is Magnifier. Turning this on allows your camera to magnify things.

I recommend taking some time and tapping through the General area, just so you know where everything is!

Cellular

If you are worried about Data caps, you can change the data settings to reduce the data used. Go to Settings > Cellular > Cellular

Data Options and then check off Low Data Mode.

Sounds

Hate that vibration when your phone rings? Want to change your ring tone? Head to the Sounds Settings menu! Here you can turn vibration on or off and assign ring tones to a number of iPhone functions. I do suggest finding an isolated space before you start trying out all the different sound settings—it's fun, but possibly a major annoyance to those unlucky enough not to be playing with their own new iPhone!

Tip: You can apply individual ringtones and message alerts to your contacts. Just go to the person's contact screen in Contacts, tap "Edit," and tap "Assign Ringtone."

Swipe Keyboard

A Swipe Keyboard was added in iOS 13. What's that? Instead of lifting your finger as you tap, you swipe across the keyboard. Some people prefer it and feel like they can type faster using it. Others can't stand it. If you want to try it out, go to Settings > General > Keyboard.

Customizing Brightness and Wallpaper

On the iPhone, wallpaper refers to the background image on your Home screen and to the image displayed when your iPhone is locked (Lock screen). You can change either image using two methods.

For the first method, visit Settings > Wallpapers. You'll see a preview of your current wallpaper and Lock screen here. Tap "Choose a New Wallpaper." From there, you can choose a pre-loaded dynamic (moving) or still image, or choose one of your own photos. Once you've chosen an image, you'll see a preview of the image as a Lock screen. Here, you can turn off Perspective Zoom (which makes the image appear to shift as you tilt your phone) if you like. Tap "Set" to continue. Then choose whether to set the image as the Lock screen, Home screen, or both.

The other way to make the change is through your Photos app. Find the photo you'd like to set as a wallpaper image and tap the Share button. You'll be given a choice to set an image as a background, a Lock screen, or both.

If you want to use images from the web, it's fairly easy. Just press and hold the image until the Save Image / Copy / Cancel message comes up. Saving the image will save it to your Recently Added photos in the Photos app.

Mail, Contacts, Calendars Settings

If you need to add additional mail, contacts or calendar accounts, tap Settings > Mail, Contacts and Calendars to do so. It's more or less the same process as adding a new account in-app. You can also adjust other settings here, including your email signature for each linked account. This is also a good place to check which aspects of each account are linked—for example, you may want to link your Tasks, Calendars and Mail from Exchange, but not your Contacts. You can manage all of this here.

There are a number of other useful settings here, including the frequency you want your accounts to check for mail (Push, the default, being the hardest on your battery life). You can also turn on features like Ask Before Deleting and adjust the day of the week you'd like your calendar to start on.

Adding Social Networks

If you use Twitter, Facebook or Flickr, you'll probably want to integrate them with your iPhone. This is a snap to do. Just tap on Settings and look for Twitter, Facebook and Flickr in the main menu (you can also integrate Vimeo and Weibo accounts if you have them). Tap on the platform you want to integrate. From there, you'll enter your user name and password. Doing this will allow you to share webpages, photos, notes, App Store pages, music and more, straight from your iPhone's native apps.

iPhone will ask you if you'd like to download the free Facebook, Twitter and Flickr apps when you configure your accounts if you haven't already done so. I recommend doing this—the apps are easy to use, free, and look great.

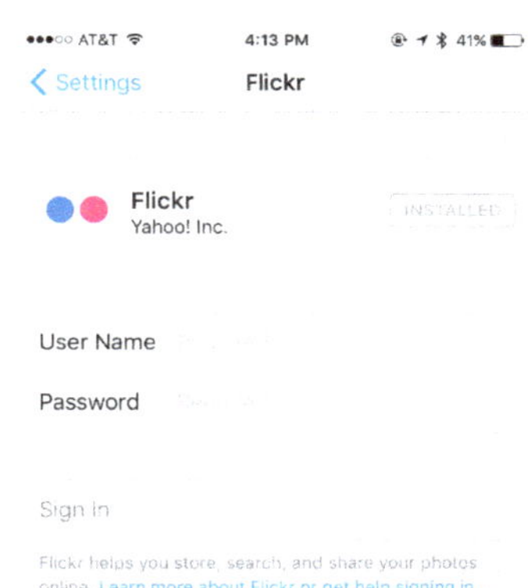

I found that when I associated my Facebook account, my contact list got extremely bloated. If you don't want to include your Facebook friends in your contacts list, adjust the list of applications that can access your Contacts in Settings > Facebook.

Family Sharing

Family Sharing is one of my favorite iOS features. Family Sharing allows you to share App Store and iTunes purchases with family members (previously, accomplishing this required a tricky and not-entirely-in-compliance-with-terms-of-service dance). Turning on Family Sharing also creates a shared family calendar, photo album, and reminder list. Family members can also see each other's location in Apple's free Find My ap. Overall, Family Sharing is a great way to keep everyone entertained and in sync! You can include up to six people in Family Sharing.

To enable Family Sharing, go to Settings > iCloud. Here, tap "Set Up Family Sharing" to get started. The person who initiates Family Sharing for a family is known as the family organizer. It's an important role, since every purchase made by family members will be made using the family organizer's credit card! Once you set up your family, they'll also be able to download your past purchases, including music, movies, books, and apps.

Invite your family members to join Family Sharing by entering their Apple IDs. As a parent, you can create Apple IDs for your children with parental consent. When you create a new child Apple ID, it is automatically added to Family Sharing.

There are two types of accounts in Family Sharing—adult and child. As you'd expect, child accounts have more potential restrictions than adult accounts do. Of special interest is the Ask to Buy option. This prevents younger family members from running up the family organizer's credit card bill by requiring parental authorization for purchases. The family organizer can also designate other adults in the family as capable of authorizing purchases on children's devices.

Continuity and Handoff

iOS includes some incredible features for those of us who work on multiple iOS and OSX devices. Now, when your computer is running Yosemite or higher, or your iPad is connected to the same Wi-Fi network as your iPhone, you can answer calls or send text messages (both iMessages and regular SMS messages) from your iPad or computer.

The Handoff feature is present in apps like Numbers, Safari, Mail and many more. Handoff allows you to leave an app in one device mid-action and pick up right where you left off on a different device. It makes life much easier for those of us living a multi-gadget lifestyle.

Continuity Camera

One of the things I love most about the Apple ecosystem is how well devices work with each other; that is becoming more and more true with each OS update. With MacOS Ventura, you can use your iPhone as a webcam.

The MacBook has a pretty decent webcam. But you know what has an even better webcam? Your iPhone! Think about that stunning camera lens on the back of your camera being able to capture you. Suddenly, your conferences went from HD to 4K! What's even nicer is now, Center Stage is on the iPhone—that means the camera stays focused on you as you move around.

A feature that cool probably requires a huge amount of setup, right? Nope! You ever hear that Apple phrase, "It just works"? Well, this feature...it just works! (as long as your Mac is running OS Ventura) All you have to do is make sure your computer and iPhone are on the same wireless network.

Let me show you how it works in Zoom. Here's how I look on my MacBook without my iPhone:

Not bad. But now I go to the video tab in Zoom and select my iPhone as the camera. You should see any available webcam listed. One will be the name of your iPhone followed by "Camera"; that's the one you want.

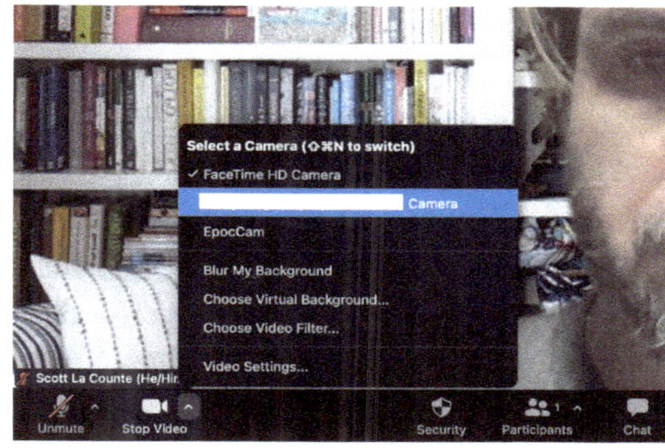

You'll hear a little bell-type noise, then after a second or two, your iPhone's camera will appear.

The difference is pretty crazy; my office doesn't have great lighting, but when I switch to my iPhone for meetings, the image not only looks clearer, the lighting looks flawless.

The example above is Zoom, but the feature works on most video conference apps (FaceTime, Microsoft Teams, etc.).

Stacked Notifications

Notifications used to come onto your locked screen one way. That's not the case anymore. If you go to Settings > Notifications, you can change between Count (where notifications are hidden and it only shows a number representing how many notifications you have), Stack (which stacks all the notifications up so only the first one shows, but you can tap it to reveal the others), or List (which is the traditional appearance of notifications).

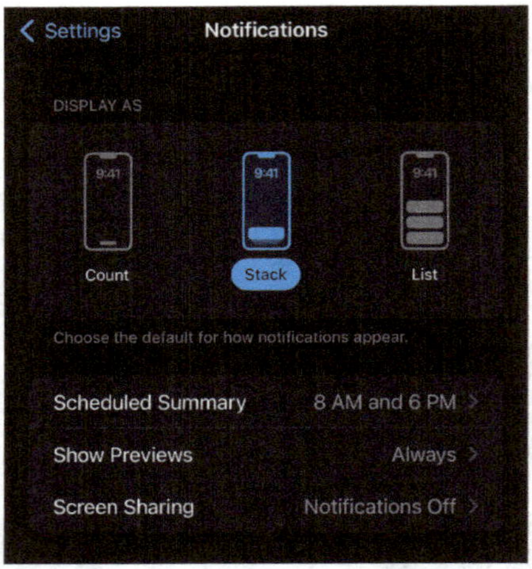

Copy and Delete Screenshot

Screenshots are nothing new on the iPhone (hold the side button and volume up), but now when you tap Done, it gives you a new option to Copy and Delete it. That means the screenshot erases but you can still go into another app and paste it in.

Creating Custom Icons

If you want to put your own fresh spin on any icon, it's "technically" possible, but there are limitations. For example, you could change the iMessage icon to your wedding photo. What are the limitations? You will not get notification indicators on it. So your icon won't light up with a new message indicator, for example. It also launches through the

Shortcuts app, which creates a delay for how quickly it opens.

To do this, you need to create a Shortcut for the app. If you don't see the Shortcuts app, then it's possible that you deleted it and need to install it again.

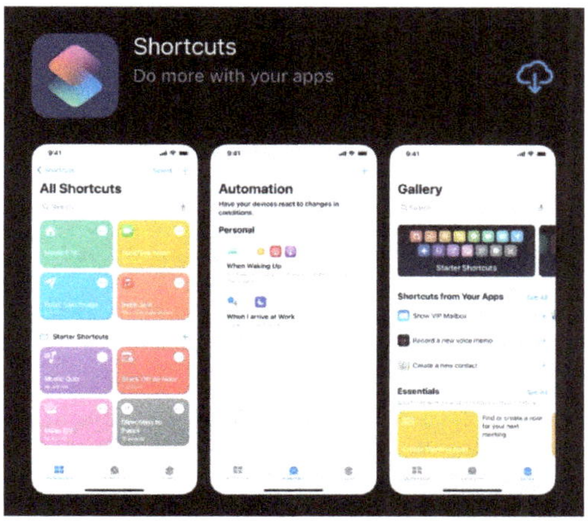

When the app launches, tap the + icon in the upper right corner.

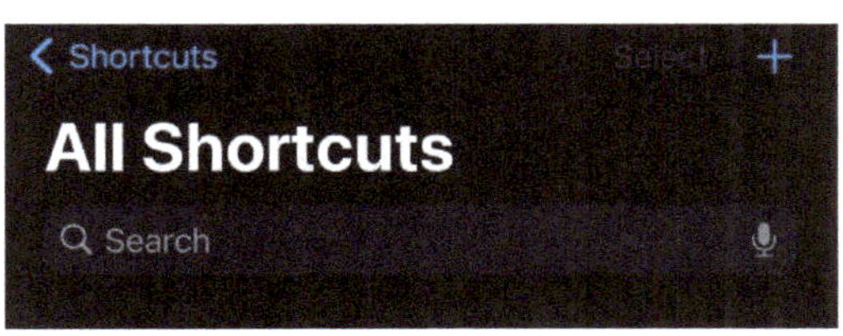

Next, select Add Action.

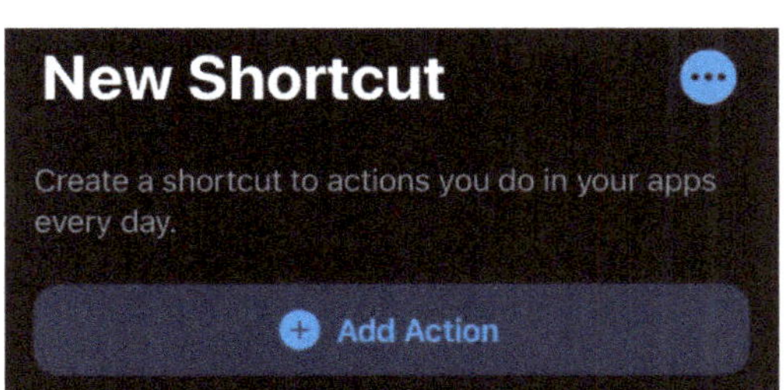

You can search for all possible actions, but it's faster just to search for the actions you want to perform. In this case: Open app.

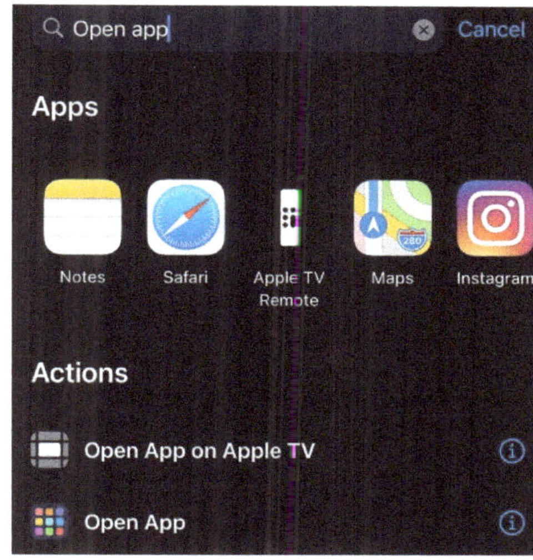

Tap Choose to select the app you want to open.

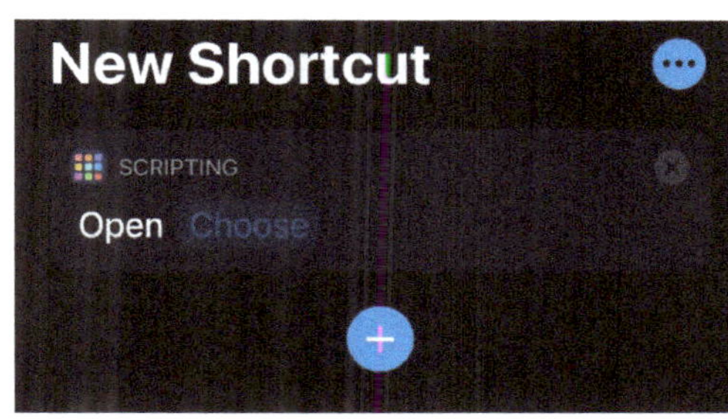

Type in the name of the app you want to open. I'm choosing the Messages app.

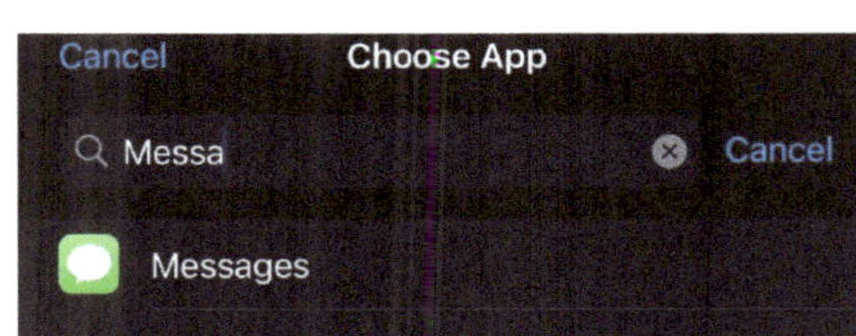

Next, tap the icon in the upper right corner with the three dots and blue circle.

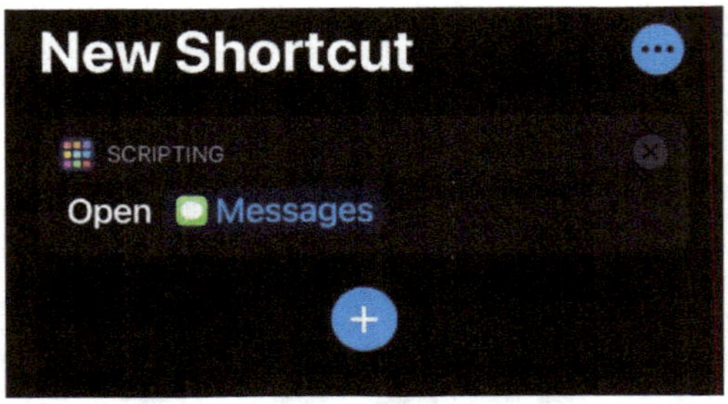

You want to create an icon for it on your Home screen, so tap Add to Home Screen.

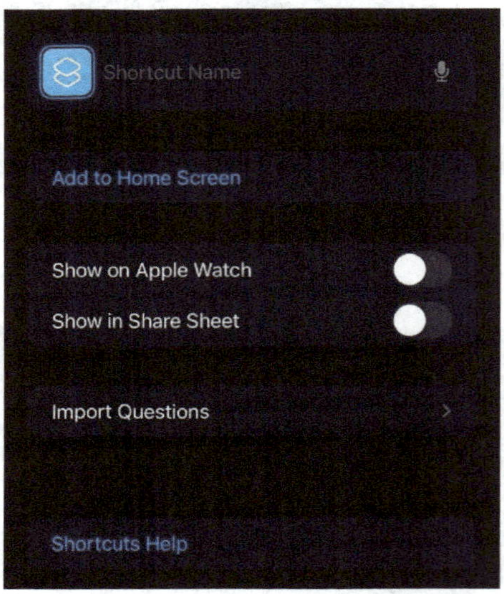

Tap the icon image, and select where the image is that you want to use, then select the image.

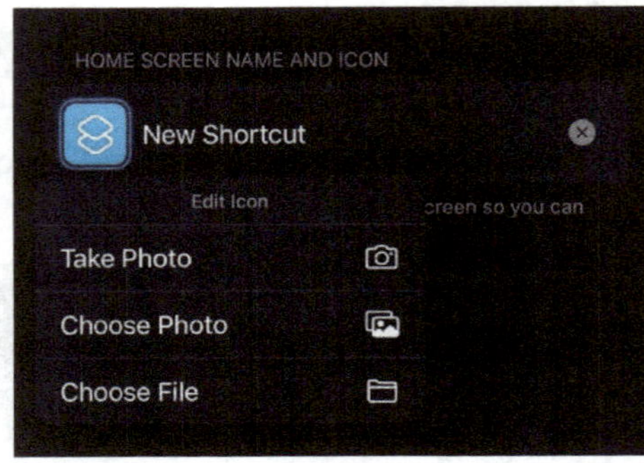

It will give you a preview of the icon. Before tapping Done, make sure and change the name from New Shortcut to whatever you want to call it.

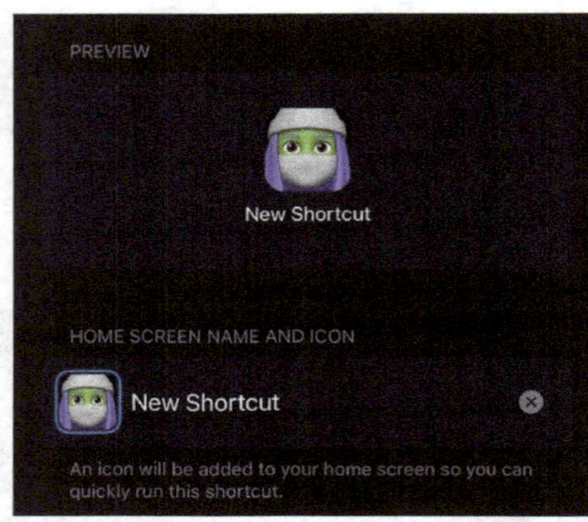

Once you finish, it will show up on your Home screen just like any other app.

Chapter 7: Taking Photos

Taking Photos

Now that you know your way around some of the settings, let's get back to the fun stuff! I'll look at using the Camera app next.

The Camera app is on your Home screen, but you can also access it from your Lock screen for quick, easy access.

The Camera app is pretty simple to use. First, you should know that the Camera app has two cameras: one on the front and one on the back.

The front camera has typically had a lower resolution and was mostly used for self-portraits; with the iPhone 11 and iPhone Pro, the front camera was upgraded to 12 MP and takes the same pro photos as the back. All the features covered in this section are on both the front- and back-facing cameras with the exception of Time-Lapse and Pano modes.

There are six modes on the camera. When you launch the app, you'll see the different modes at the bottom just above the shutter. Use your finger to slide to the mode you want; the mode in yellow is the mode that is active.

The six modes are as follows:

- Time-Lapse – Time-lapsed videos
- Slow-Mo – Slow-motion videos
- Video
- Photo (the default mode)
- Portrait – For studio-like photos that give a blurred background effect
- Pano – For panoramic photos

Using the lenes

- The iPhone Pro comes with three lenses:
- Ultra-wide
- Wide
- Telephoto

When you take a normal photo or video (not portrait or slo-mo video) you will see three numbers: .5, 1x, and 2. These represent the lens. Tapping them will make the preview either zoom in or out.

If you tap and hold one of the numbers, you'll get more precise numbers—so if you don't want to zoom all the way in or out, you don't have to. You can also pinch in and out on your screen to zoom in and out.

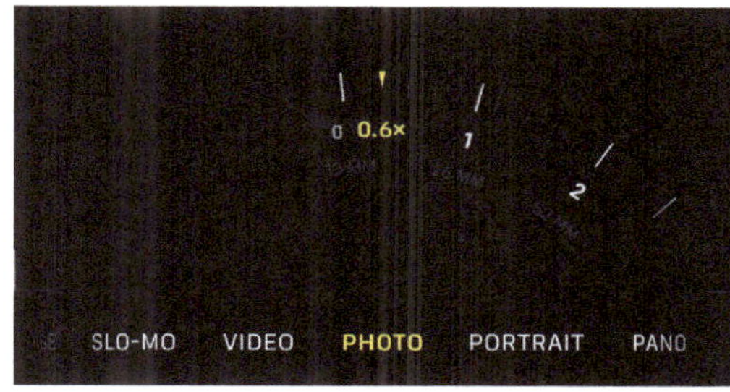

What does all this mean in practice? To give you an example, below are three photos taken at the same spot with each lens.

Ultra-Wide (0.5)

Wide (1x)

Telephoto (2)

Different Camera Modes

At the top of the app are three buttons: flash, night mode, and live mode. Night mode comes on automatically in low-light settings.

Tapping on the arrow in the middle of this will give you an expanded list of options.

The options appear at the bottom after you expand it. The options are as follows: flash, night mode, live mode, frame, timer, and color.

If you tap on any of these options you get more options to either toggle them on and off or, when applicable, make adjustments to them.

Night Mode is a new feature on the iPhone 11 and Pro, and the manual controls here might seem a little unfamiliar; Night Mode will come on automatically (if activated, the icon will be yellow and indicate the number of seconds it will shoot for), but when you press the Night Mode icon, you can manually adjust the settings it would automatically capture.

What Night Mode is doing automatically behind the scenes is simulating a longer exposure. That basically means it's taking longer to capture the image. The slider in Night Mode adjust the number of seconds it will be exposed—the longer it's exposed the more light you are letting in.

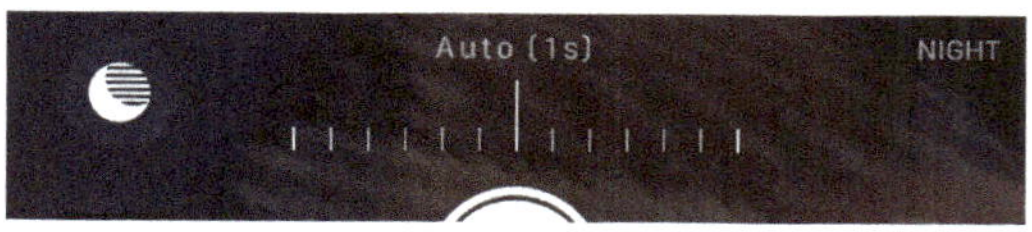

The gyroscope inside your iPhone is smart enough to detect if the iPhone is resting on a tripod. If it is, it will allow for even longer exposures.

As you take a photo, you can tap a person or object to focus on. As you do this, you'll see a yellow box. If you move your finger up or down, it will adjust the brightness of the photo.

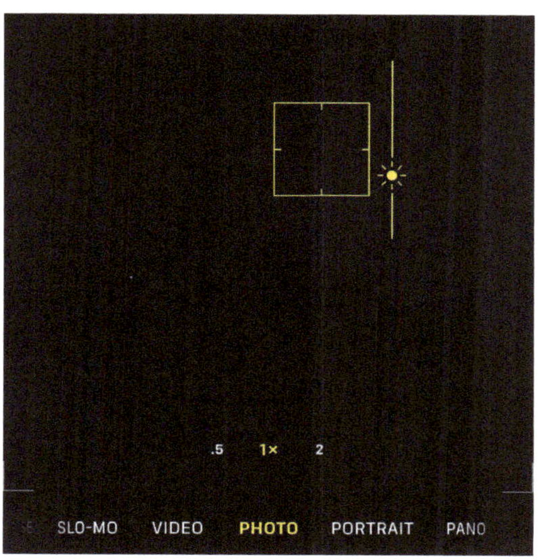

As you take photos, you can capture quick videos without leaving the photo. Tap and hold the shutter and drag it to the right, then release it when you are done recording the quick video. This effect can also be performed when you are shooting a video and want a quick photo.

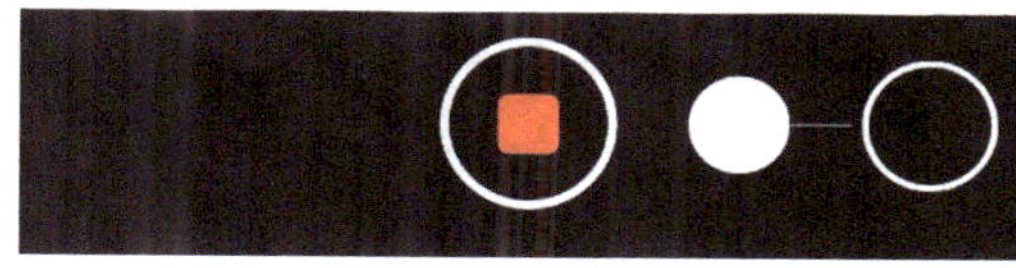

Burst Mode

Previous iPhones let you take a "Burst" of photos by holding the shutter; this was ideal for things like action shots—you could take dozens of photos in seconds and then later pick the one you like best.

Holding the shutter not lets you slide to take a quick video. Burst, however, can still be accomplished. The new method is tapping shutter and sliding your finger to the left.

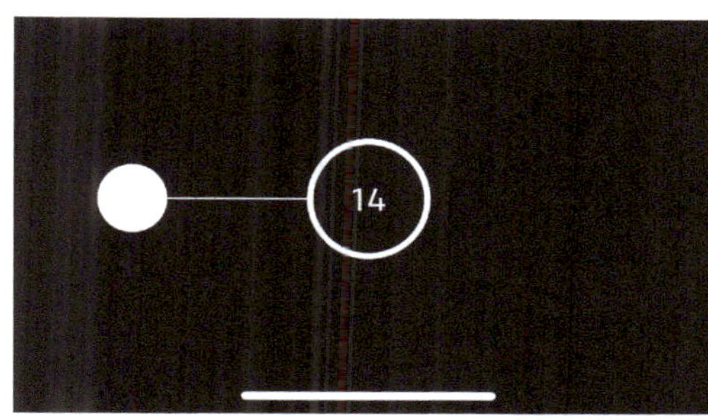

Portrait Mode

One of the most popular camera modes is portrait mode. Portrait mode captures images that really pop by blurring everything but the subject.

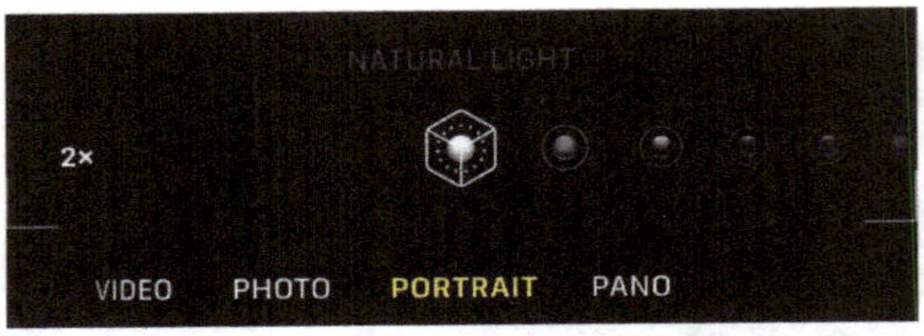

When you drag your finger over the boxes just above Portrait, you can see all the different modes within Portrait mode. They are: Natural Light, Studio Light, Contour Light, Stage Light, Stage Light Mono, and High-Key Light Mono.

When you take a Portrait photo, you can change the mode when you edit the photo. So, for example, if you take it with Studio Light, but decide later that you want Natural Light, it won't be too late to change it. I'll cover this in the next section.

Pano Mode

Pano mode lets you patch several photos together to create one giant landscape photo. You can switch lenses before taking the photo.

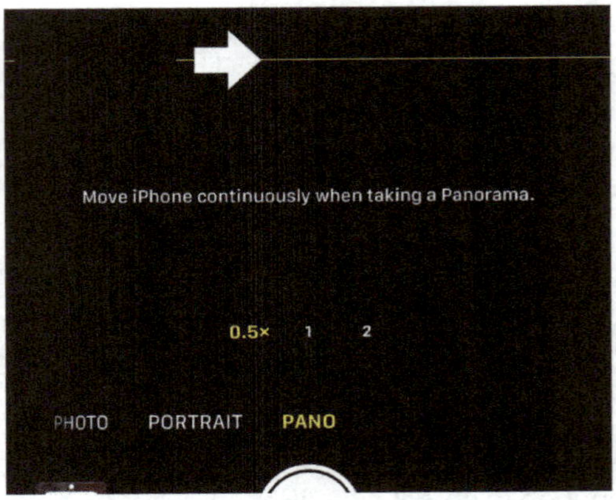

Exposure Setting In the Camera

In addition to all the other controls in the Camera app, iOS 15 added an exposure icon.

When you tap this icon, a slider appears to let you manually change the exposure of the picture you are taking.

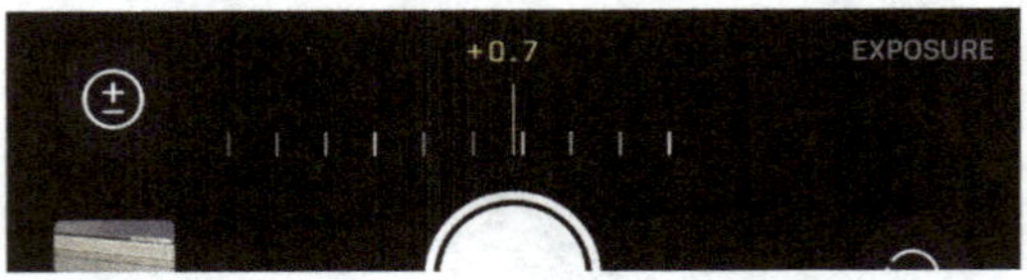

Quicktake Video

Quicktake video has been added to all devices; not just the iPhone 11 and up.

Cinematic Mode

Cinematic is a highly touted new mode on the iPhone; it's supported across all iPhone 13's (standard and pro). What is it? Think of it kind of like the Portrait mode--only with video. What it does is let's you put a focus on one person in the shot and blue everything else, then when another person speaks, change the focus to bring attention to them. The transitions are pretty seamless and it's fun to play around with.

To get started, open your camera app and choose the Cinematic mode, then tap record.

As it records, the yellow frame will indicate the current person of focus that it's detected; gray frame indicates that it sees another person, but they are not the focus.

Tap the grey box to make them the focus. If it doesn't see the person, then just tap them.

You can also tap and hold the screen to lock the focus.

When you are done, just tap the record button again.

Editing Cinematic Videos

Where things get even more fun with Cinematic mode is editing. You can even do it on an older phone (iPhone X and up--as long as iOS 15 is on it).

To get started, open the Photos app and find the video. Next tap Edit, then tap the Cinematic at the top of the screen--that turns the effect on and off.

To change the focus in a video, do the steps above. As you go through the video, tap the subject you want to switch focus to or double tap to automatically focus on a subject.

Under the video time bar you'll see white and yellow dots--white dots are automatic changes; yellow indicate any manual changes.

You can turn manual tracking on and off by tapping on the square with the dot in the center in the upper left corner.

Camera Settings

You can access camera settings by going to the Settings app and Camera.

Mirror Front Camera is useful if you take a lot of selfies; it flips the image so if your shirt has text, for example, it won't appear backward.

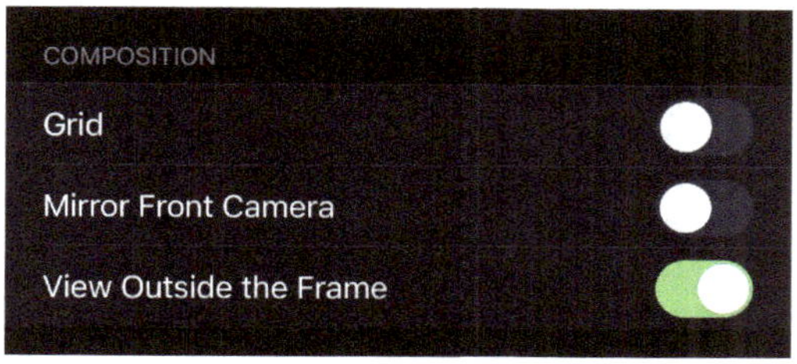

Smart HDR will use the brain of the phone to blend photos together to create a single image with the best exposure.

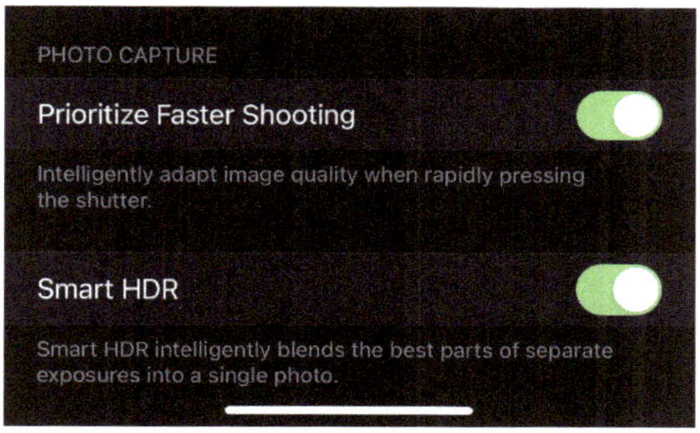

QR Codes

Have you ever seen one of those boxes on a business telling you to scan it for more information? That's a QR Code.

In the past, you would need an app to open that. iPhone's native camera now has that function built in. Hold up your phone to a QR Code and act like you are going to take a picture. As soon as it focuses on it, a drop-down notification will appear asking you if you'd like to open the link Safari.

Macro Photography

The pro lineup of iPhone's (starting with the iPhone 13 Pro) support macro photography (and video). As of this writing, there is no button to activate it. To take a macro photo, just move your phone close to the object and the phone will automatically focus it and recognise the type of shot you are taking.

Photographic Styles

Photographic Styles is a new feature added to all iPhone 13 models (standard and Pro); it's a quick way to add a preset style to a photo--rich contrast, vibrant, warm or cool. So if you like really bright photos, you can have that preset style and quick apply it to new photos every time you take a photo.

Pick A Style

To get started with styles, open the camera app then tap the up arrow.

This will bring up an option row just above the shutter.

Tap the cascade icon.

Next swipe through all the available styles: rich contrast, vibrant, warm, and cool.

Below each style is Tone and Warmth; you can tap either of those to make further adjustments to the style.

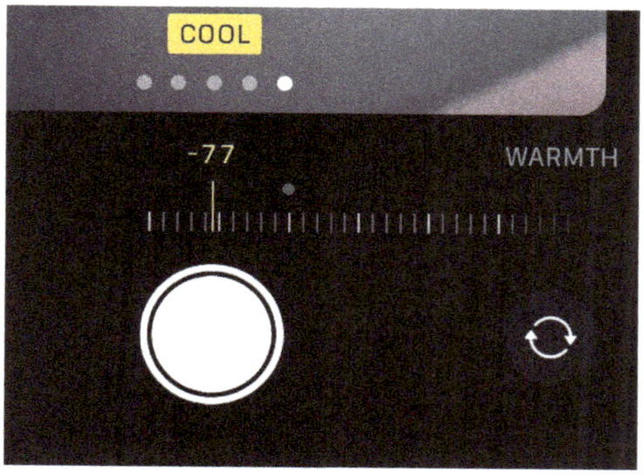

When you are done, tap the cascade icon again. To turn it off, follow the same steps, but when you pick the style, select standard. You'll see a line through the icon indicating that it is turned off.

You can also pick your styles in the Settings app. It's under Camera > Photographic Styles.

Raw Photography

If you are a hobbyist or professional photographer, then you probably know all about the Raw file format. If you have an iPhone 14 Pro, then you have the option to shoot photos in Raw format. Raw maintains more capabilities for editing on professional software, but on the phone it takes up a lot of space--about 25MB ro 75MB per photo you take. That doesn't sound like much. But let's say it's Christmas and you took 100 photos throughout the day. That's 25GB of storage for a single day.

By default, Raw mode is turned off. You can turn Raw Photography on and off in settings. Go to the Settings > Camera > Formats.

Finally toggle on Apple ProRAW.

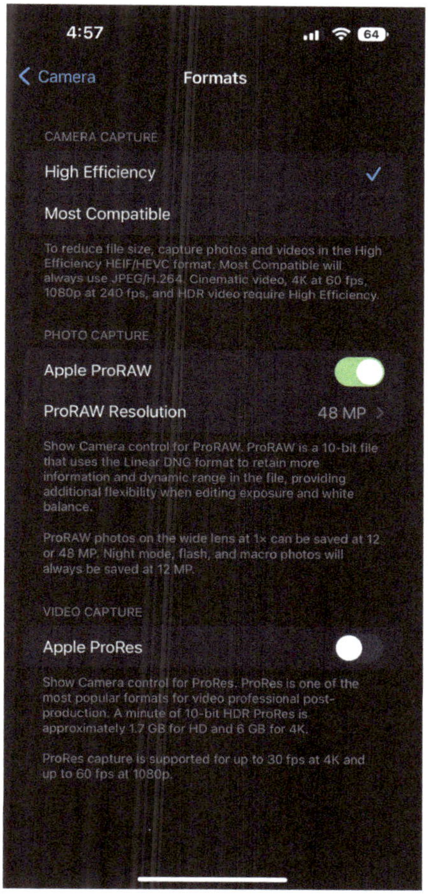

To change 12MP to 48 MP on the ProRAW camera, go to Settings > Camera > Formats.

If you have ProRes turned off the camera app looks like the image below.

When you have it turned on, you'll see a Raw icon appear.

This makes it easy to turn on and off Raw photography, so you aren't taking massive photos with every shot.

ProRes

One of the touted stand out features of the 2021 Pro mode phones is something called "ProRes"; sounds fancy, right? In theory, it is. It's not so much about recording in a very high resolution--though it does do that--as it is recording in a standard that can be edited on high end video software--like Apple's own FinalCut.

For most users, ProRes probably won't be for them for one pretty big reason: storage. When you use ProRes, a single minute could mean several gigabytes of storage. Recording your child's 30 minute school performance might come pretty close to eating up all your phones free storage!

Editing Photos

Now that you've captured your masterpiece, you'll want to edit it to really make it shine. There are thousands of photo editor apps on the App Store. Some, like Adobe Lightroom, will let you make professional changes to the photos, while others are just for fun.

For this chapter, I'm going to stick to making basic edits with Apple's built-in editor. This isn't to say the edits won't be professional—or even fun; there's a lot you can do with the editor.

Regular and Live Photos

The options in editor change based on the kind of photo you took. If you took a Live photo, then there will be a few extra edits you can do; the same is true if you captured in Portrait mode. This first section is going to cover the most common photos: regular (non-Live) and Live.

How do you know what kind of photo it is? When you go into the photos app and view the photo, it will tell you right below the back arrow in the upper left corner. The below example is a Live photo.

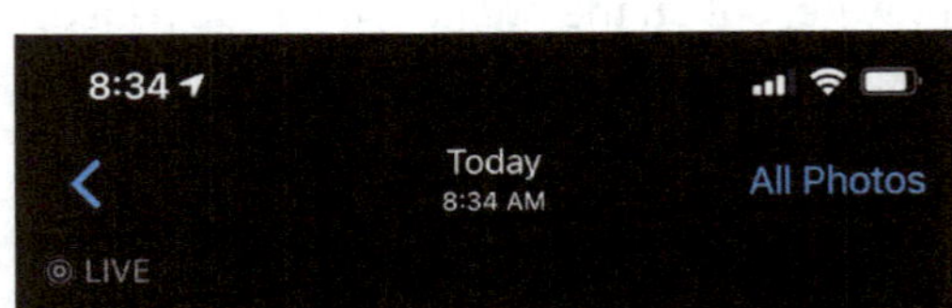

At the bottom of the photo is a list of all options available for editing the photo. The first is the Export button. This option lets you alter the photo outside of the photo app. What does that mean? For starters, you can share via text, email, AirDrop, or upload it to another app, but there's a lot more you can do here: print, add to Wallpaper, add to an album, assign to a contact, and more. The next option is the favorite button (I'll cover where these photos go in the next section); the last options are to Edit and Delete the photo.

When you select Edit, you'll see several new options on the bottom in the Now Open photo editor. The first option is the Live button (if it's a Live photo). When you take a Live photo, you'll have several photos within that photo; by tapping on the Live button, you can select the photo you want to use. The phone automatically picks what it believes is the best photo, but this isn't always the case.

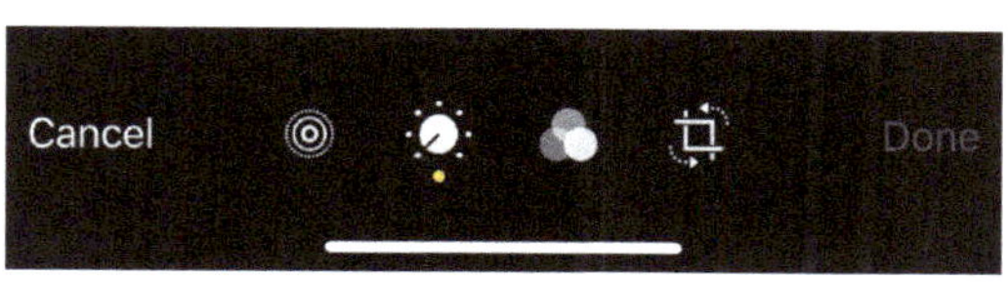

Next to the Live button is the option to make corrections to the photo's overall look. The first option is to Autocorrect (this adjusts the lighting and color levels to what the phone believes is best). Next to that are all the manual corrections: Exposure, Brilliance, Highlights, Shadows, Contrast, Brightness, Black Point, Saturation, Vibrance, Warmth, Tint, Sharpness, Definition, Noise Reduction, and Vignette.

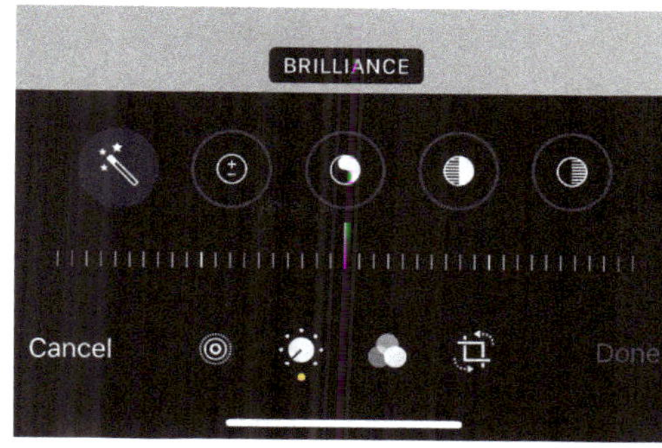

As you slide your finger to the correction you want to perform, you'll notice a slider bar beneath it; you use your finger to move left and right to define the intensity of the correction.

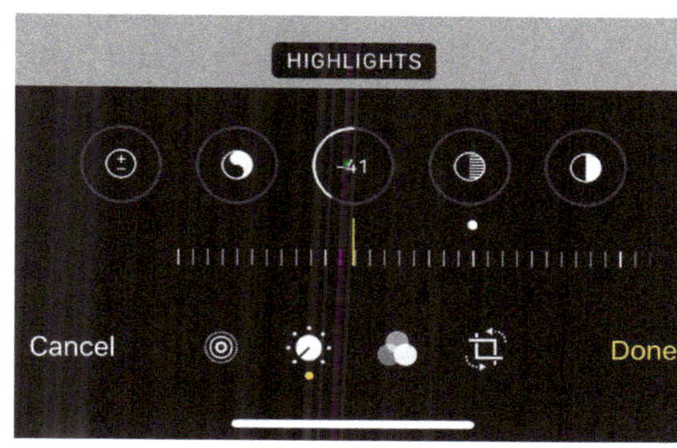

Next is the option to apply Filters to the photos. This works in a similar way: select the filter you want to apply, and then use the slider below to increase or decrease the intensity of the filter. The available filters are Vivid, Vivid Warm, Vivid Cool, Dramatic, Dramatic Warm, Dramatic Cool, Mono, Silvertone, and Noir.

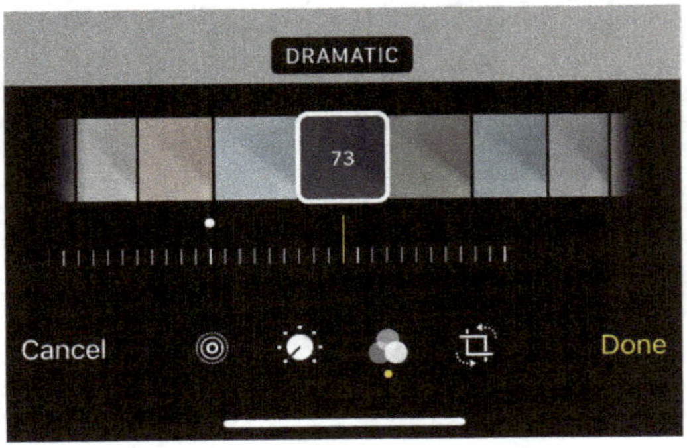

The last option is to Crop. Notice, when you select this option, there are small, white, corner lines around the photo? You can use these to drag to the areas you want to crop—slide in and out, up and down, or left and right.

At the bottom of the cropped area are options to straighten the photo.

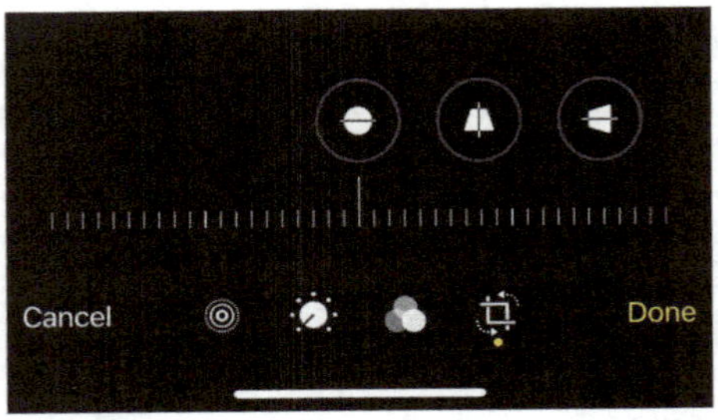

In the top left corner are options to rotate or flip the photo.

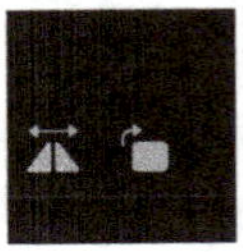

The top right has options to crop to a pre-defined size.

When you select the pre-defined size button, you'll see several new options; these are helpful if you are creating for something in particular—like a frame.

When you finish all your edits, tap the Done button; additionally, you can undo everything and keep the original photo by selecting Cancel.

At any point, you can also tap the three dots in the upper right corner of the screen. This brings up the options menu.

If you have other photo apps, you might see them here; the option most people will likely use, however, is the Markup option.

Markup lets you draw and add shapes to the photo—think of it like note taking on a photo.

The bottom has all your choices for color and writing instrument. You can also use the ruler to help you draw a straight line with any of those choices.

You can additionally tap the plus button to add shapes, text, a signature, and more.

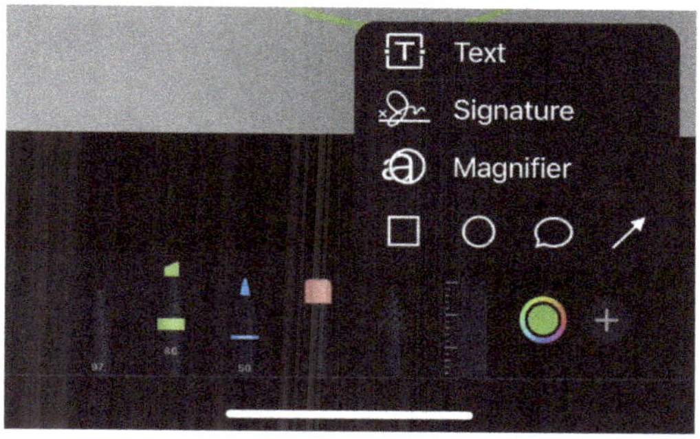

Once you're done with the Markups, tap Done to save your creation or Cancel to erase everything.

Portrait Photos

Editing a portrait photo is exactly the same—with a few exceptions covered in this section.

You know it's a Portrait photo by the indication at the top of the photo.

Once you tap that you want to edit the photo, select the first button, which brings up the Portrait edits available. Use your finger to slide to the Portrait edit you want to make to the photo. Available filters are Natural Light, Studio Light, Contour Light, Stage Light, Stage Light Mono, and High-Key Light Mono. Once you make the filter selection, a slider appears below it to adjust the intensity of it.

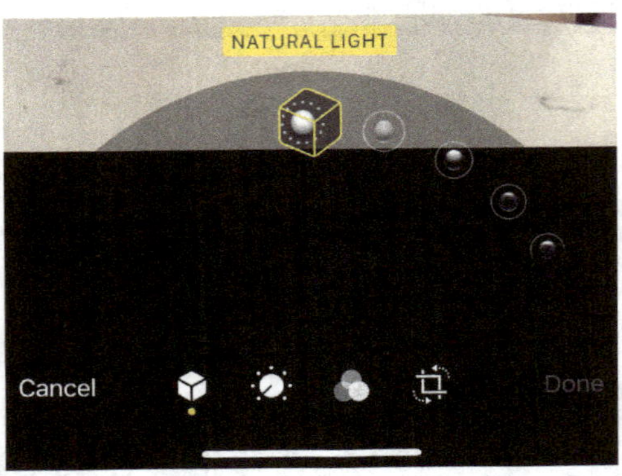

In the upper left corner of the screen, you'll see a button that says f 4.5; this option adjusts the depth of the photo (or the background blur).

When you tap this option, you'll see a slider appear at the bottom of your screen where you can adjust the depth of the photo.

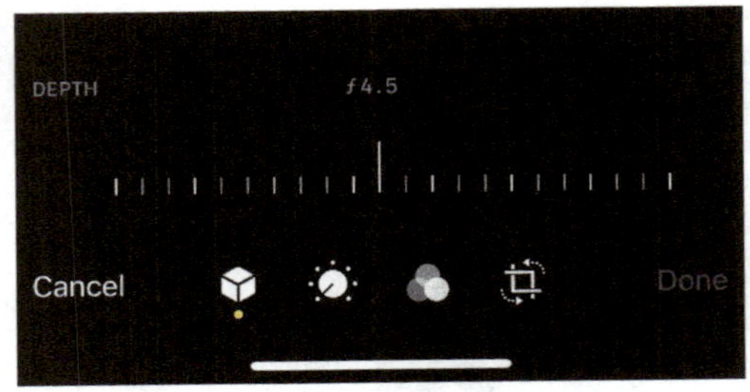

Camera Settings You Should Know

If you go into you Settings, then Camera, there are several settings you should know about (even if you decide not to use them right now).

The setting that I believe is most useful is Composition. Toggling on Photos Capture Outside the Frame means when you take a photo, you can capture more than what you see when you thumb through all of your photos.

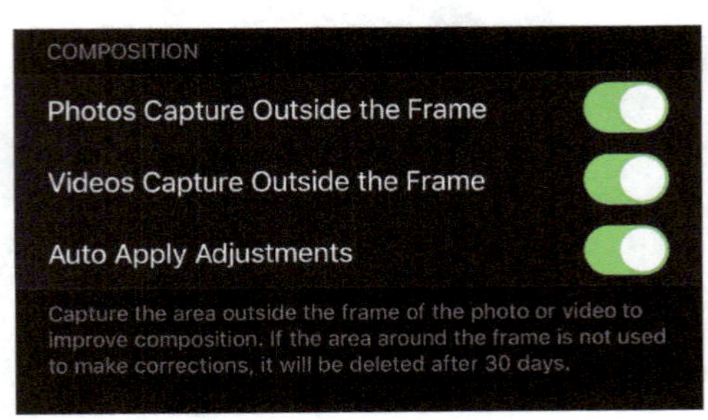

What does that mean? Look at the image below. The image in the center is what I see in my library, but when I go to Edit and Crop, notice how the area is larger? I can drag over to show even more of the photo.

If you don't like that the camera goes back to the default settings whenever you open it, then you can toggle on the Preserve settings.

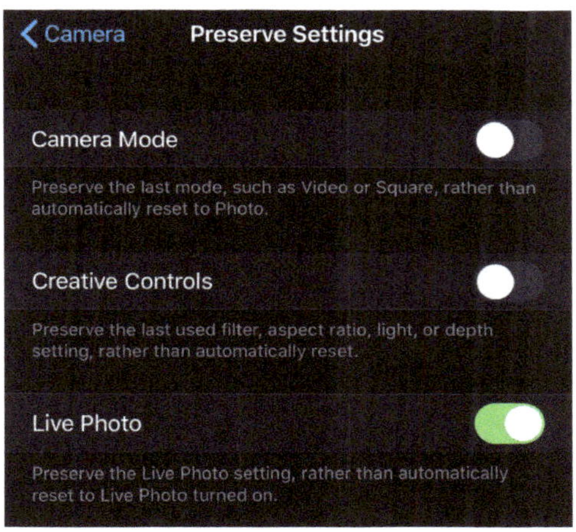

When you record a video, you can shoot as high as 4K. However, doing so creates very large videos. You can record in a lower setting. Tap on Record Video to update your preferences.

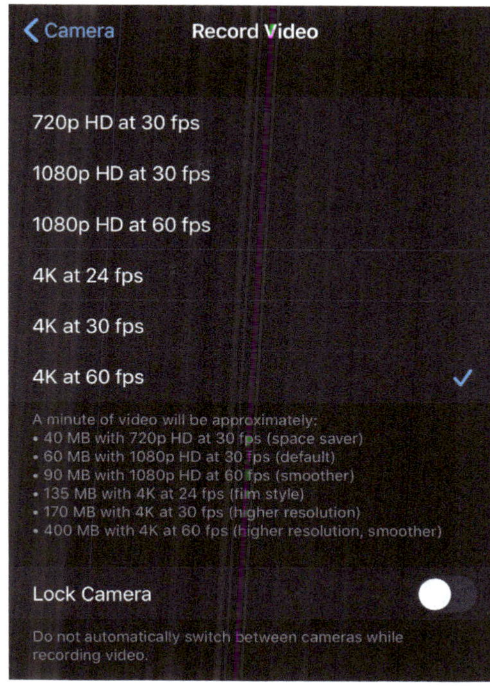

You can also change the Slow-mo camera settings.

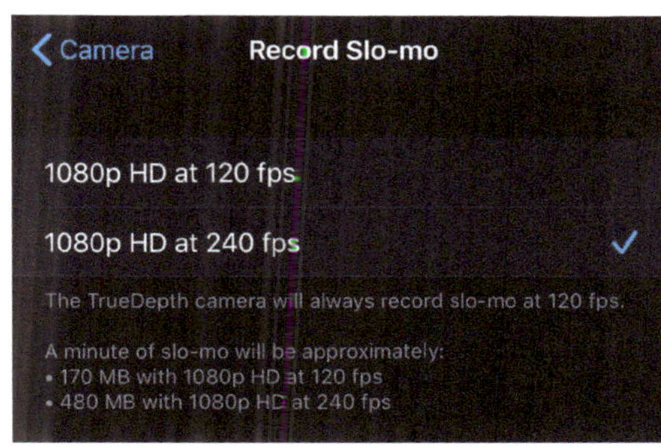

Finally, toggling on Grid will put a grid over your photo app to help you take straight photos and videos.

Lift Photo out of Background

Pictures in texts and documents are fun. You know what's better? Remove the background so the image really stands out!

Open up a photo, then tap the portion you want to pull out from the background. Next, select copy.

Next, go to the application you want to paste it into. I'm using the Notes app, but you can use a text message, email, or lots of other apps. From here, you'll tap and hold, then select paste.

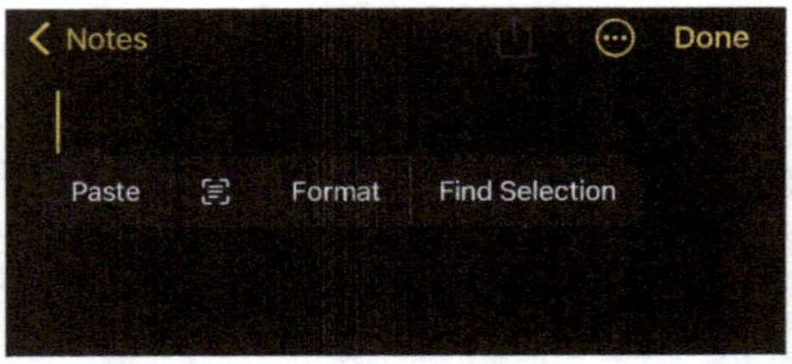

Look at that! A photo is pasted with the background removed!

Viewing, Organizing, Searching and Sharing Photos

Remember the olden days when you got a roll of film with just a dozen or two shots on it? You were careful with what pictures you took because you were limited on how many moments to capture. Smart phones have changed that. Today you can take dozens of shots in seconds. That means most people have thousands of photos on their phone. It didn't take Apple long to realize people would have a problem organizing and finding all those photos.

Now that you have made changes to your photos, how do you find and organize them? This section will cover that.

When you open the Photos app, there are four tabs available: Photos (where you see all photos), For You (curated collections of photos—like On This Day memories), Albums (where private shared albums live), Search (where you search for your photos).

Viewing Photos

When you select the first tab (Photos) you'll notice a new option appears at the bottom: Years, Months, Days, All Photos. If you are like most people, you probably have thousands and thousands of photos on your phone. This just makes it easier to find what you are looking for.

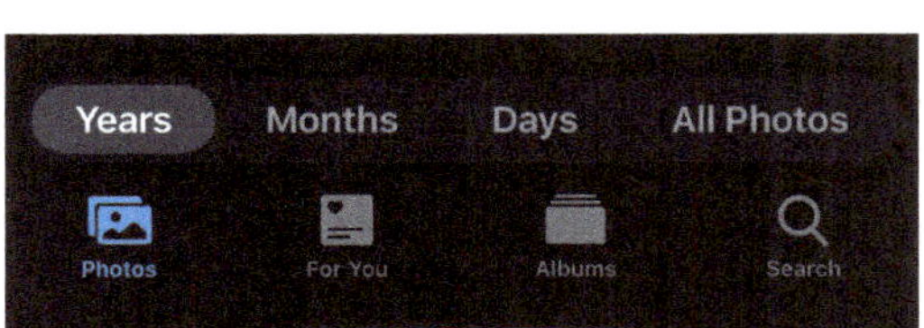

It also makes it easier to share memories. For example, if I want to share all the photos I took on New Year's Day with my wife. I just go to Years, and go to the year I want, then slide to Months, and find January. Slide again to Days and find January First, and finally in the top right corner tap the tree dots to bring up the options for the photos. This collects all the photos together and gives me a few options: Share them, put them in a movie, or show them on a map.

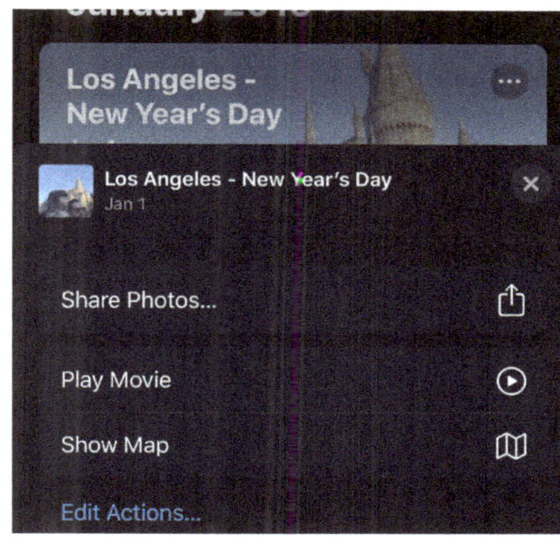

When I select share, it asks me how I want to share them, and I just pick Messages to text my wife the pictures.

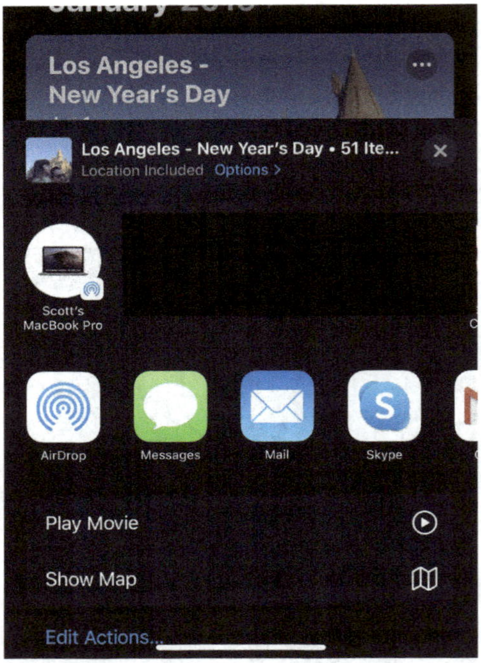

From here, they are all assigned an iCloud link, and that link is inserted into a text message. When my wife gets it, she won't see fifty-one photos appear; she'll see a photo with a link to the location for all. That way she can either view them, download them, or select only a few photos to download.

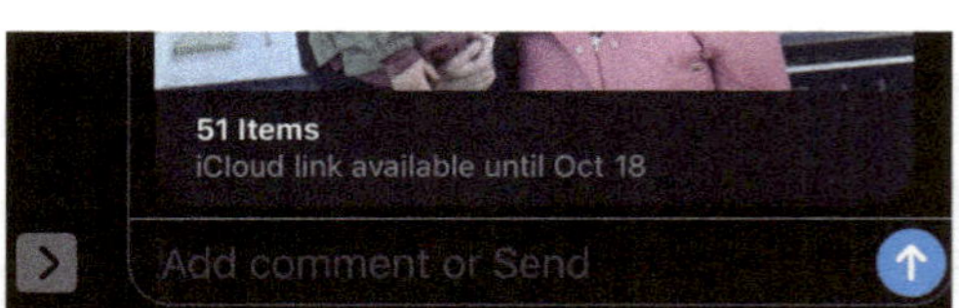

For You

You probably noticed by now that your phone is pretty smart. It has all sorts of things running in the background to figure out who you are and what you like; For You is one area that shows this off. It recognizes when you take a lot of photos in a particular area and marks them as memories, then starts assigning them to this section. You can do all the things you did in Photos, such as share them and turn them into movies.

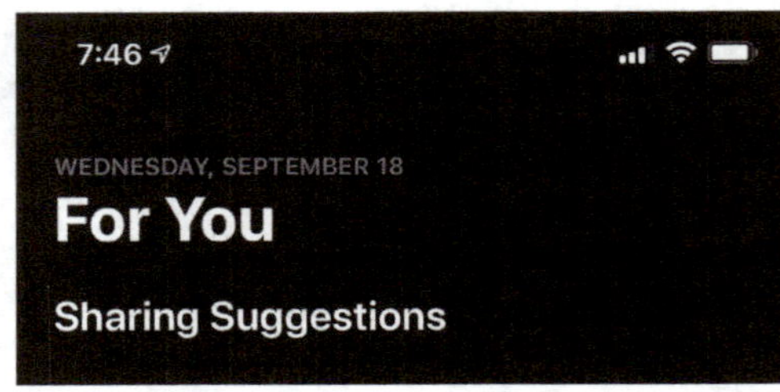

Not all memories are happy ones; when you open up memories, you can tap the options in the upper right corner to either block or delete a memory.

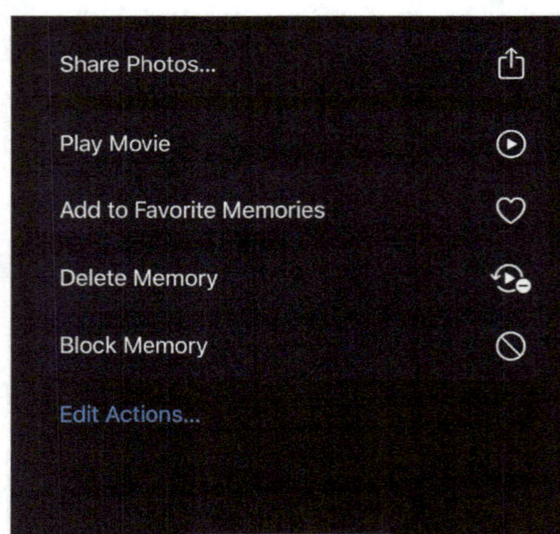

If you decide to play a movie with the memory (and this also applies to any album you turn into a movie), you can edit how it will show—a short or medium clip, and what kind of effects (like music) it has.

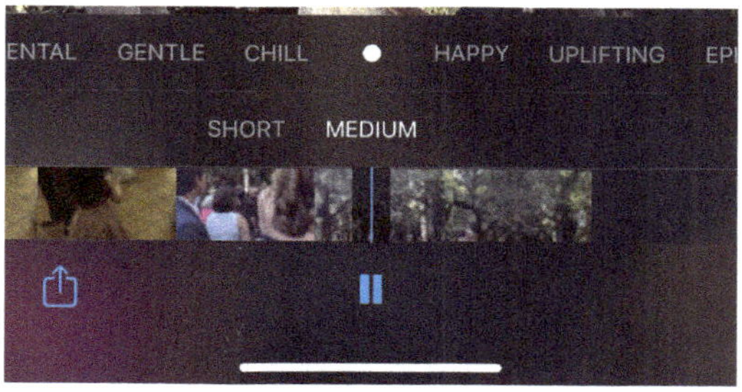

Albums

Albums is where you can really start to organize things. Remember when I said above that when you press the like button on a photo it goes to the Favorites folder. This is where you'll find that folder. To add an album, tap the + button.

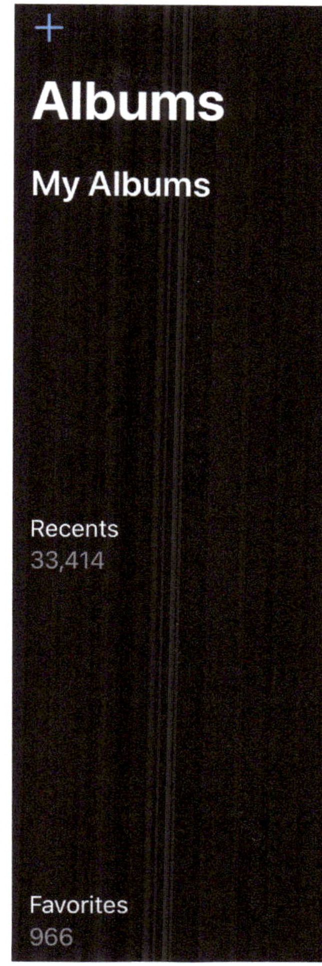

This will ask if you want to create a New Album or New Shared Album; the first option is something you see and the second is something you make available to others.

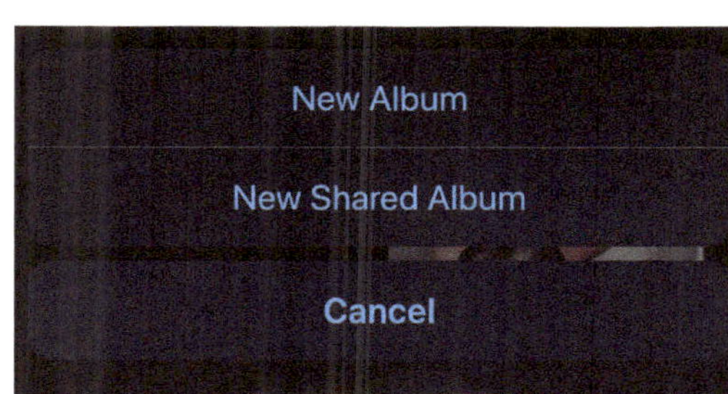

When you create a Shared Album, it will first ask you to give it a name.

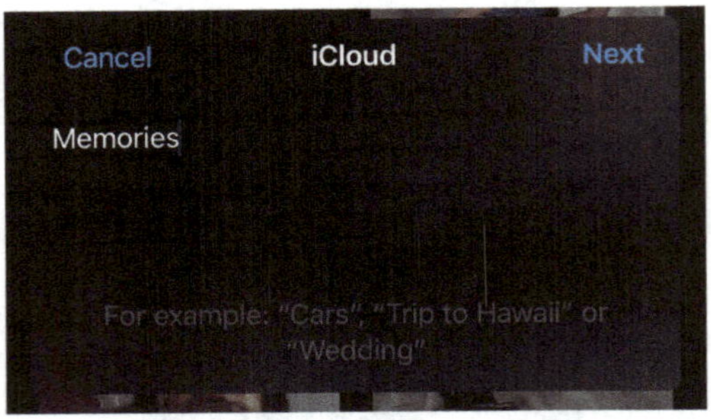

Next, you select who you want to share it with (you can also leave it blank for now).

After this you'll see a blank shared album.

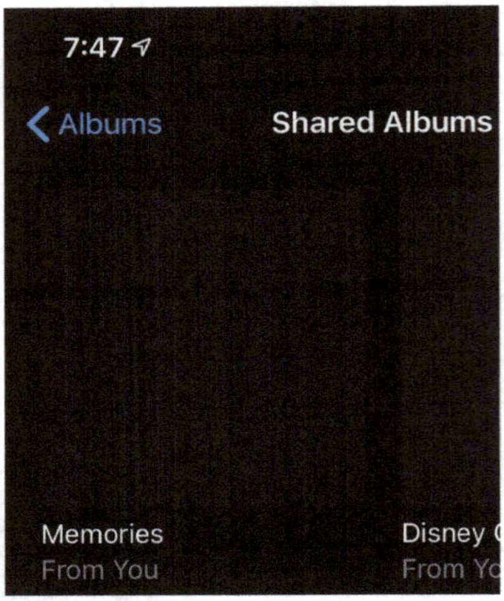

Once you tap on the album, you can start adding your photos.

Selecting People on the bottom allows you to invite people to view it. Under People, you'll also see settings to let people share photos to the album—so, for example, if you just had a wedding, you can share an album with everyone that was there and ask them to add in all of the photos they took. You also go to People to delete an album.

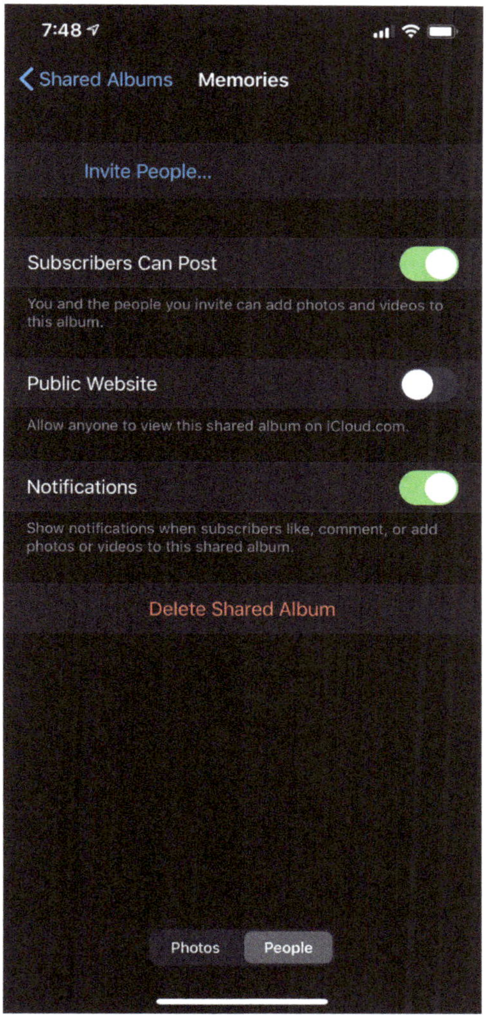

At any time, you can also go into People and tap a person's name who is a member of the album and remove them.

Search

Search is pretty smart. You may wonder how you can search for photos when there is no text. There are a number of ways.

When you take a photo, it geotags the location (in other words, it labels where it was taken—either the city or in some cases the actual name of a place; for example, if you were at a museum, then it would know the name of the museum based on the geotag).

Another way is through facial recognition. When you take a photo, the AI inside your phone scans it to see if it notices a person or even an animal.

One of the first things you see when you tap the search option is People; in the example below, I can tap on Dad and see all the photos I've taken that have my dad in them; I can also search in the box above for a location and Dad, which would find any photo of my dad at that location.

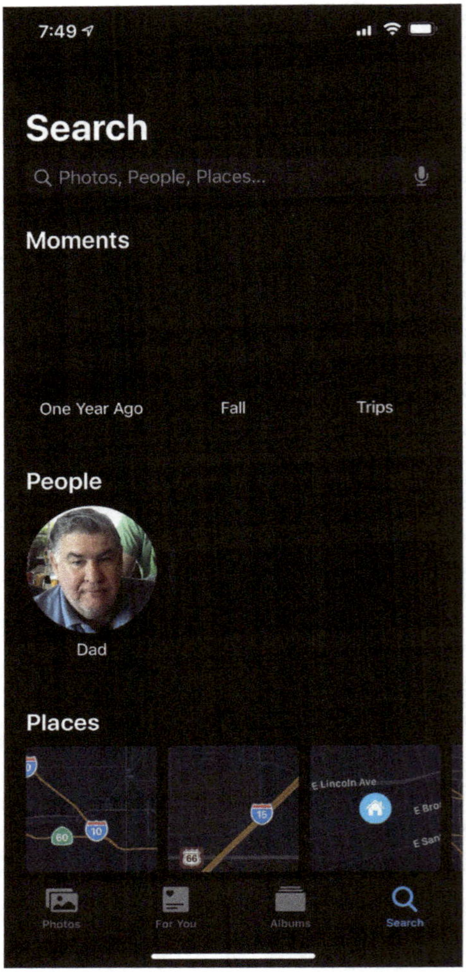

To give you an example, I go to Disneyland a lot because I live in Southern California and have a kid. When I search Disneyland, it will show me every photo I've taken there—over 6,000! Like I said, I go there a lot.

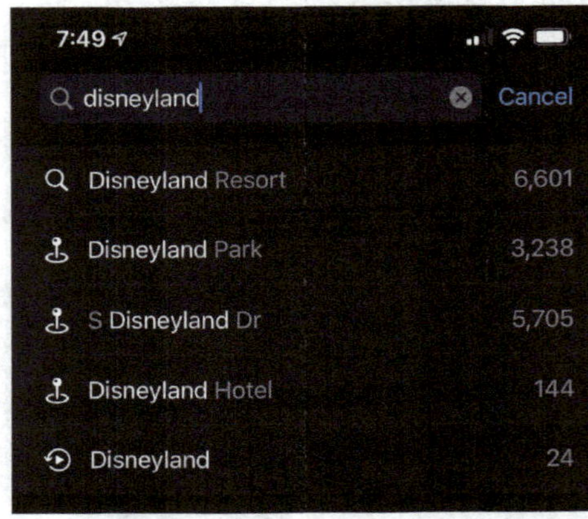

Because there are so many results, I can start adding other things to the search. For example, I can search for Nashville, and then I can also search for just photos with food in them, or just photos taken in the Winter.

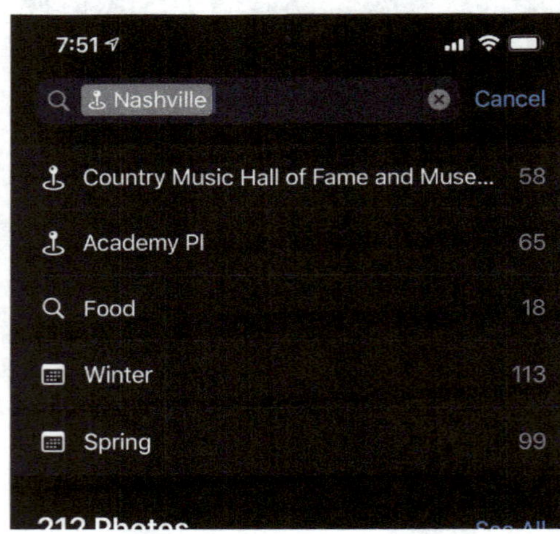

The search isn't quite as smart when it comes to other things, but it's evolving. It can detect objects, for example, but not quite as accurately as people. It does do a pretty good job with animals, however.

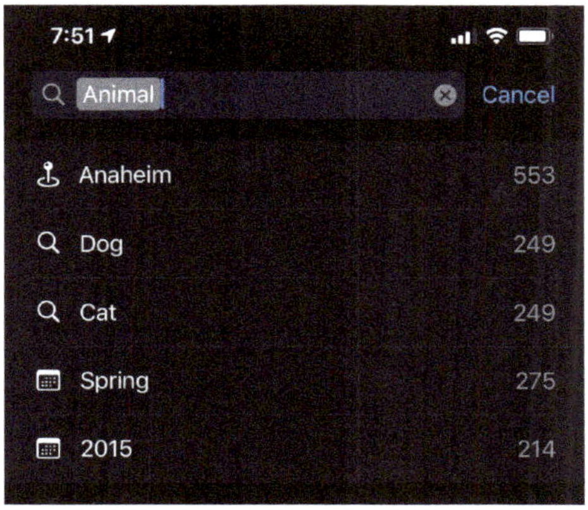

When there is a person it notices in a lot of your photos, it will come up as Unnamed Person; once you give the person a name, it will start showing all photos with that person with that name.

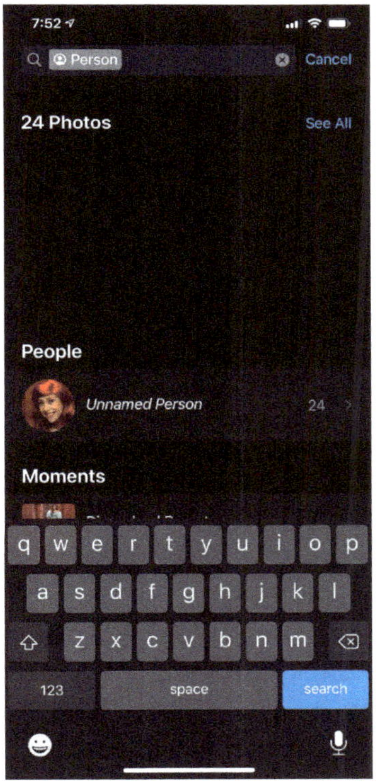

When you tap on a person, you can select the options in the upper right corner to see further options; you can share the photos, turn them into a movie, and more. There's also an option to confirm additional photos, which lets you see photos the AI might not be too sure about.

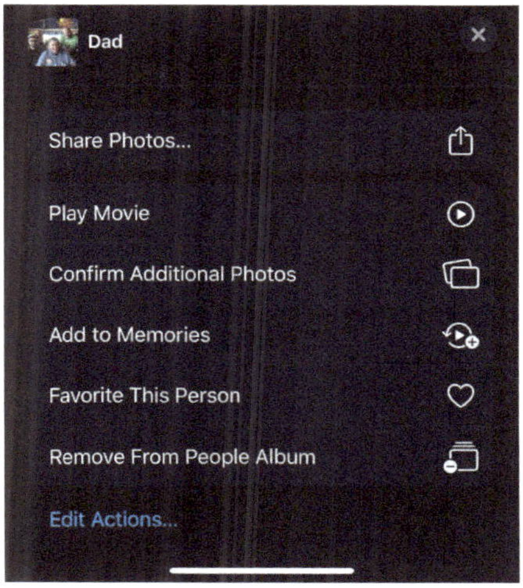

Hide Photos

We all have embarrassing photos—you know, the ones with you dressed in a tutu while riding a unicorn? Or is that just me?!

If you want to hide "certain" photos so only you can see them, then that's an option. It used to be you could hide them, but they would show up in your albums. They were "kind of" hidden, but I think most people would agree that they weren't so much hidden as harder to find.

In iOS 15, the ability was added to completely hide that folder. Go to the Settings app, and then Photos; scroll to Hidden Album. If it's toggled on, the Hidden Album will be in the Utilities area of albums (like I said, harder to find, but not really hidden); if it's toggled off, it's gone. Like nowhere to be found. The images are saved and stored in the cloud—even though you can't see them. To see them, toggle it back on, then go to Albums and scroll to Utilities. If you know a celebrity, then pass this information on to them, so we can stop hearing about all those "accidental" shares of photos meant to be private.

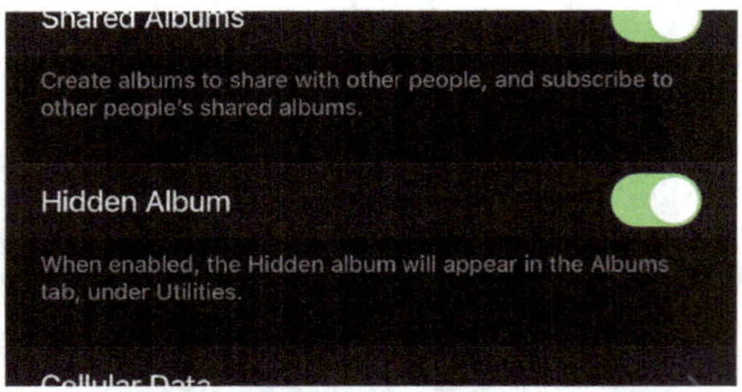

To hide a photo, find it, then select it and tap the Share icon; this brings up how you want to share it (kind of a misleading name, isn't it—you're hiding it because you don't want to share it!); one of the options is Hide—tap that.

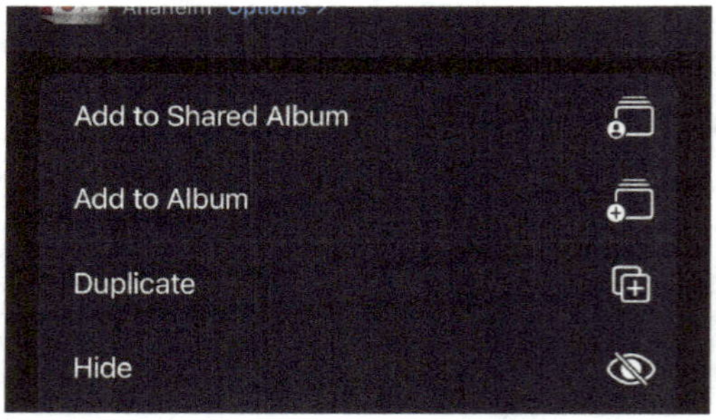

It will confirm that you actually want to hide it. If you change your mind later, then you go into the hidden album and unhide it the same way. You can also select several images at a time to hide them as a group.

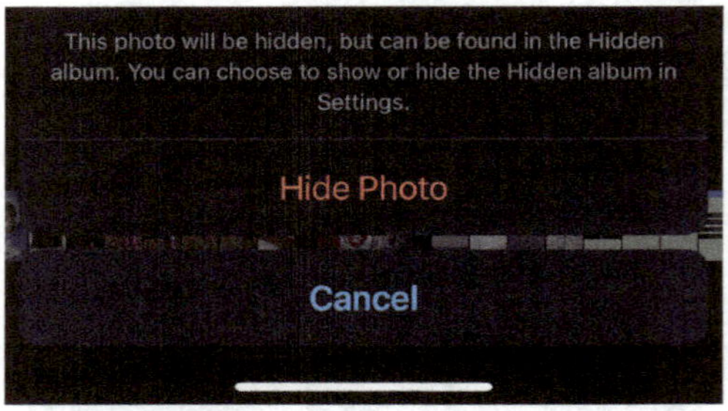

Caption Photos

Swiping up on a photo lets you make changes and add filters, and it also lets you add a caption; captions can later be searched. So you can add something like "Grand Canyon Vacation" and later search for that term.

Duplicate Photos

Photos and videos will probably quickly take the most amount of space on your phone. What's more, many photos will be duplicates. There are lots of reasons this happens. If you look at the image below, you'll see that I have over 1,000 duplicates! You can clean this up by opening the photos app, tapping on

Albums, going to the bottom to utilities, and selecting Duplicates.

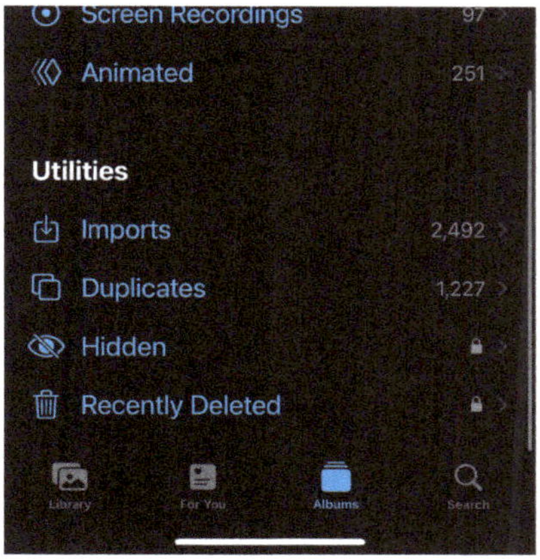

This shows you all the duplicates on your phone. Don't need two copies? Just tap merge. It will merge them. It will keep the highest quality image if the two images are different sizes.

Shared Library

Sharing an album is nothing new in iOS. Sharing a library is something quite different, however. Sharing a library gives people access to all of your photos—or photos that you give them permission to see—a date range, for example. One of the cool features to this is you can share directly to that folder when you take a picture. Let's take a look at how to set it up and how it works.

To get started, you have to go into your Settings. From Settings, navigate to Photos, then click the Shared Library option.

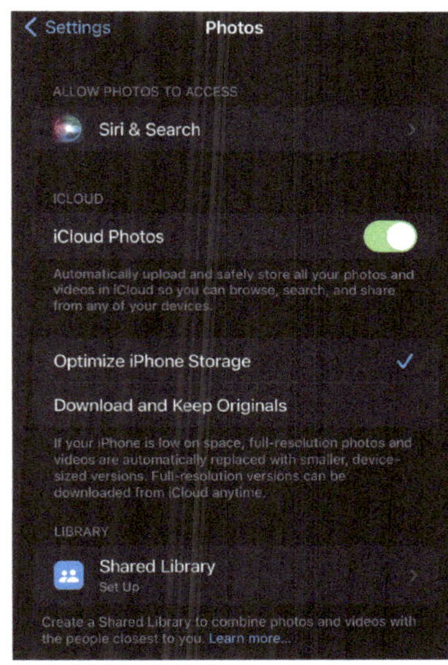

This brings you into a very simple set of instructions for setting things up; just tap the blue Get Started option to get started.

Next, you'll add the contacts you want to add to sharing—be careful here: since it's sharing all of your photos, you probably will only want to select immediate family.

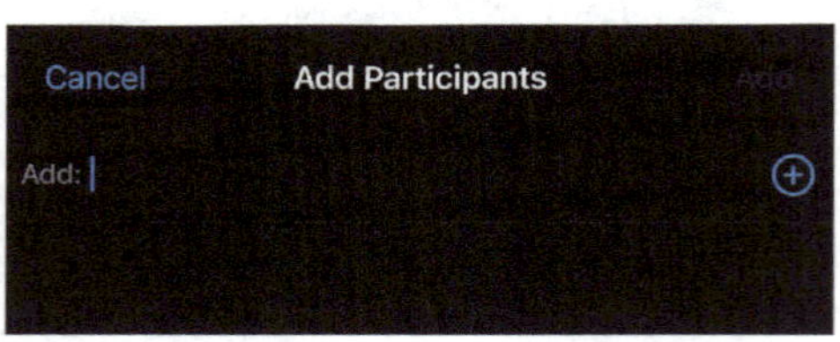

Next, select what you want to share: all of your photos, a date range of photos, or manually choose.

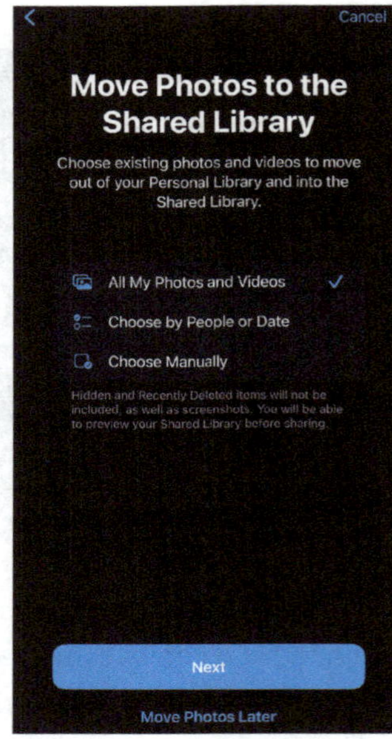

Next, it will give you a preview of what you are sharing. If you have been an iPhone user for a while, it might be quite large—you can see in my case that I am sharing nearly 50,000 photos, and 4,000 videos. If you are sharing something similar, you'll probably see a processing screen for an extended amount of time.

From here, you'll decide how you are inviting them to see the photos.

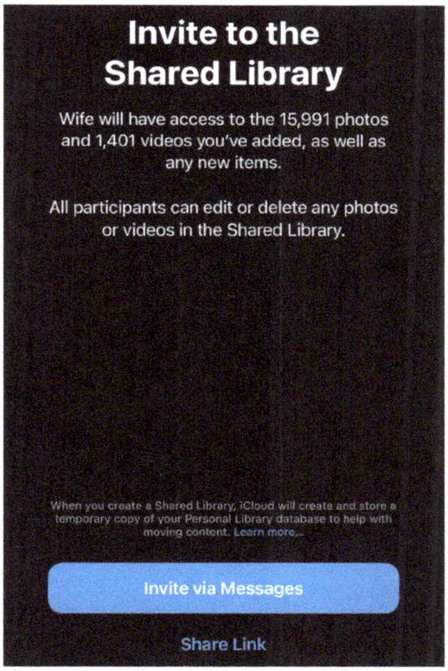

It will just put a small thumbnail with the link in the message that you send.

It will also ask you if you want to share directly from the camera—that means it shares what you take a photo of.

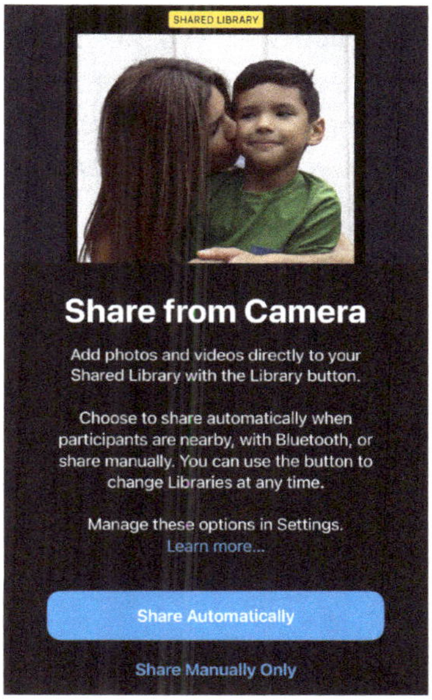

Once you answer the question about the camera, you are ready to start sharing.

You'll now notice when you go into photos that when you click the little three dots in the upper right corner of all photos, there's an option to view your different libraries.

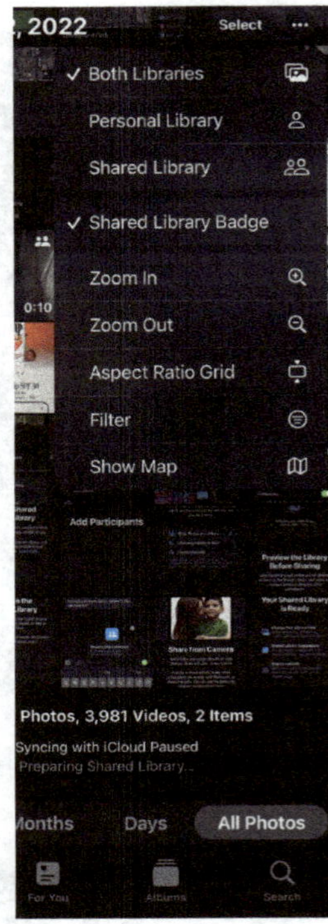

Head into your camera app, and you'll also see a little person icon either toggled on or off.

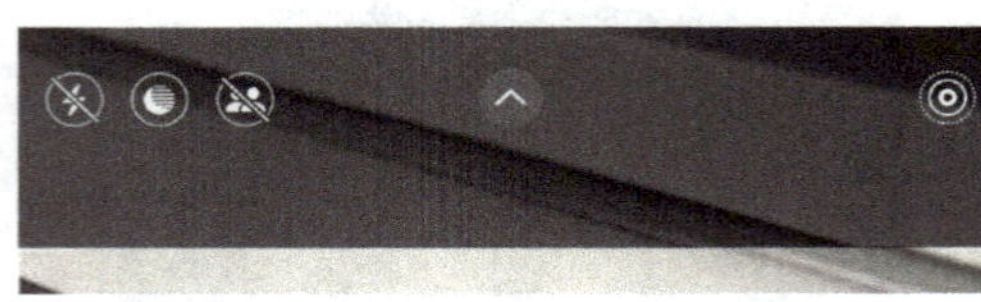

Off means you aren't sharing the photos that you take pictures of in your Shared Library; toggled on means that you are.

Photos (Memories)

iPhone has always shined at how it makes doing things effortless; remember the old days when sharing a slideshow of your vacation required skill? In iPhone? It requires a few seconds of your time! You can create a movie memory complete with transitions and music that you can share over email or text in a matter of seconds! And they look great!

To get started, go to the Photos app, then tap Albums, and select the + icon to create a new album—or you can use an existing album.

Next select New Album.

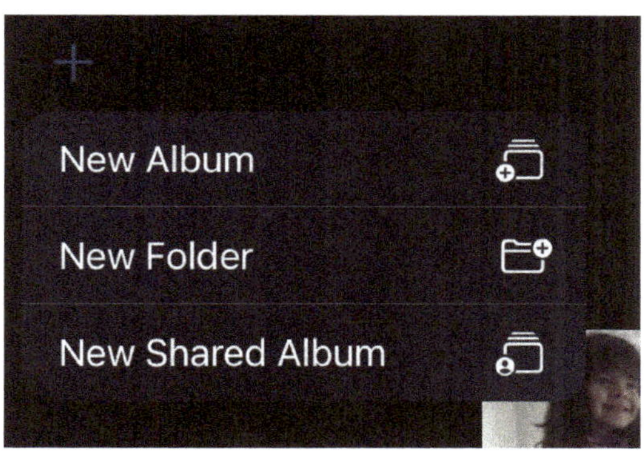

And finally, name your album and select the photos that go into it.

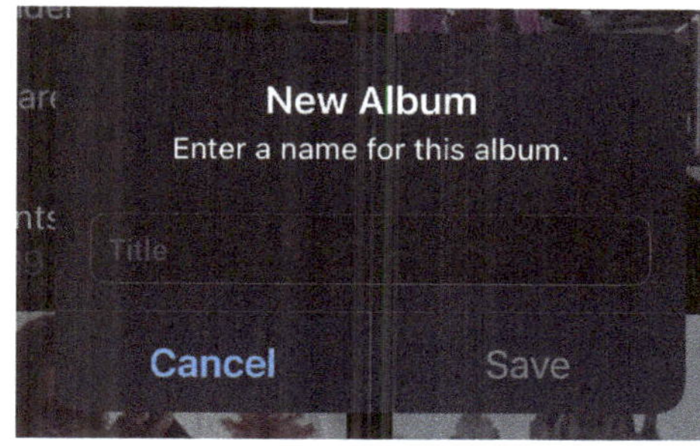

I created one called Christmas through the years.

To create a video of this album, tap on the three dots in the upper right corner, then select Play Memory Movie.

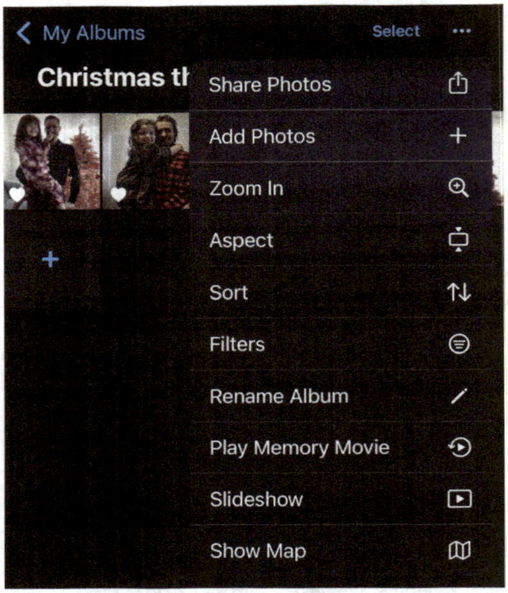

It's all generated automatically, and even finds music to go with it—without telling Apple anything, it recognizes that these photos were over the holidays and it attaches Christmas music to the video. If you want to share it with someone, tap the Share in the upper right corner.

Next, select how and who to share it with, and let iPhone do the rest!

To change the music, select the Music icon in the lower left corner, then select the add music icon.

Apple will suggest a few that it thinks would fit well with the photos. If you want to search for a song, tap the magnifying glass.

When you tap the music icon, there's also three circles to the right of the add music icon. You can use that to adjust how the movie looks.

There's several different looks to pick from. Tap the one you want and it will change instantly.

Look Up

Photos on the iPhone are smart—like really smart! Take a look at the photo below. You know it's a dog, but what if you want to know what kind of dog (i.e. the breed of dog)?

When you swipe up, if Apple recognizes something significant in the photo (this won't always work), then it will say "Look Up" and next it, it will say what it is. In the photo below it's a dog—but it could be food, other types of animals—lots of things!

Tap the Look Up and it will tell you what it sees in the photo and give you a page to see more.

Smart Text

The iPhone doesn't just recognize important places. It sees text. Tap and hold your finger over text and you can copy it, look it up, or even translate it. If it's a phone number, you can call the person from tapping on the photo!

Chapter 8: Using Siri

By now, you probably know all about Siri and how she can remind you of things. If not, press and hold the Side button.

Siri works the same as always, but she's gotten a few under-the-hood updates to make her faster.

The biggest change to Siri is the look. The theme of many of the changes to iOS is how do you minimize what already works. With Siri that means having a smaller look. It now launches in a more nonintrusive way.

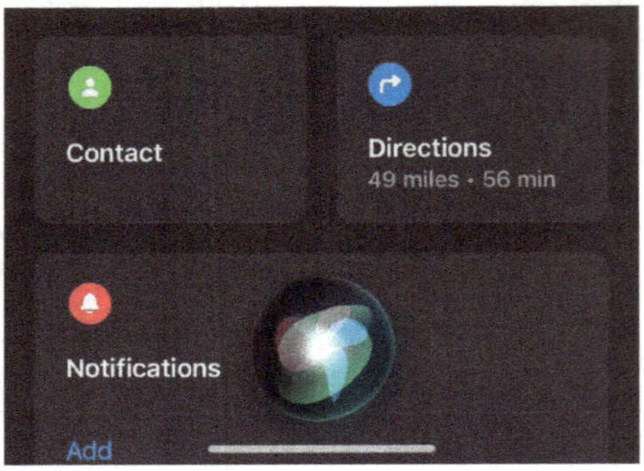

Her replies also go with fewer distractions. She used to launch full-screen replies that took you out of what you were doing to see the answer. Now it just takes a little bit of space.

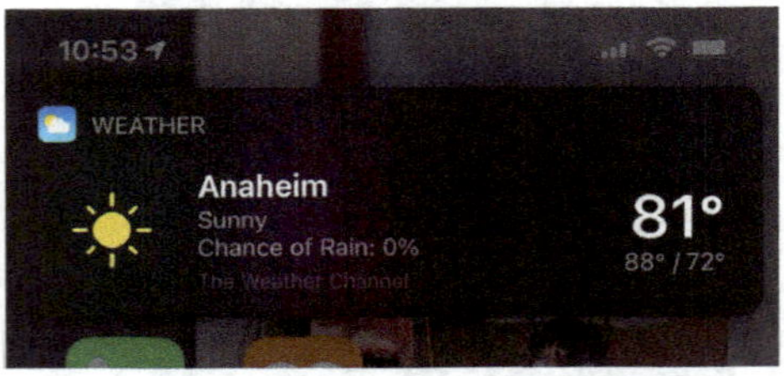

So, what exactly do you do with it? The first thing you should do is introduce Siri to your family. Siri is pretty smart, and she wants to meet your family. To introduce her to your family, activate Siri by pressing and holding the Home button and say: "Brian is my brother" or "Susan is my boss." Once you confirm the relationship you can now say things like: "Call my brother" or "Email my boss."

Siri is also location-based. What does that mean? It means that instead of saying, "Remind me to call wife at 8 AM" you can say, "Remind me when I leave work to call wife," and as soon as you step out of the office you will receive a reminder. Siri can be a bit frustrating at first, but it's one of the phone's most powerful apps, so give it a chance!

Everyone hates to deal with waiting. There's nothing worse than being hungry and having to wait an hour for a table. Siri does her best to make your life easier by making reservations for you. For this to work, you'll need a free app called "OpenTable" (you'll also need a free account), which is in the Apple App store. This app makes its money from restaurants paying it, so don't worry about having to pay to use it. Once it's installed, you will simply activate Siri (press the Home button until it turns on) and say, "Siri, make me a reservation at the Olive Garden," (or wherever you want to eat). Note that not all restaurants participate in OpenTable, but hundreds (if not thousands) do, and it's growing monthly, so if it's not there, it probably will be soon.

Siri is ever evolving. And with the latest update, Apple has taught her everything she needs to know about sports. Go ahead, try it! Press and hold the 'Home' button to activate Siri, and then say something like: "What's the score in the Kings game" or: "Who leads the league in homeruns?"

Siri has also gotten a little wiser in movies. You can say, "Movies directed by Peter Jackson" and it will give you a list and let you see a synopsis, the review rating from Rotten Tomatoes, and in some cases even a trailer or an option to buy the movie. You can also say, "Movie show times" and nearby movies that are playing will appear. At this time, you cannot buy tickets to the movie, though one can imagine that option will be coming very soon.

Finally, Siri, can open apps for you. If you want to open an app, simply say, "Open" and the app's name.

The new iOS lets you add shortcuts to Siri; you can see this in Settings > Siri & Search > Short cuts.

Siri Shortcuts

Siri Shortcuts is one of the most powerful apps on your phone. And probably the one most people never use. What is it?

Shortcuts might not be the best way to describe it. Automation does it more justice, in my opinion. It's a way to teach Siri how to automate the things you do often in life.

Let me give an example:

Let's say you have a playlist when you plug your phone into CarPlay. You always play it on shuffle. You stop it when you get to your location.

The old way of doing this was manually. The new way to do this is just plug in the phone and let your phone do the rest.

Absolutely nothing for you to do.

Siri Shortcuts becomes easier in iOS because it's all built into the phone with a native pre-installed app.

SHORTCUTS VS. AUTOMATION

When you first open the app, you'll see three menus on the bottom: shortcuts, automation, gallery. What's the difference?

Shortcuts are things you can actually add to your phone, sort of like apps—so you could have an icon representing your shortcut right on your Home screen. "Automation" is actions your phone takes when something happens—you plug it into CarPlay, for example, the phone does X. "Gallery" is pre-made automations that you can add.

Using Shortcuts

To create a shortcut, go to the shortcut menu and tap "Create Shortcut."

Next, select: "Add Action."

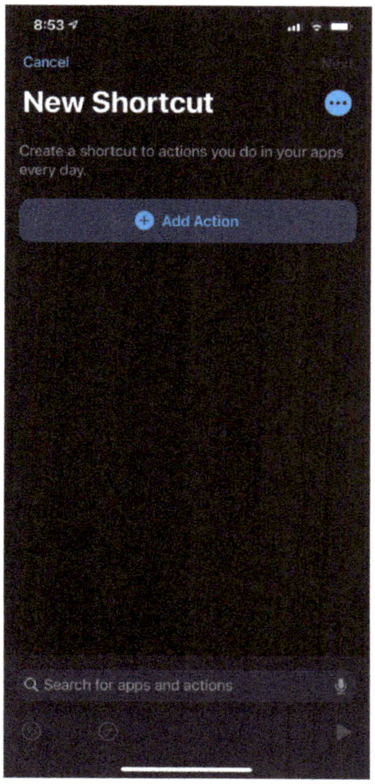

From here, you define the shortcut. Do you want to have a shortcut whenever you want to play your workout playlist, for example? Tap "Media." I'm going to create a shortcut to call my wife, so I don't have to go into the phone app to do it. Under suggestions, I'm selecting "Call" and "Wife."

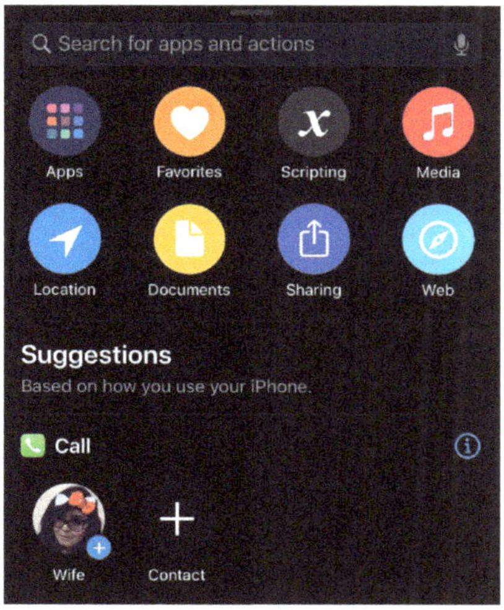

The shortcut is created. From here I can tap the '+' button to create an additional action. For example, whenever I call her, get the current driving time so I can tell her how far I am from home.

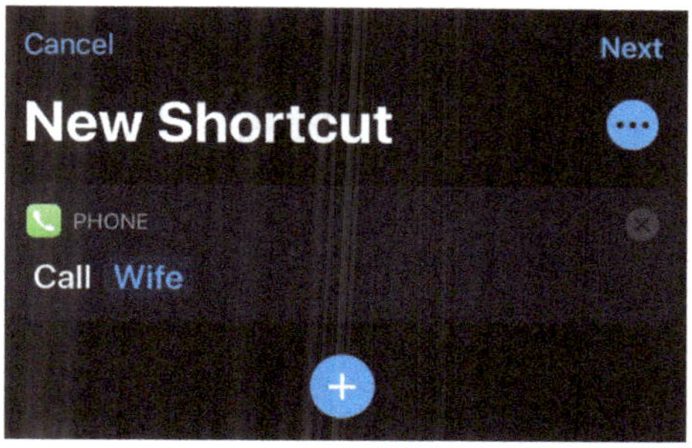

If I tap the three dots, I can customize the Shortcut.

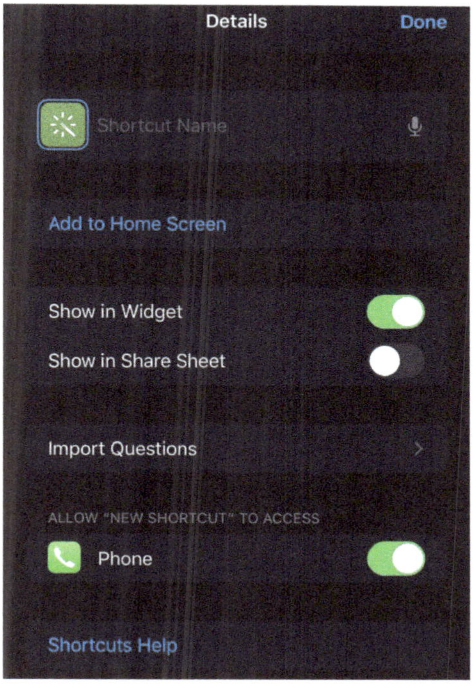

Once I give it a name, I can add it to my Home screen with "Add to Home Screen."

From here, if I tap on the small icon, I can choose a custom photo to assign to it.

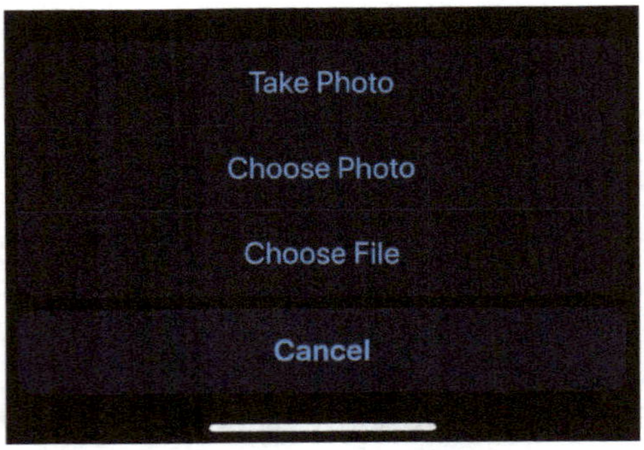

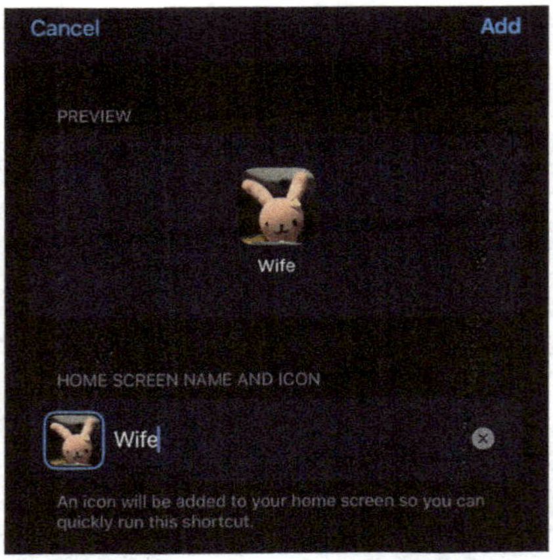

Once you add it, it will appear on your Home screen.

The shortcut also appears in your Siri Shortcut app.

To remove it, long press it. Then tap "Delete."

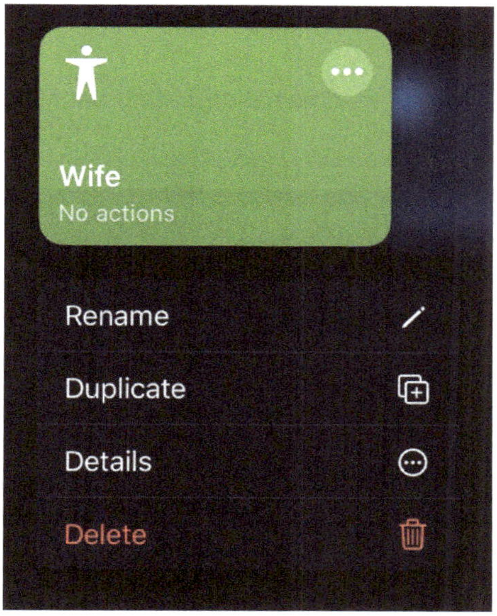

Using Automation

Adding an automation is similar to the method used for shortcuts. Select "Automation" from the Siri Shortcut menu. You have two options. Personal automation and Home automation. Personal is an automation that would be on your iOS device for you to use. Home automation would be something accessible to anyone in your home and is ideal for something like the Homepod.

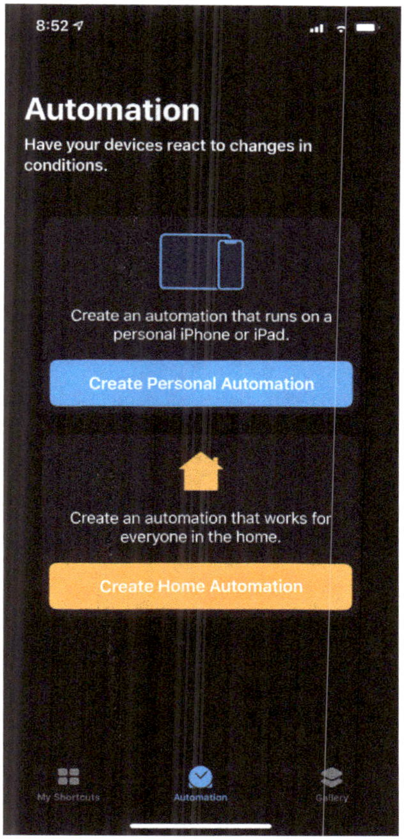

Once you select "Create," you'll see a series of suggestions. Select the ones you want and follow the steps.

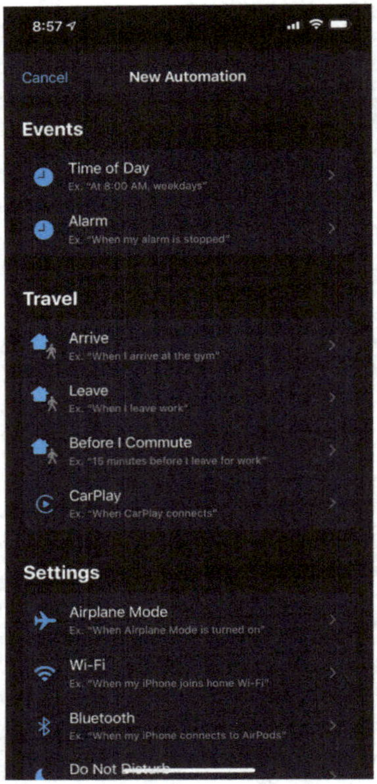

To remove the automation, swipe over it and select "Delete."

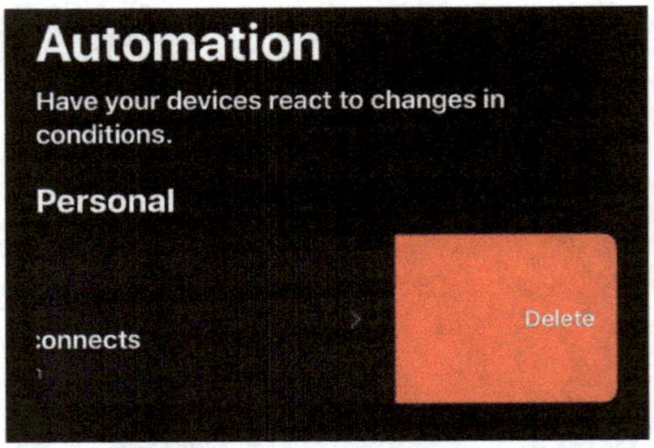

CHAPTER 9: APPLE SERVICES

It used to be a few times a year Apple would take the stage and announce something that everyone's head exploded over! The iPhone! The iPad! The Apple Watch! The iPod!

That still happens today, but Apple also is well aware of the reality: most people don't upgrade to new hardware every year. How does a company make money when that happens? In a word: services.

In the past few years (especially in 2019) Apple announced several services—things people would opt into to pay for monthly. It was a way to continue making money even when people were not buying hardware.

For it to work, Apple knew it had to be good. They couldn't just offer a subpar service and expect people to pay because it said Apple. It had to be good. And it is!

This book will walk you through those services and show you how to get the most out of them.

iCloud

iCloud is something that Apple doesn't talk a lot about but is perhaps their biggest service. It's estimated that nearly 850 million people use it. The thing about it, however, is many people don't even know they're using it.

What exactly is it? If you are familiar with Google Drive, then the concept is something you probably already understand. It's an online storage locker. But it's more than that. It is a place where you can store files, and it also syncs everything—so if you send a message on your iPhone, it appears on your MacBook and iPad. If you work on a Keynote presentation from your iPad, you can continue where you left off on your iPhone.

What's even better about iCloud is it's affordable. New phones get 5GB for free. From there the price range is as follows (note that these prices may change after printing):

- **50GB: $0.99**
- **200GB: $2.99**
- **2TB: $9.99**

These prices are for everyone in your family. So, if you have five people on your plan, then each person doesn't need their own storage plan. This also means purchases are saved—if one family member buys a book or movie, everyone can access it.

iCloud has become even more powerful as our photo library grows. Photos used to be relatively small, but as cameras have advanced, the size goes up. Most photos on your phone are several MB big. iCloud means you can keep the newest ones on your phone and put the older ones in the cloud. It also means you don't have to worry about paying for the phone with the biggest hard drive—in fact, even if you have the biggest hard drive, there's a chance it won't fit all of your photos.

Where Is iCloud?

If you look at your phone, you won't see an iCloud app. That's because there isn't an iCloud app. There's a "Files" app that functions like a storage locker.

To see iCloud, point your computer browser to iCloud.com.

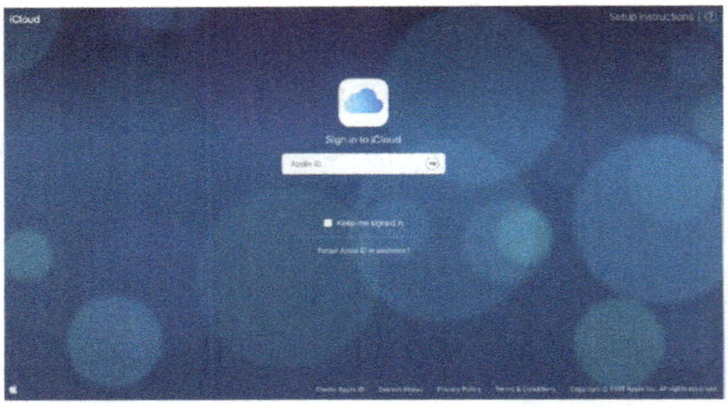

Once you sign in, you'll see all the things stored in your cloud—photos, contacts, notes, files; these are all things you can access across all of your devices.

In addition, you can use iCloud from any computer (even PCs); this is especially helpful if you need to use Find iPhone, which locates not only your iPhone, but all of your Apple devices—phones, watches, even AirPods.

Backing Up Your Phone With iCloud

The first thing you should know about iCloud is how to back up your phone with it. This is what you will need to do if you are moving from one phone to another.

If there's no iCloud app on the phone, then how do you do that? While there is no native app in the traditional sense that you are used to, there are several iCloud settings in the Settings app.

Open the Settings app; at the top you will see your name and profile picture; tap that.

This opens my ID settings where I can update things like phone numbers and email. One of the options is iCloud. Tap that.

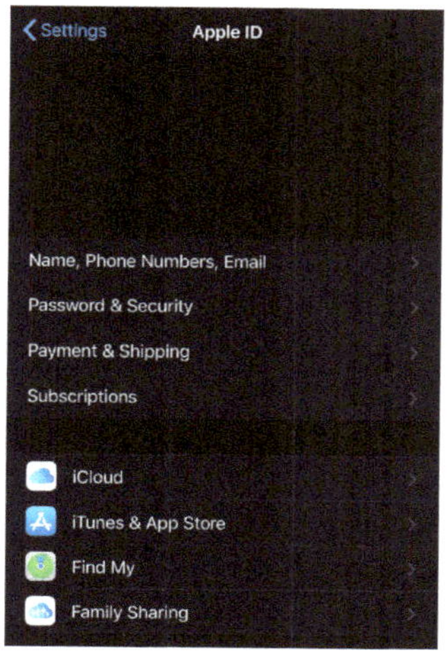

Scroll down a little until you get to the setting that says iCloud Backup, and tap that.

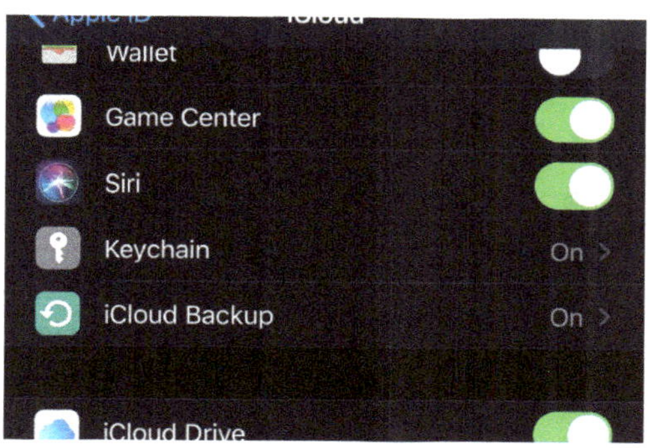

It will probably be on (the toggle switch will be green); if you'd rather do things manually, then you can toggle it off and then do Back Up Now. If you turn it off then you'll have to do a manual backup each time.

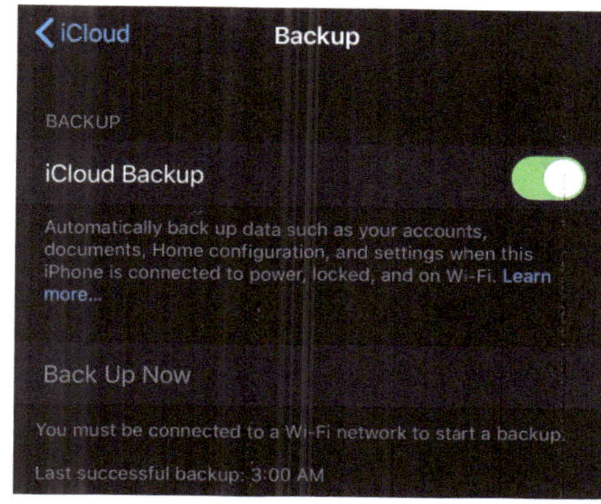

From the iCloud, you'll also be able to change what apps use iCloud and see how much space you have left. In my case, I have the 2TB plan, and we've used about half of it.

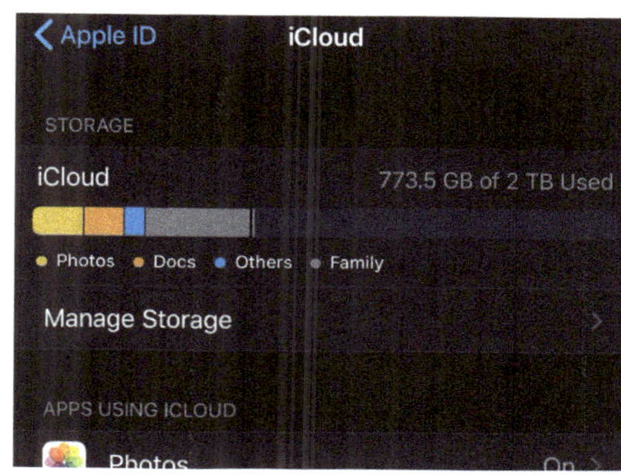

If you tap Manage Storage, you can see where the storage is being used. You can also upgrade or downgrade your account from this page by tapping on Change Storage Plan.

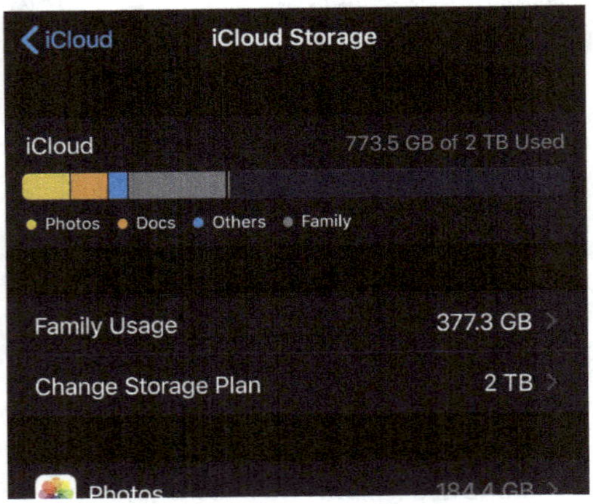

Tap on Family Usage and you can see more specifically what family members use what. You can also stop sharing from this page.

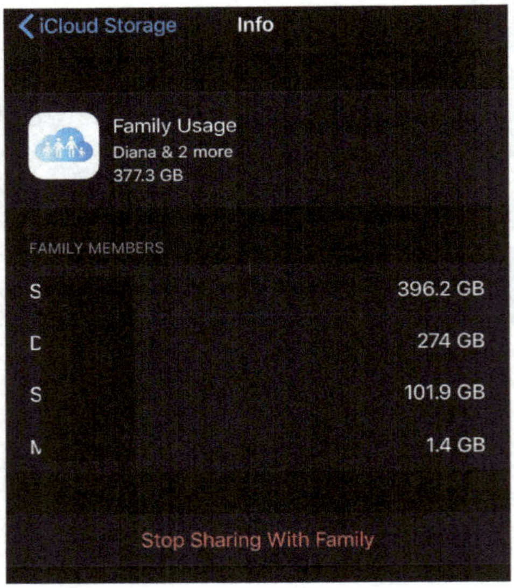

Moving to a New Device

When you get a new device, you will be asked during the setup to log in with your Apple ID associated with your previous device, and then get the option to recover from a previous device.

Sharing Photos With iCloud

To share and backup photos with iCloud, go into Settings > Photos and ensure iCloud Photos is toggled to green. If you are short on storage, you can check the option below to Optimize storage.

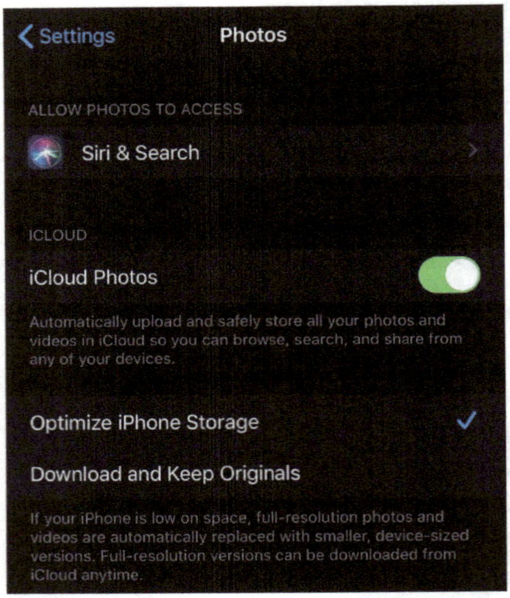

Files App

To see your cloud files, open the Files app.

The first thing you'll see is all your recent files.

If you don't see what you are looking for, then go to the bottom tabs and switch from Recents to Browse.

This opens a more traditional looking file explorer.

If you want to create a new folder, connect to a server, or scan a document, tap the three dots in the top left corner to open your app options.

Scan Documents lets you use your camera like a traditional flatbed scanner to scan and print documents.

You can tap on Sort by Name to change how files are sorted.

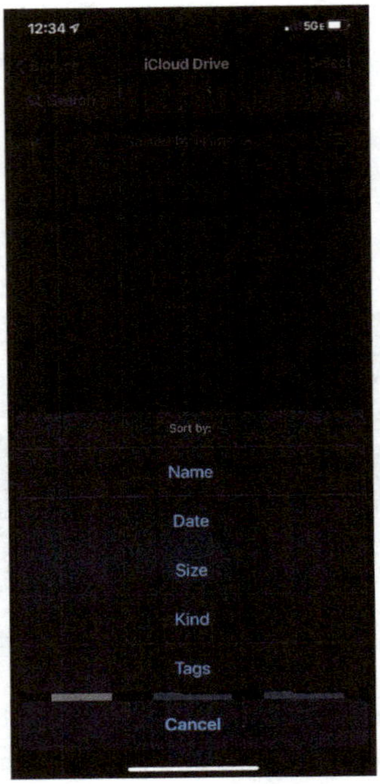

iCloud Settings

One other important set of iCloud settings is in Settings > General > iPhone Storage.

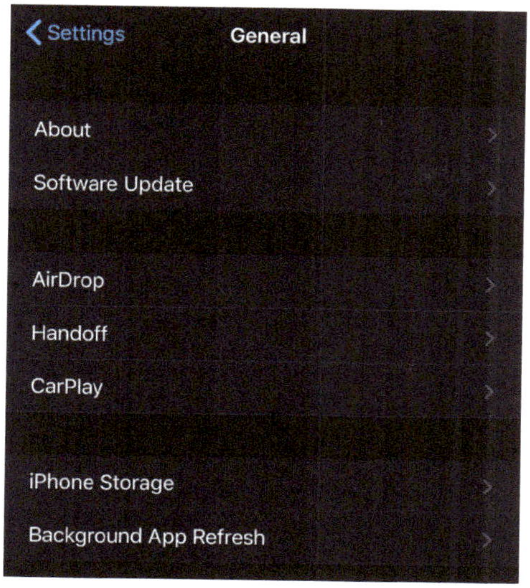

When you tap this, it will show you how much storage apps are using and also make recommendations.

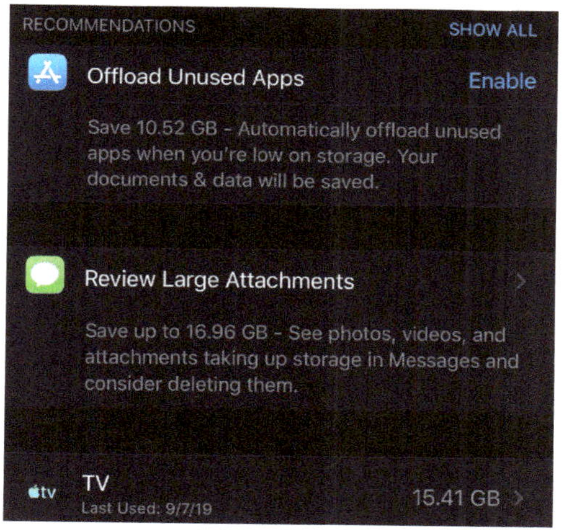

Apple Arcade

Apple Arcade is sort of like Netflix for games. It's $4.99/month (nothing extra for other members of your family—share it with up to five members).

The price gives you access to 100+ games. Unlike some streaming services where you have to play the games online, Apple Arcade lets you download the games to play them offline. You can play them on all your Apple compatible devices: iPhone, iPad, and Apple TV. When you stop playing on your phone, you can start playing where you left off on your TV or iPad.

There are no ads and you can use it with parental controls.

How to Sign Up

Apple Arcade isn't an app. It's a Service. You only download what you want. You sign up by visiting the app store and tapping on Arcade. This brings you to the main Arcade menu where all you have to do is tap Subscribe.

Once you subscribe, you'll see a welcome menu.

The Arcade menu is now replaced by games you can download. Tap "Get" for any game you want. $4.99 is for everything—not per app.

When you read about the game, be mindful of the app size; if you have data restrictions, make sure you download it over Wi-Fi.

The app looks like every other app on your phone. The only difference is the splash screen, which says "Arcade."

Cancelling Arcade Subscription

All subscriptions are cancelled the same way. Go to the app store, and tap your account. Next, tap Subscriptions.

This shows you all of your active subscriptions, including Apple Arcade.

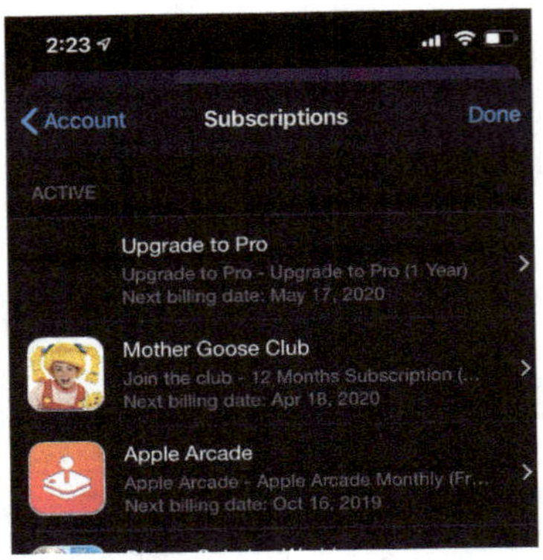

Once you click on it, there is an option to cancel on the bottom.

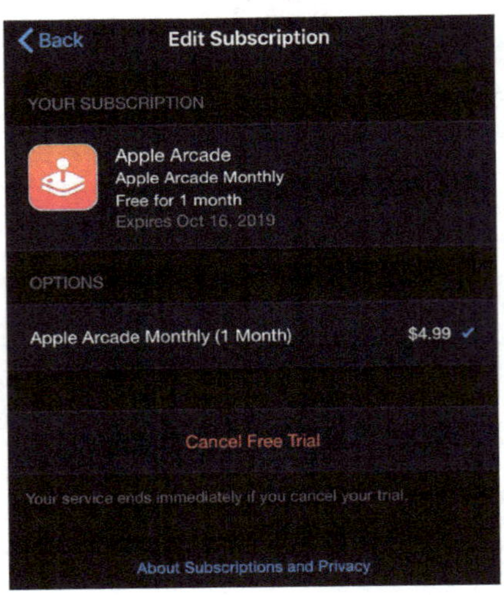

You will get a notification that all of your games will be erased after your subscription expiration (note: it expires on the original expiration date—not the date you cancel).

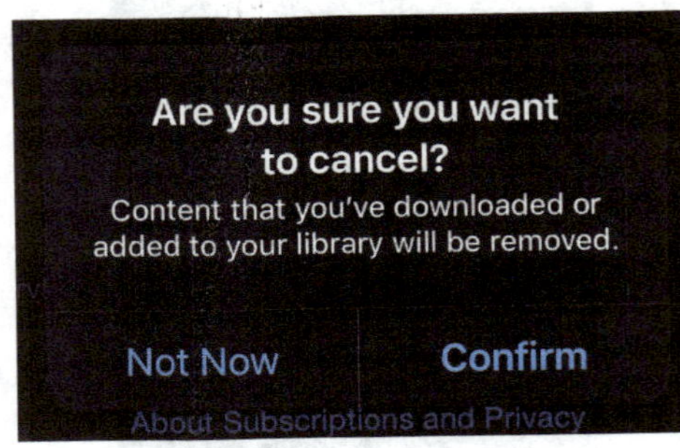

The subscription details now tells you when it's cancelled.

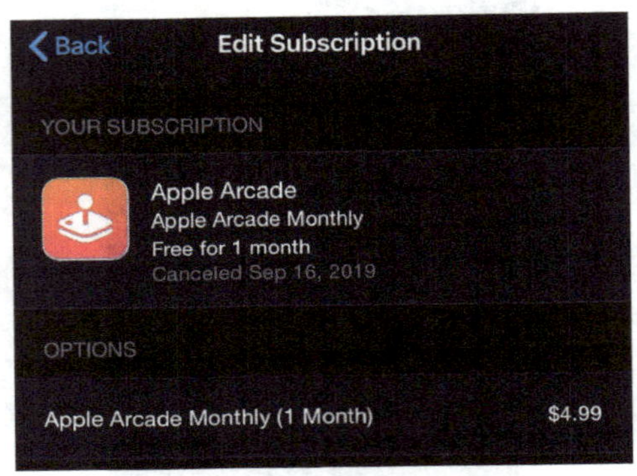

Apple TV+

Apple has been quietly working on a TV service for quite some time. In 2019, they finally revealed the details. It is $4.99 a month (free for a year if you buy an iPhone, iPad, Apple Watch, Apple TV, or Mac—note that this may change in the future), and launched November 1.

To watch any of these shows, go to the TV app. It's available on Apple TV, iPad, and iPhone; it remembers your place, so if you pause it on one device, you can pick up where you left off on another.

Shows and films are being added monthly, and current shows are getting future seasons, so look for this area to rapidly change.

Apple Music

Apple Music is Apple's music streaming service.

The question most people wonder is which is better: Spotify or Apple Music? On paper it's hard to tell. They both have the same number of songs, and they both cost the same ($9.99 a month, $5 for students, $14.99 for families).

There really is no clear winner. It all comes down to preference. Spotify has some good features—such as an ad-supported free plan.

One of the standout features of Apple Music is iTunes Match. If you are like me and have a large collection of audio files on your computer, then you'll love iTunes Match. Apple puts those files in the cloud, and you can stream them on any of your devices. This feature is also available if you don't have Apple Music for $25 a year.

Apple Music also plays well with Apple devices; so, if you are an Apple house (i.e. everything you own, from smart speakers to TV media boxes, has the Apple logo), then Apple Music is probably the best one for you.

Apple is compatible with other smart speakers, but it's built to shine on its own devices.

I won't cover Spotify here, but my advice is to try them both (they both have free trials) and see which interface you prefer.

Apple Music Crash Course

Before going over where things are in Apple Music, it's worth noting that Apple Music can now be accessed from your web browser (in beta form) here: http://beta.music.apple.com.

It's also worth noting that I have a little girl and don't get to listen to a lot of "adult" music, so the examples here are going to show a lot of kids music!

The main navigation on Apple Music is at the bottom. There are five basic menus to select from:

- Library
- For You
- Browse
- Radio
- Search

Library

When you create playlists or download songs or albums, this is where you will go to find them.

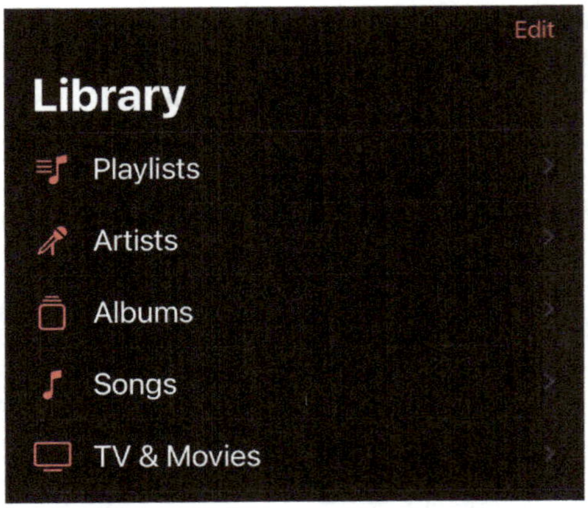

You can change the categories that show up in this first list by tapping on Edit, then checking off the categories you want. Make sure to hit Done to save your changes.

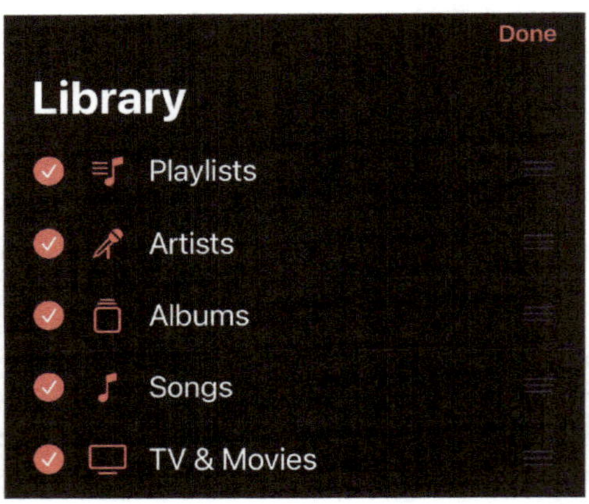

When you tap on the playlist you want to play, you can also share it with your friends by tapping on the three dots that show the options menu, and then tapping on Share Playlist.

Listen Now

As you play music, Apple Music starts to get to know you more and more; it makes recommendations based on what you are playing. In Listen Now, you can get a mix of all these songs and see other recommendations.

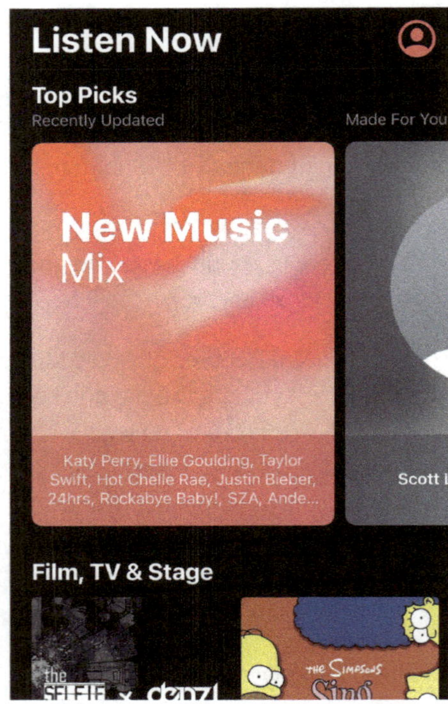

In addition to different styles of music, it also has friends' recommendations so you can discover new music based on what your friends are listening to.

Browse

Not digging those recommendations? You can also browse genres in the Browse menu.

In addition to different genre categories, you can see what music is new and what music is popular.

Radio

Radio is Apple's version of AM/FM; the main radio station is Beats One. There are on-air DJs and everything you'd expect from a radio station.

While Beats One is Apple's flagship station, it's not its only station. You can scroll down and tap on Radio Stations under More to explore and see several other stations based on music styles (i.e. country, alternative, rock, etc.). Under this menu, you'll also find a handful of talk stations covering news and sports. Don't expect to find the opinionated talk radio you may listen to on regular radio—it's pretty controversy-free.

Search

The last option is the search menu, which is pretty self-explanatory. Type in what you want to find (i.e. artist, album, genre, etc.).

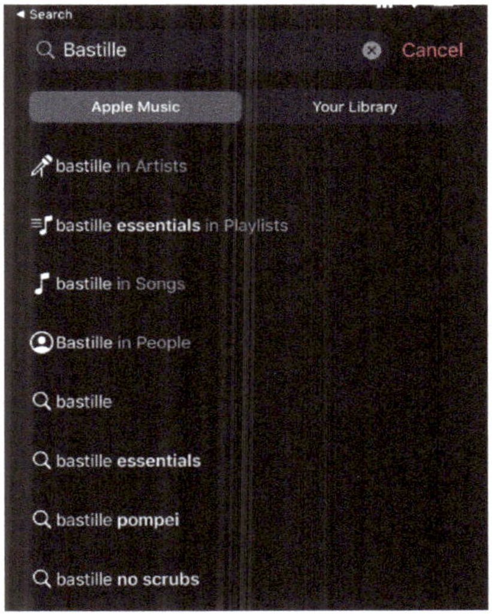

Listening to Music and Creating a Playlist

You can access the music you are currently listening to from the bottom of your screen.

This brings up a full screen of what you are listening to with several options.

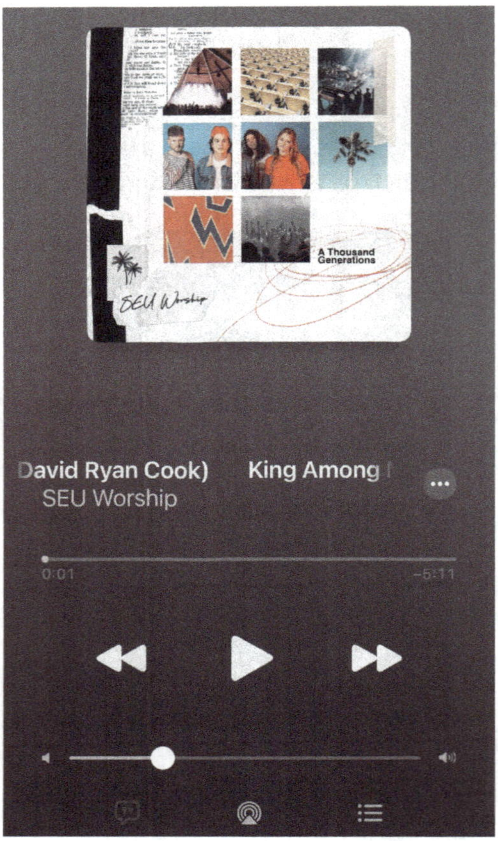

The play, back/forward, and volume buttons are pretty straightforward. The buttons below that might look new.

The first option is for lyrics. If the song is paused, then you can read through the lyrics; if the song is playing, then it will bold the lyrics to the song it is currently playing. If you ever caught yourself wondering if the singer is saying "dense" or "dance" then this feature is a gamechanger.

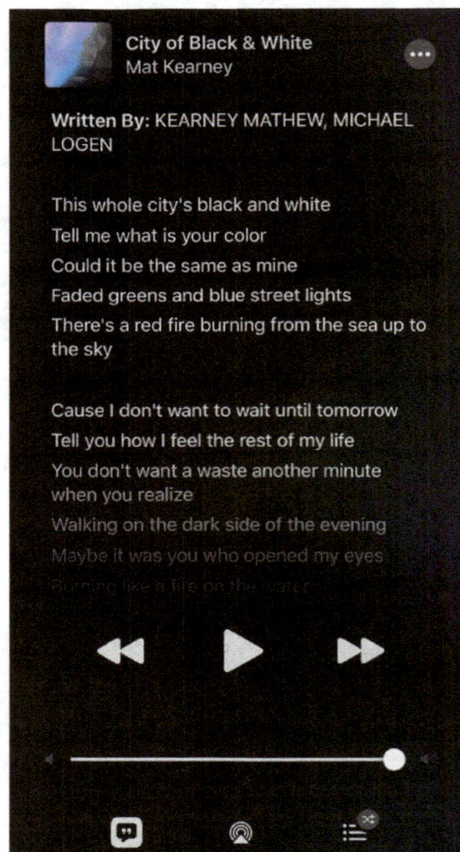

The middle option lets you pick where you play the music. For example, if you have a HomePod and you want to listen wirelessly to the music from that device, you can change it here.

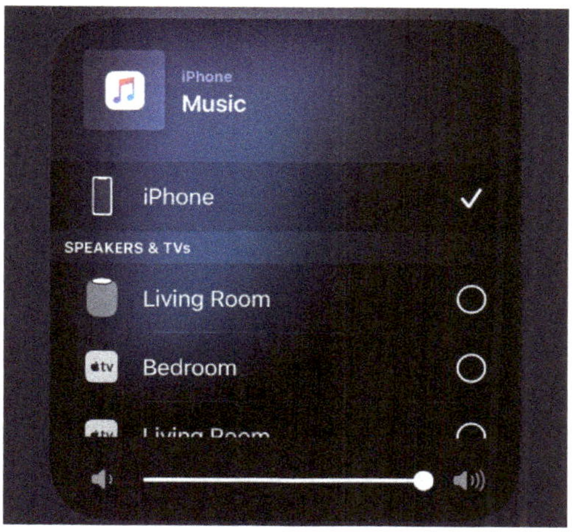

The last option shows the next song(s) in the playlist.

If you want to add a song to a playlist, then click the three dots next to the album/artist name. This brings up a list of several options (you can also go here to love or hate a song—which helps Apple Music figure out what you like); the option you want is Add to a Playlist. If you don't have a playlist or want to add it to a new one, then you can also create one here.

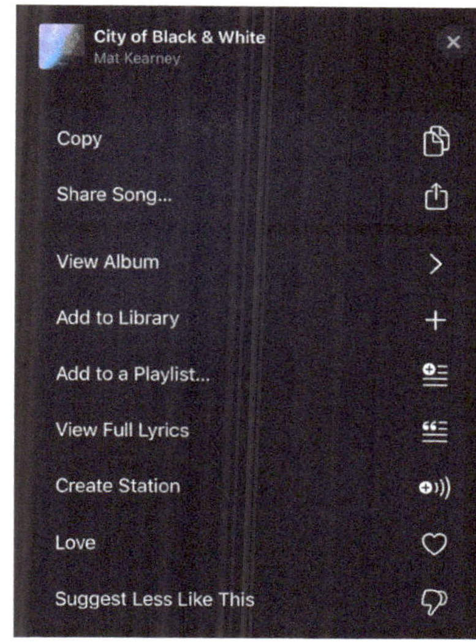

At any point, you can tap the artist's name to see all of their music.

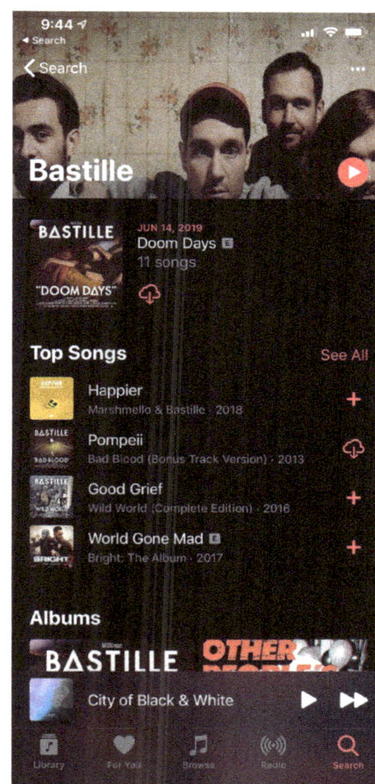

In addition to seeing information about the band, their popular songs, and their albums, you can get a playlist of their essential songs or a playlist of bands that they have influenced.

If you scroll to the bottom, you can also see Similar Artists, which is a great way to discover new bands that are like the ones you are currently listening to.

Tips for Getting the Most Out of Apple Music

Heart It

Like what your hearing? Heart it! Hate it? Dislike it. Apple gets to know you by what you listen to, but it improves the accuracy when you tell it what you think of a song you are really into…or really hate.

Use Settings

Some of the most resourceful features of Apple Music aren't in Apple Music—they're in your settings.

Open the Settings app, and scroll down to Music.

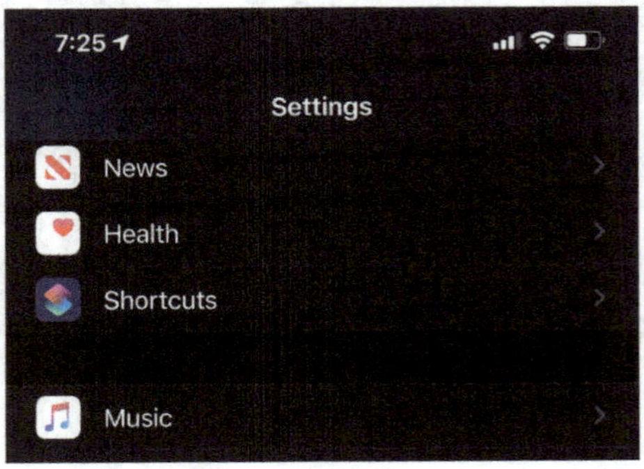

There are a few things to note here.

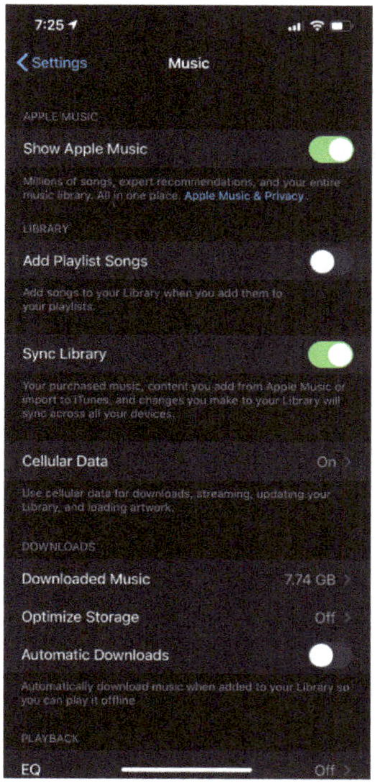

The first is under Cellular Data. Tap that and you'll see an option to turn high quality streaming on and off. If you want the best quality even when you are using data, then turn it on.

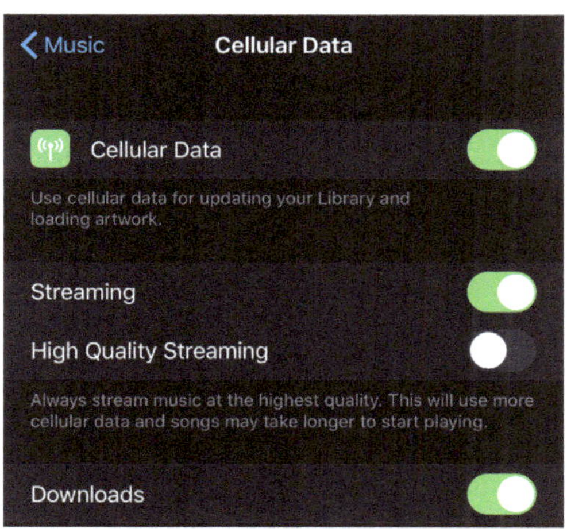

Next, go to Optimize Storage. If you are running short on space, then make sure and tap to toggle off.

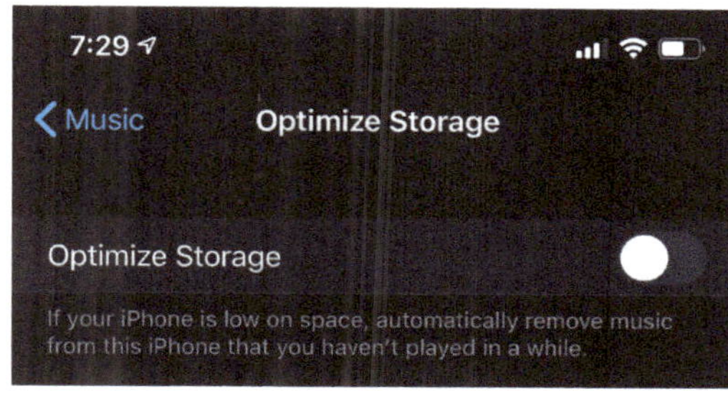

Want to change the way your music sounds—such as more or less bass—go to EQ in the settings.

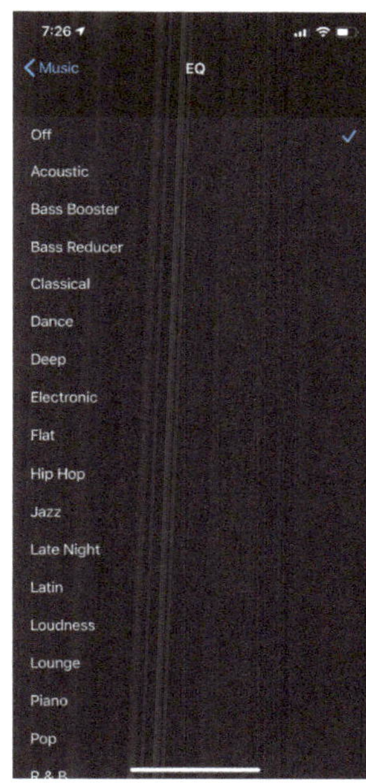

Download Music

If you don't want to rely on data when you are on the go, make sure and tap the Cloud on your music to download the music locally to your phone. If you don't see a cloud, add it to your library by tapping the plus, which should change it to a cloud.

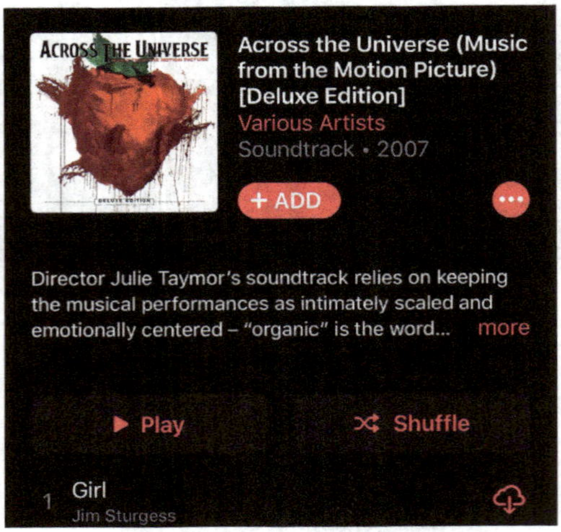

Hey Siri

Siri knows music! Say "Hey Siri" and say what you want to listen to, and the AI will get to work.

Wake Up to Music

If you'd like to wake up to a song instead of a buzzing noise, open your alarm. Next, tap "Sound."

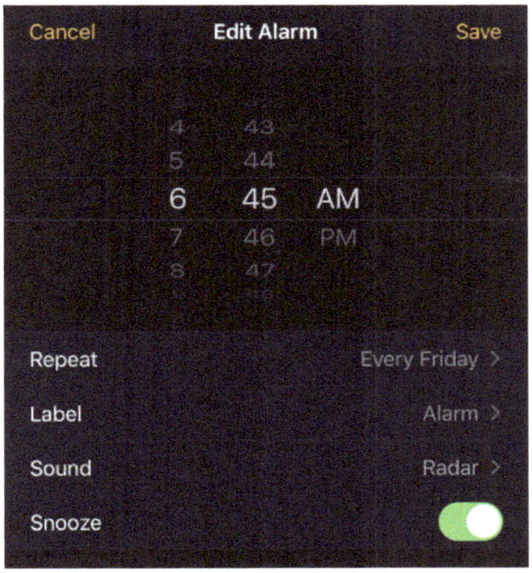

From here, select "Pick a Song."

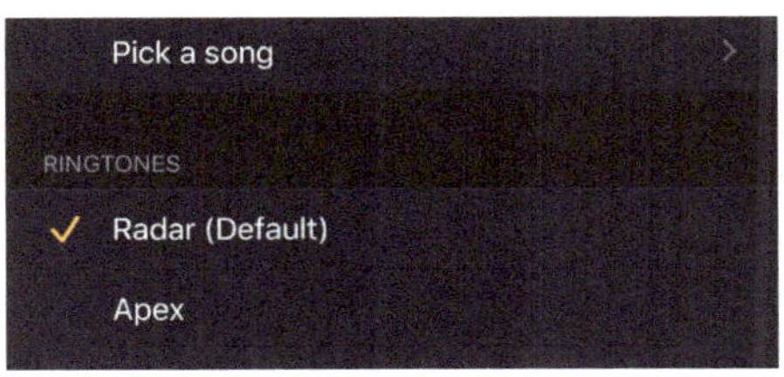

Finally, pick your music.

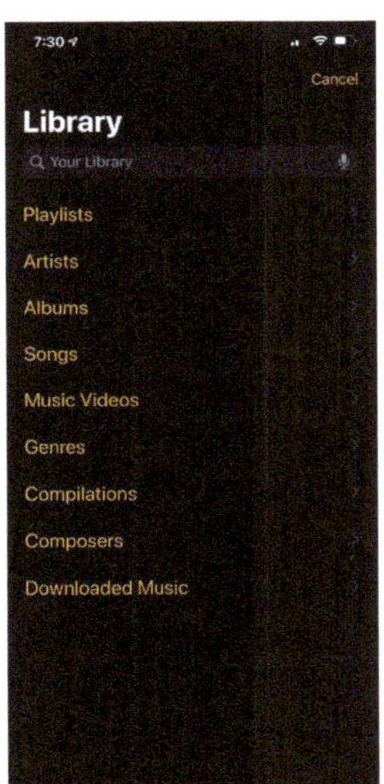

Lockscreen Music

If you want the music cover art to show on the home screen, tap the thumbnail of the image and it will enlarge.

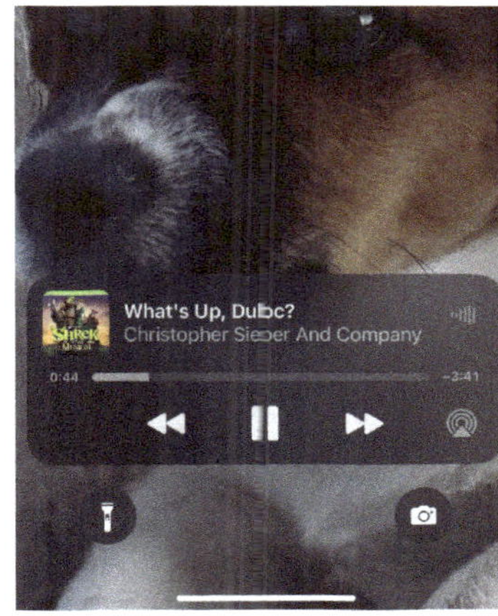

Tap the enlarged cover and it will shrink.

Sort Playlist

If you grow tired of shuffling your playlist or listening to it in the order you created it, you can sort the playlist by the date the song was added, artist, and more.

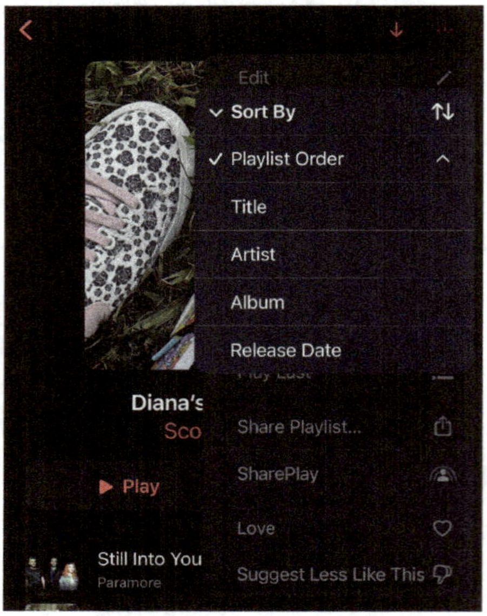

Apple News+

In 2012, a little app with big ambitions called Next (it was later changed to Texture) disrupted the magazine industry by creating the Netflix of magazines. For one low price, you could read hundreds of magazines (and their back issues too). They weren't small indie magazines—they were the big ones: People, Time, Wired, and more.

Apple took notice, and, in 2018, they acquired the company. The writing was on the wall: Apple wanted to get into print services.

In 2019, it was announced that Texture would close because Apple would release a new service called News+. News+ does everything that Texture did, but also combines newspapers (Los Angeles Times and The Wall Street Journal).
There is a free version of the service that curates news for you; the paid version that carries the magazine subscriptions is $9.99. (You can have five family members on your plan.)

What really makes Apple News stand out is it's curated for you and your tastes. If you have other family members on your plan, it will be curated for them as well—it's based on the user's tastes, so if you have a family member into entertainment news and you are into game news, you won't see their interests —only yours.

Apple News Crash Course

To get started, open the News app from your phone (if it is not on your phone, it's a free download from the app store)

The UI for the app is pretty simple. There are three menu options on the bottom:

Today—This is where you'll find your curated news

News+—Where you'll find magazines

Following—This is where you can change your interests and unfollow certain news.

Today

The Today menu gives you all your news (starting with the top news/breaking news) in a scrolling format.

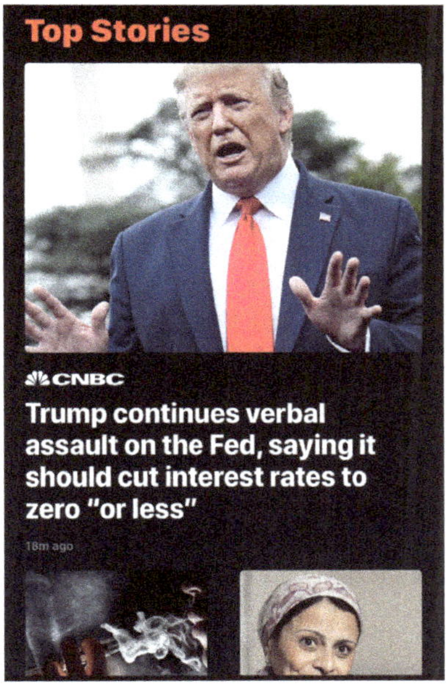

The app relies a lot on gestures. Swipe left over a headline/story and you'll get options to suggest more stories like it, share the story, or save the story for later.

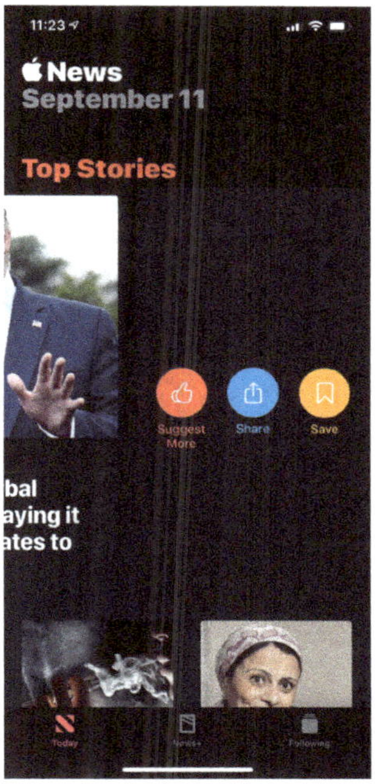

Swipe right over a story, and you can dislike it (so it stops showing similar stories) or report it. Typically, "report" in a news app means you find it somehow inappropriate in nature; that's true here, but there are other reasons to report it—such as, it's dated wrong, it's in the wrong category, it's a broken link, or something else.

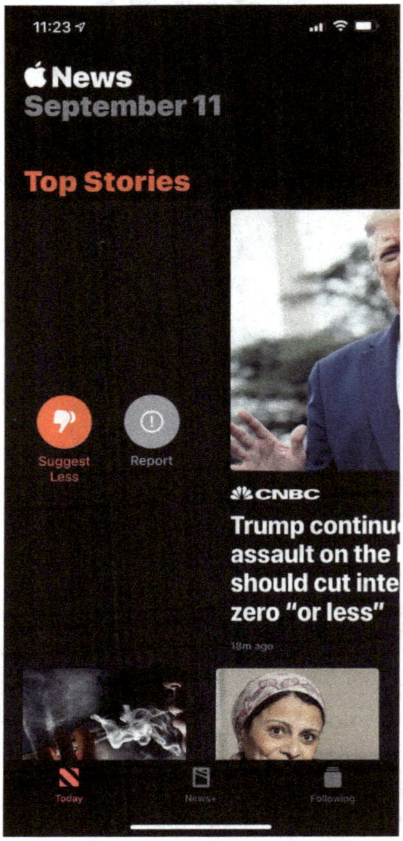

As you scroll down, you start seeing different categories (Trending Stories in the example below); when you tap the three dots with a circle, you'll get an option to block it so it won't show in your feed any longer.

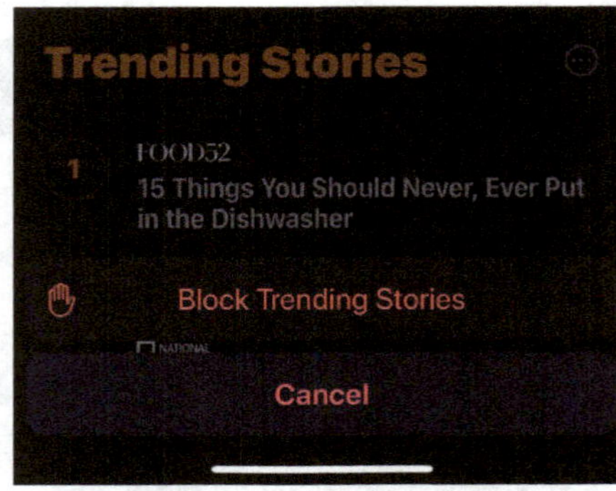

When you tap to read a story, there are only a few options. At the top, there's the option to make the text larger or smaller; next to that is the option to share the story with friends (assuming they have Apple News). To get to the next story, there's an option in the lower right corner (or swipe left from the right corner of the screen); to get back to the previous page, tap the back arrow in the upper left corner or swipe right from the left side of the screen.

One criticism of Apple News by some has been its UI; when Apple announced the service along with its partnership with the Los Angeles Times and Wall Street Journal, many expected a format similar to what you have seen with the magazines section—a full newspaper type layout.

Worse, many didn't even know how to find the newspaper. And if they did find it, they couldn't search for stories. While the app is pretty resourceful, this is still an early product and some of the features you want might not be there yet.

That said, you can "kind of" read the Los Angeles Times (or any newspaper in Apple News) in a more traditional way. First, find an article in your feed from the publication you want to see more from, and then click the publication's name at the top of the story.

This will bring up the publication along with all the topics from that publication.

If you want to search for a particular story or publication, then head over to Following on the tab at the bottom of the screen, and search for what you want to find.

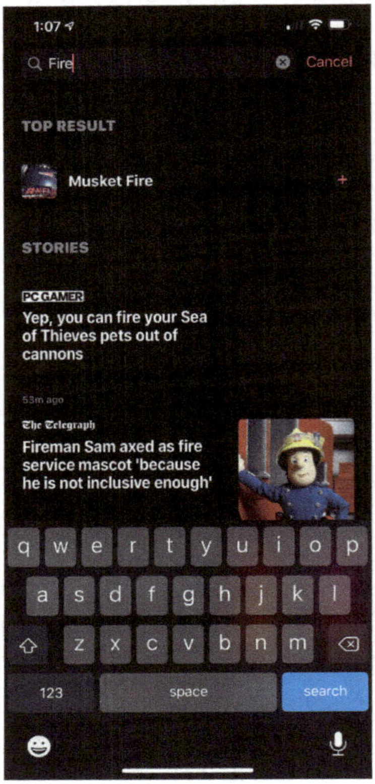

Following

Since we are on the Following tab, let's talk about it for a minute, and then go back to the middle tab (News+).

This is where you are going to be able to look at your history, read saved stories (as noted above), search for stories and publications, and follow or unfollow topics.

To unfollow a category, swipe left over it and select unfollow.

To add a new category, scroll down a little. You'll see suggested topics. Tap the + for any you want to follow.

You can move your categories around by tapping on the Edit button at the top right.

News+

The last section to cover is News+; this is where you'll find all the magazines you love.

The format is similar to the Today screen; magazines you read are at the top; below that are stories pulled from several different magazines that the app thinks you'll be interested in. There's also a more personalized For You section.

When you read articles from the list, it opens in the actual magazine and looks a little different from articles in the Today area.

Anytime you want to read more from a magazine (or see back issues) just click the logo from an article you are reading.

That brings up a list of all the issues you can read as well as some of the latest stories from the magazine.

Tapping the + button in the upper right corner will let you follow the publication.

If you long press (press and hold) the magazine cover from your My Magazines section, you can also unfollow, delete, or see back issues from the publication.

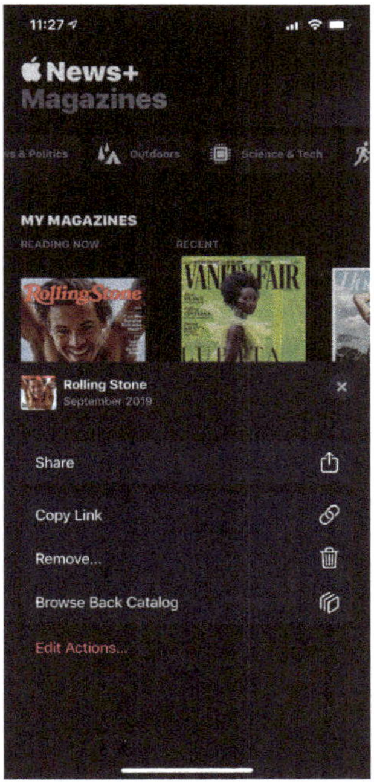

To browse all the magazines available, select Browse the Catalog from the main screen (or browse by a category that you are interested in).

This brings up a list of all the magazines you can read (at this writing, there are around 300).

Long press any of them and you can download the magazine, follow it, block it, or browse the back-issue library.

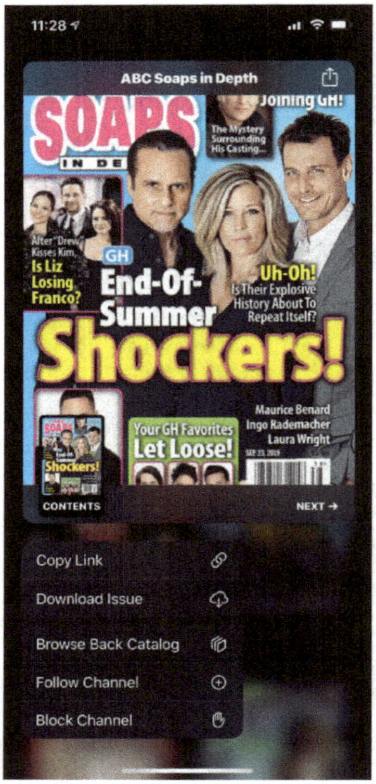

Apple Card

One of Apple's most talked about new products is Apple Card. Apple Card is a credit card that, at first glance, doesn't differ from most credit cards. It may not have the best rewards (1% to 3% cash back depending on your purchase) or best interest rate, but that doesn't mean it's not disrupting the industry; it's definitely something you should consider getting.

On the surface, the advantage of Apple Card is receiving your rewards the next day—not waiting for them. That's nice. But where it excels is in security and how it helps you keep track of purchases.

Getting Your Card

Getting an Apple Card will probably be the easiest credit card sign up you have ever experienced in your life. To get started, go to the Wallet app on your iPhone.

When the app opens, click the + button and follow the application. It will just ask you a series of questions and then tell you if you are approved.

If you're approved, your card will appear in your Wallet app with other cards.

When There Is No Apple Pay

Once you are approved for the card, you can start using it! There's no need to wait for the card—in fact the rewards are better if you don't use the card!

But sometimes you need a card. Not everyone accepts Apple Pay, after all. Fortunately, you can request a card.

You'll probably be surprised by the card. It's thick. Like really thick. Like probably the thickest card in your wallet! You can't even bend it. It doesn't feel like a plastic card. It feels like metal. That's because it's made of metal. It's not heavy at all, fortunately.

It takes about a week to arrive, and activating it is probably going to impress you. There's no number to call. No number to input on a website. None of that stuff.

It comes in a stylish envelope; when you lift the flap of the envelope and put it next to the bottom of your iPhone, it will recognize the card and start the activation process. It looks a bit like the screen below—the card in the illustration was already activated, so the steps no longer are there. The whole process is quick, stylish, and seamless—everything you'd expect from Apple.

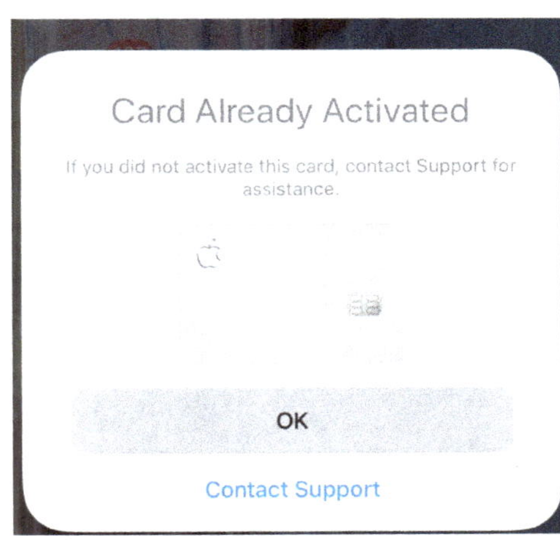

Many people think they have to wait for their card to use it online where Apple Pay isn't accepted. That's not true. You just need the credit card number. I know, I know—there is no credit card number! That's where you are wrong. There's no visible number, but there is a number.

To see it, tap the card in your Wallet app, and then tap the three little dots near the top.

This opens up your account information where you can see your credit limit, interest rate, make payments, and contact support. One of the options is "Card Information."

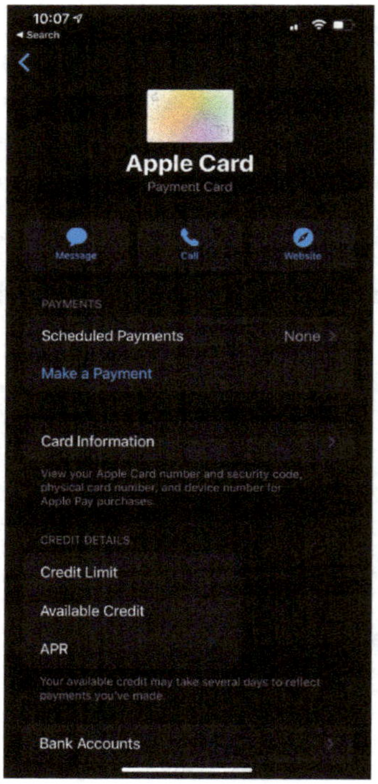

Here you'll be able to see your card number, expiration, and security card. Worried someone has your number? Just request a new number.

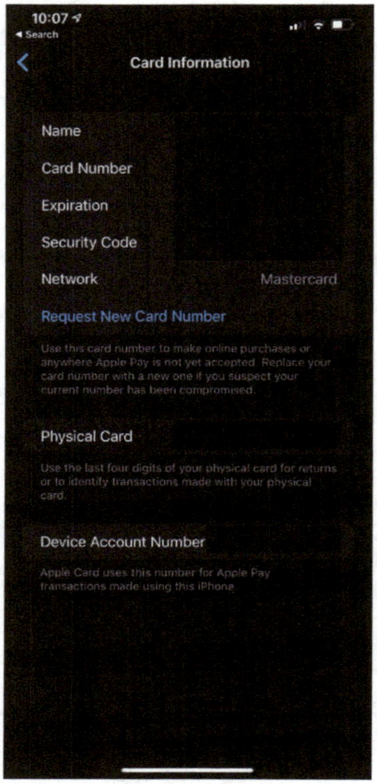

Requesting a new number doesn't affect your physical card. If someone steals your physical card, then make sure you deactivate that, and request a new card. How do you do that? Hit the back arrow to go back to your account menu. Scroll down to "Request Replacement Card." This will suspend your account to stop any future transactions and a new card will be sent.

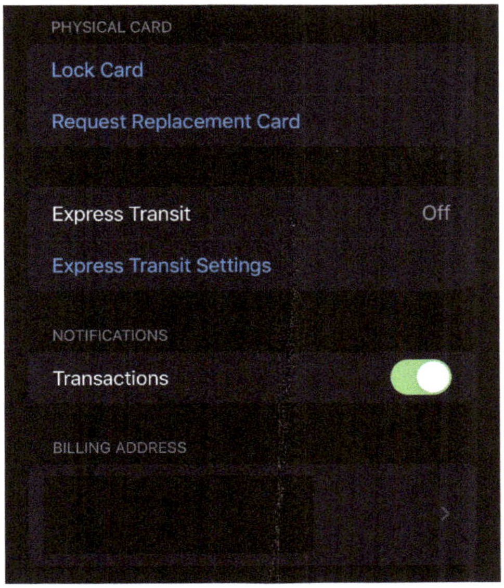

What if you want to remove the card? Go back a screen, and then go to the bottom of the screen and tap Remove This Card (remember, however, that this won't close out your account).

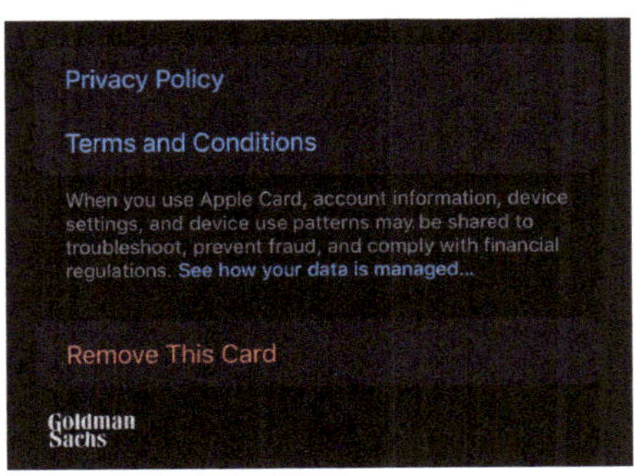

Seeing Card Activity

When you tap your card from the Wallet app, you can see all your activity, such as balance, when the payment is due, and recent transactions.

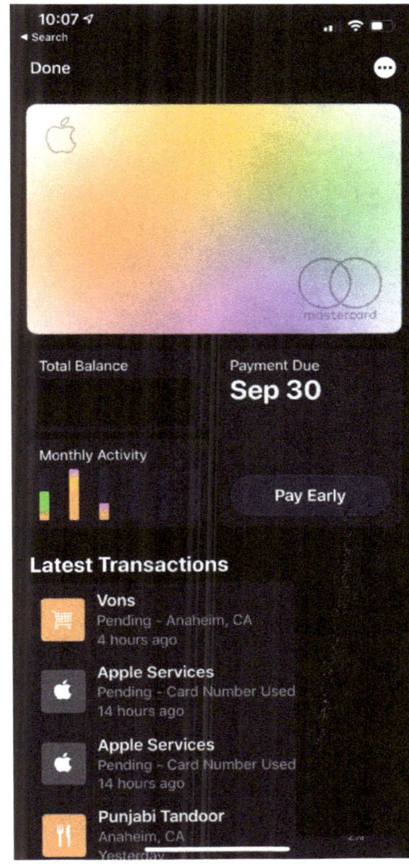

Not sure what a transaction is? Tap on it and you'll get more information about the store, and, in many cases, see a map of where it was purchased. This is helpful when tracking down mystery payments, which appear on other credit cards with weird names that don't make any sense and seem more like codes than businesses.

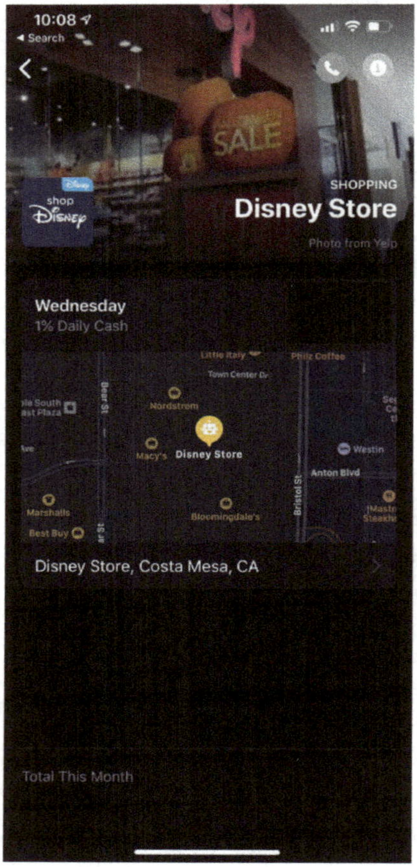

If you tap on Monthly Activity from the previous screen, you can see the categories in which you are spending money. You can also see your rewards.

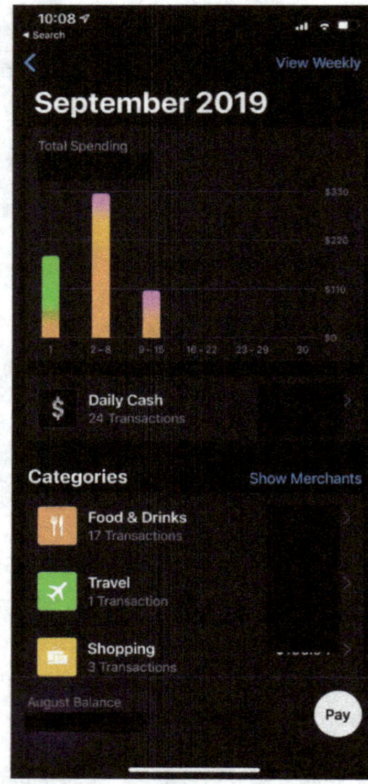

The big question on your mind might be how you spend those rewards. The rewards money is on a separate card called a Cash Card that you can access from your Wallet app. You can spend the money by using it anywhere that takes Apple Pay, or you can transfer the money straight to your bank account. You can also use the Cash Card to text money to friends.

Making Payments and Seeing Statements

To make a payment to your card, go to your main card page and tap the Payment Due box. This brings up your payment information. Interest is very transparent on Apple Card. See those dots on the circle? Tap the check mark and drag it to one of those dots; this tells you what your interest charge would be by only making a portion of the payment. Drag to the area you want to pay and then select Pay Now (or Pay Later to schedule the payment). If you don't have your bank account set up, then you'll have to do that at this point—you'll need your bank account number and routing information.

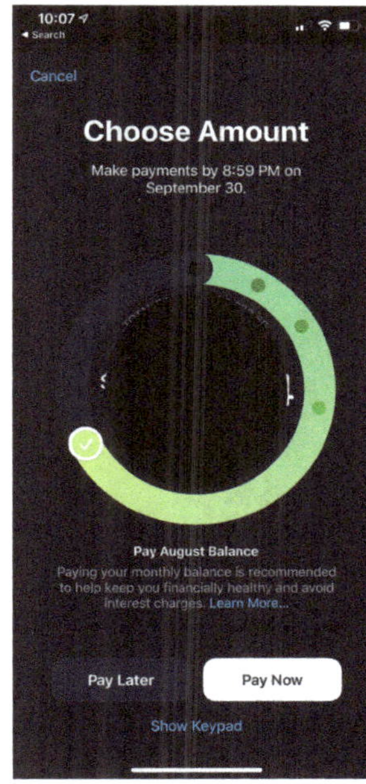

To see your credit card statement, tap Total Balance from the main menu. Go to the bottom and select the statement you want to see.

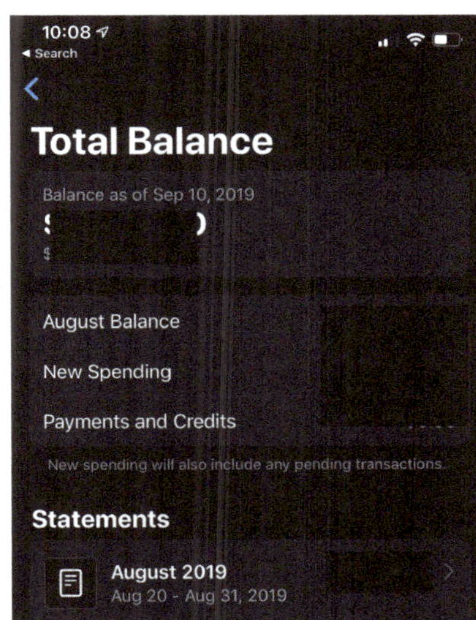

This brings up a brief, high-level, digital statement.

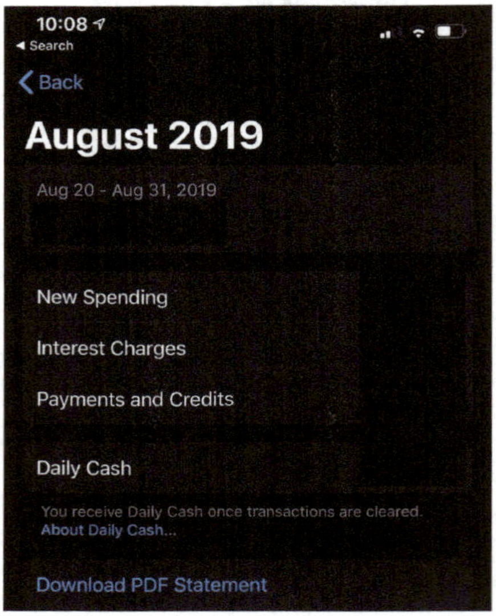

If you want to see your full statement—the long paper one you'd typically get in the mail from other credit cards—then tap Download PDF Statement.

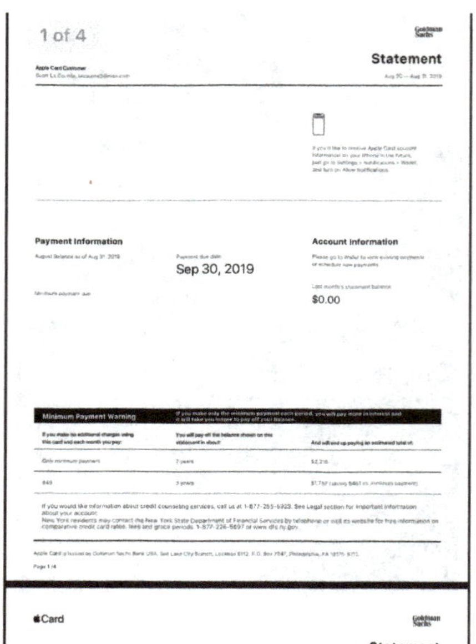

Fitness+

One of the biggest improvements coming to Apple Devices is Fitness+. This is going to be a new Apple Service that is set to disrupt the fitness industry.

It will cost $9.99 a month or $79.99 a year (with three months free if you buy a new Apple Watch); Fitness+ will also be bundled into the new Apple One Premier service ($29.99 / month), which gives you and your entire family access to all Apple Services.

The way the services will work is you pick the type of workout you want to do using either your Apple TV, iPad, or iPhone; this will sync up instantly with your watch. So while the video workout is playing, you'll see things like your heart rate on the video.

The workouts will change every week, and you can use them with or without exercise equipment. There are workouts for beginners and advance users, and Apple's AI will recommend different workouts and trainers based on your workout regiment.

You can even filter the workouts by time (from 5 minutes to 45 minutes); so if you only have a few minutes in your schedule, you can find a workout routine that fits into that schedule.

If you have used (or are familiar with) Peloton, then its a very similar concept. The biggest difference is it can work with more devices (or no device at all); that makes it great for traveling.

You'll also be able to choose the type of music that plays during your workout.

Chapter 10: Accessibility

When it comes to accessibility on the iPhone, there's a lot you can do. To simplify things, I'll break it up into four short sections:

- **Vision**
- **Interaction**
- **Hearing**
- **Media & Learning**

This will make it easier to skip whatever isn't relevant to you.

Before I get to any of that, where exactly do you find Accessibility? What's great about Apple products is you find things almost the same on any Apple device—which means the way we find accessibility here is the same way you find it on Apple Watch and iPad.

So where is it?!

First, tap the Settings icon.

Next, go to General.

And finally, tap on Accessibility.

Vision

Vision accessibility features have more options than any other feature. If you're sitting there thinking, "I can see just fine" I'd still recommend checking out this section. There's more here than just seeing—you may see perfectly fine, but prefer text a little larger or bolder.

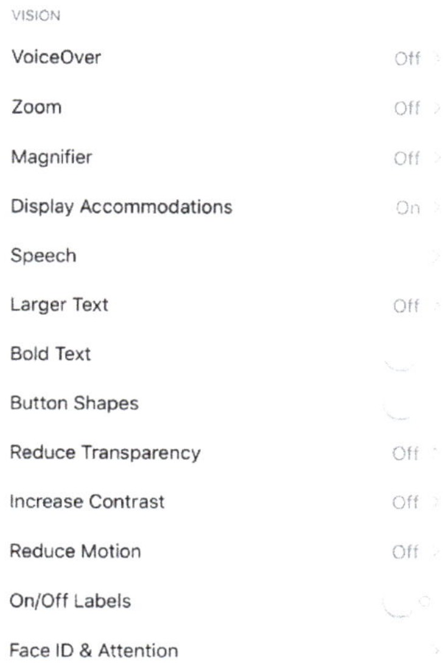

Below, I'm going to go through the list of accessibility features you should know about, and, if necessary, how to use it. Some will be pretty self-explanatory.

First up: VoiceOver. To access it, just tap VoiceOver.

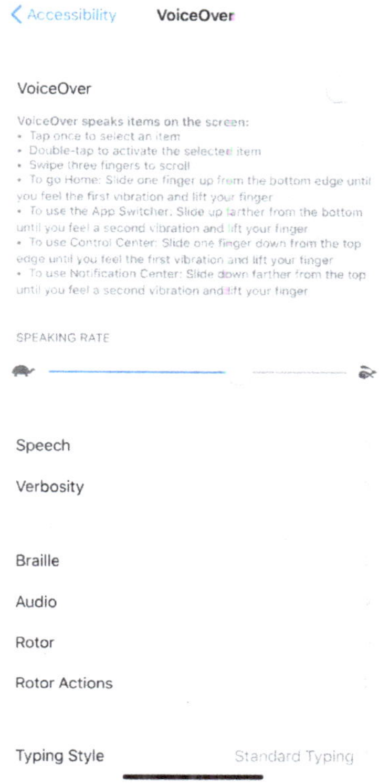

VoiceOver dictates everything on your screen. What do I mean by "everything"? Exactly that! If you adjust the volume up, then VoiceOver will tell you that the volume has turned up.

To turn this feature on? Flick the toggle. Controlling this feature? Not quite as simple. Turning it on means several of the normal gestures on the iPhone are changed a little.

To go to Home, for example, you swipe up until you feel a vibration; if you want to switch apps, you swipe up a little further until you feel a second vibration.

The voice reading things back is probably a little too fast by default. To slow it down a bit, use the slider under "Speaker Rate." The closer to the turtle icon you get, the slower it will be.

If you like VoiceOver, but don't like how long it takes to read something back, you can make it a little less wordy by tapping on Verbosity.

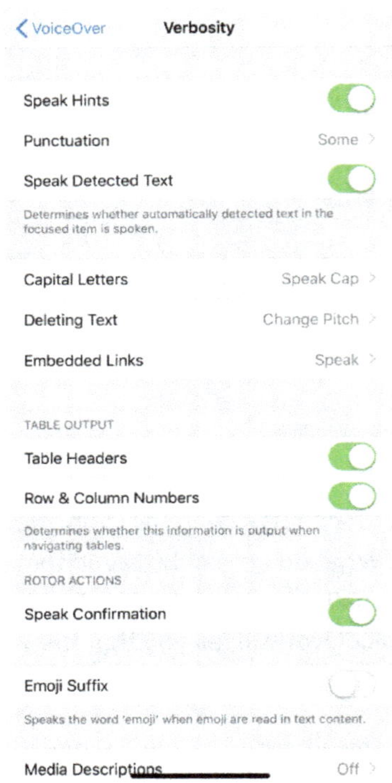

Braille is an interesting feature on the iPhone. You can't exactly feel braille on your phone, after all. So how does it work? To use it, you need a braille reader that connects to your phone (usually via Bluetooth).

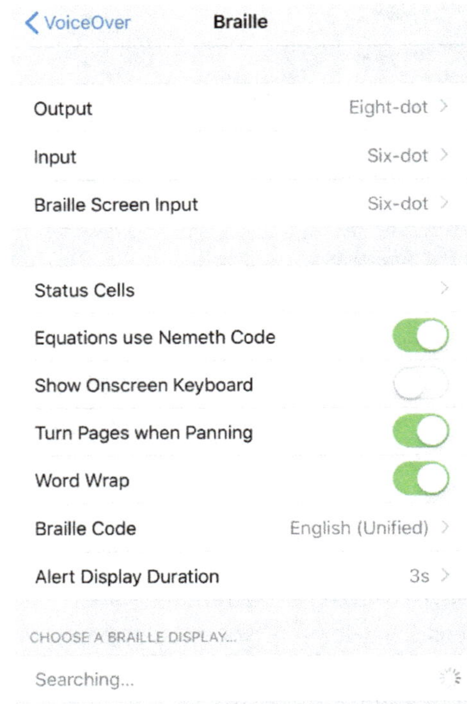

What else about VoiceOver do you need to know? The features under Braille will be a little less commonly used. Rotor controls actions you'll take to receive VoiceOver; Always Speak Notifications toggled on will automatically read back any message you get.

If you decide to use this feature, there's a number of third-party apps that are built for it. Just a few: TapTapSee, Seeing AI, Voice Dream Writer, and Read2Go.

Below VoiceOver is Zoom. Zoom is a bit less intrusive than VoiceOver; it turns on only when you tap the assigned gesture, so you might forget that it's even on.

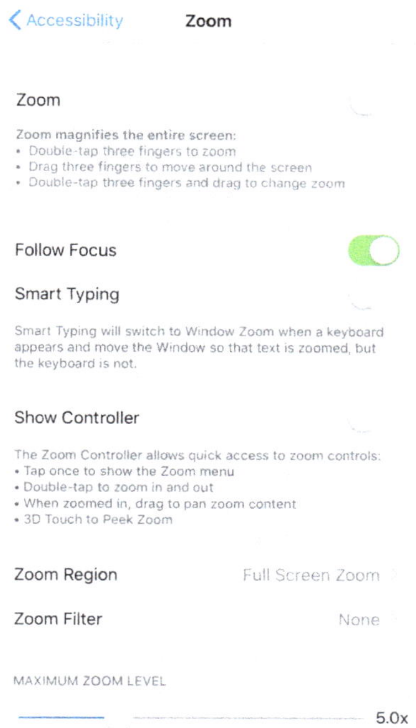

Once you toggle Zoom on, you can activate it at any time by double-tapping with three fingers. Take note here: three fingers! Use one finger and this isn't going to happen—three fingers have to touch the screen. To exit zoom, repeat this.

At the bottom of the screen, there's a slider to adjust the zoom level; by default, it's 5x. You can go up to 15x.

By default, when you tap with three fingers, you'll get a small zoomed in window; want to see the entire screen? Go to Zoom Region, and select Full Screen Zoom.

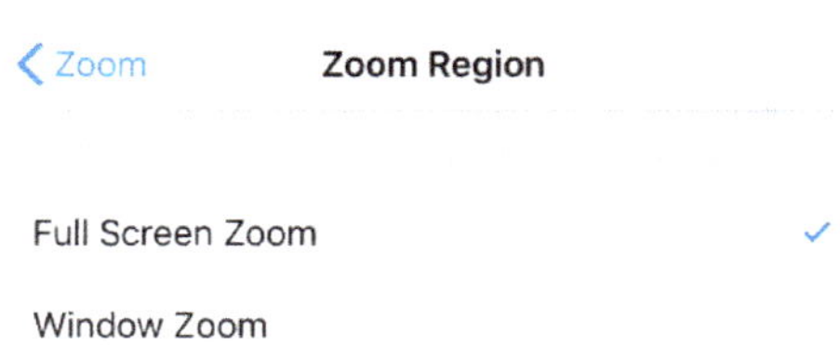

If your phone is in color, but when you zoom, you want it in greyscale—or any other filter—you can change that in Zoom Filter.

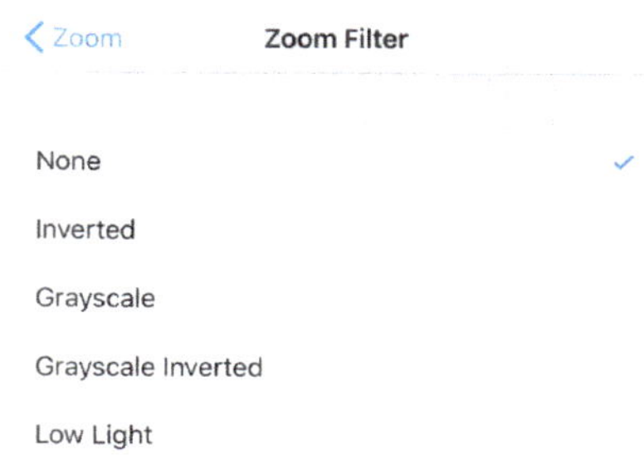

Below Zoom is a handy little feature called "Magnifier."

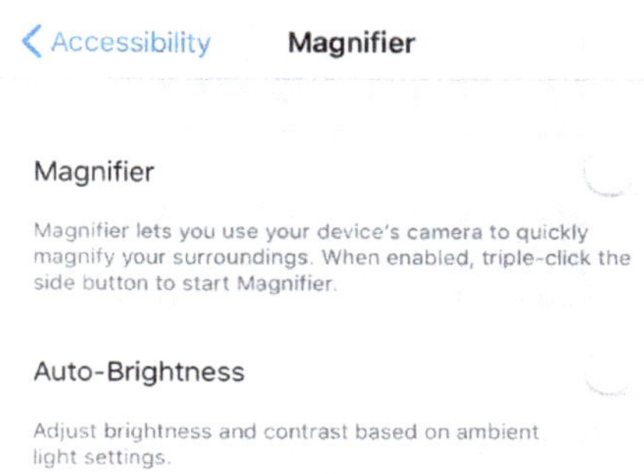

When you switch the toggle to on, a shortcut is added to use your phone as a magnifying glass. Triple-click the side button and a magnify app opens up.

Near the bottom of the screen is a slider to adjust the zoom.

Display Accommodations is where you can make your screen black and white—or a number of different settings. Just go into Display Accommodations, select Color Filters, toggle Color Filters to on, and select your color scheme.

In Display Accommodations, you can also reduce the intensity of bright colors, turn off auto brightness, and invert colors.

One of the most common accessibility features is Larger Text; when turned on, this increases the font size for all compatible apps. On the bottom of this feature is a slider—adjust it to the right to make the font bigger, and to the left to make it smaller.

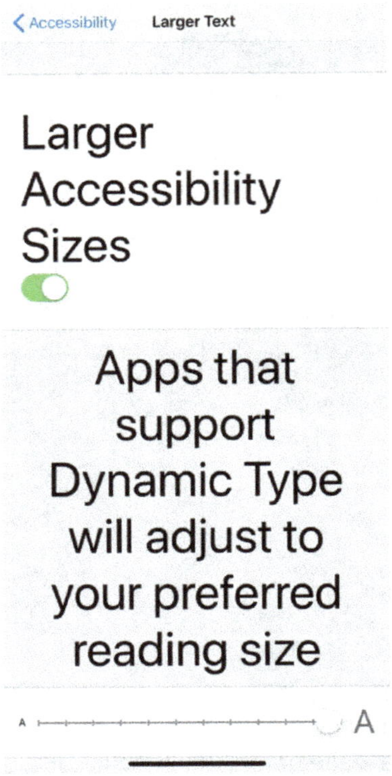

Finally, reduce motion makes the interface a little less—motion-y! What do I mean? The easiest way to explain this is for you to go to your Home screen. Move your phone around. See how the icons and background appear to be moving? If that annoys you or makes you dizzy, then toggle this on.

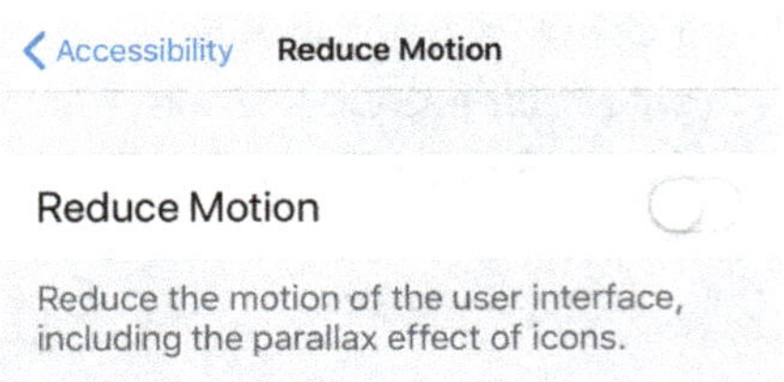

INTERACTION

Interaction is the area that pertains to gestures and the things you touch on the phone to launch different apps and widgets. Some of these require special accessories that do not come with your phone; it will note this when you tap on the feature.

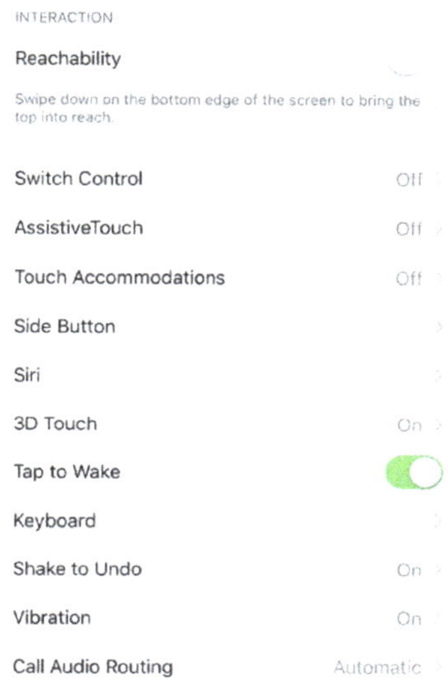

For the most part, these features will help you if you have difficulty touching the screen and find that you often open or type the wrong things as a result.

The first thing you see in this section is Reachability. This is a very important feature especially if you have the largest iPhone. Have you ever tried to get to those top icons with one hand? If you have large hands, it's doable, but even with large hands, it is a stretch. If you toggle Reachability to on, then you can swipe down on the bottom edge of your screen to bring the rows down.

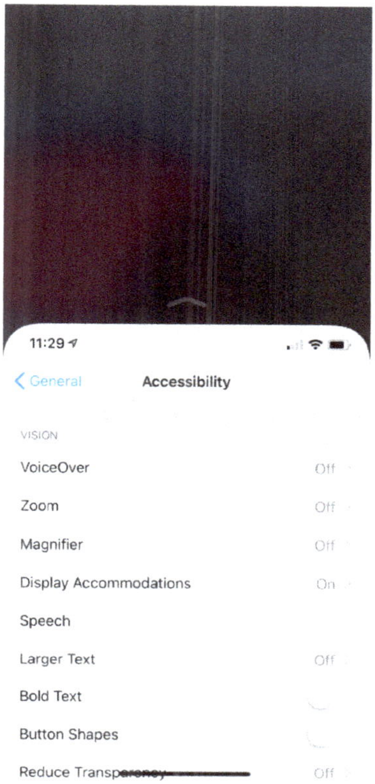

Swipe back up or tap the top in that greyish area to bring the view back to normal.

AssistiveTouch can use a special accessory, but it doesn't require one. When activated, it becomes a round shape on your screen that works a bit like a large cursor. Tapping it opens up the box below and holding it will close the app. If you really miss that home button on the phone, then you can think of it like a virtual home button—it even looks like one. Tap it once to bring up the menu and hold it to return to the home screen.

The side button is another area some people have difficulty with. This is where you go if you want the side button to respond slower (or quicker).

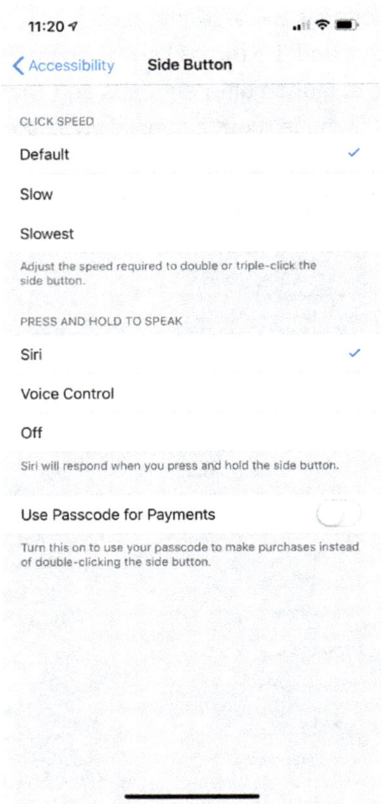

Does Siri never understand you? You aren't alone. I once asked Siri to call my wife and she tried to call John. No idea who John is or how it sounds like "wife"! If you'd rather type to Siri to prevent that kind of mishaps, you can turn it on here.

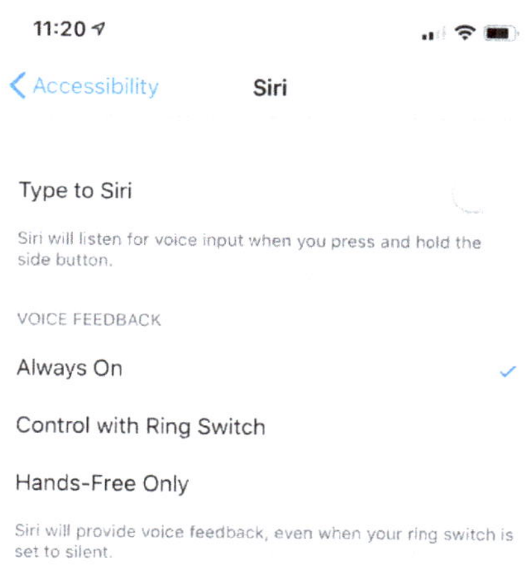

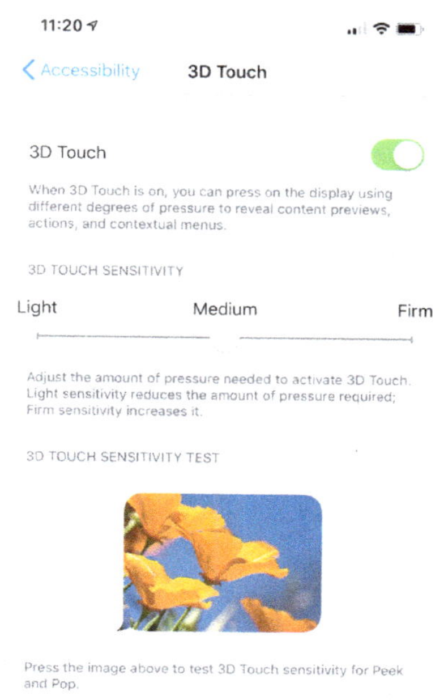

3D Touch is how hard you have to push down to activate it. If you find it too difficult to use, then you can adjust the sensitivity here.

Hearing

If you are using a hearing aid with your phone, then you'll add it and make adjustments to it in this setting. If you are looking for an alternative to a hearing aid, some people use Apple's own AirPods. If you want to do this, then it's recommended that you use third-party apps such as Petralex Hearing Aid. My suggestion, if you want to try this route, is to find cheaper headphones, and see if you even like it before investing in AirPods.

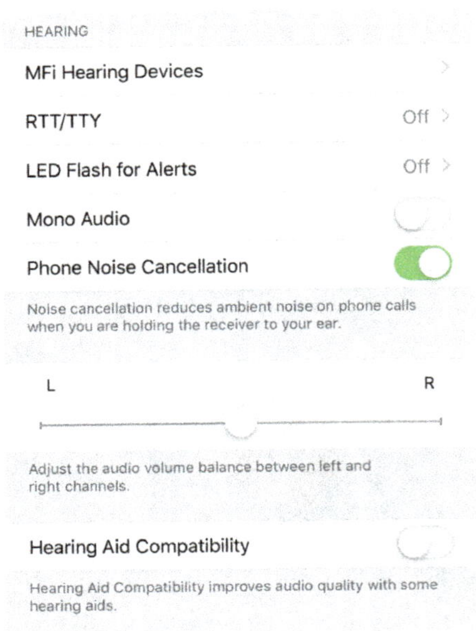

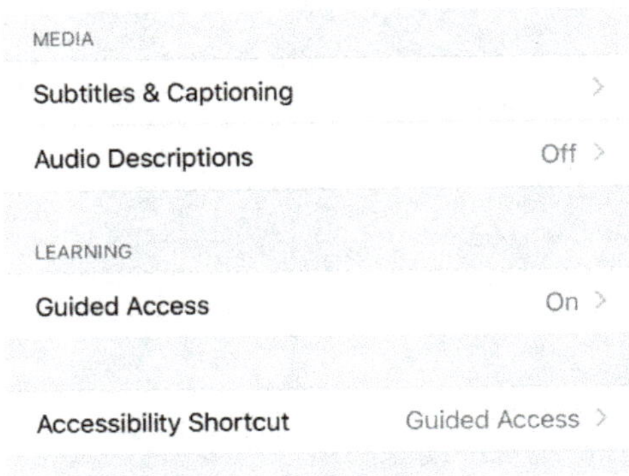

Media & Learning

Media and Learning are where you will go to turn on closed captioning for things like movies and TV shows that you purchase, or Audio Descriptions—which means it will read back what is happening in the video.

Bonus Book: Using AirPods

iPhone is great for listening to music…sort of. To get the most out of the iPhone, it helps to have wireless headphones or air buds. Yes, you could use the sound that comes directly out of the phone, but that's not ideal when you are exercising, in public, or in an otherwise loud place. This section will cover one of Apple's most popular solutions to this problem: AirPods.

What's Right For Me? AirPods or AirPods Pro

AirPods Pro is $50 more than the normal AirPods's. What exactly are you paying for?

Both, afterall have a H1 chip; both have wireless cases, and both have 24 hours of charge time with the case—the AirPods actually lasts longer than the Pro (5 hours of listening vs. 4.5).

What gives?!

There's a couple of advantages that the Pro has and that is what you are paying for. For starters, the Pro comes with three tips for a better fit. The AirPods's have a universal fit. My wife, for example, can't wear the normal AirPods's because her ears are too small; the Pro's fit perfectly.

The AirPods Pro is also sweat / water resistant—that's not to say you should go swimming with them (don't!), but it is to say if you are having a heavy work out and start to sweat, or it starts raining a little on your walk home, you don't have to take them out.

Noise cancellation and transparency modes are exclusive to the AirPods Pros.

The Pro also has Adaptive EQ; if you want to know what that means, look it up. It's a technical way of saying it sounds better—noticably better.

If you like charging the old fashion way (not wirelessly), the AirPods has what "some" might consider an advantage: it's normal USB where the Pro is USB-C. Everything is changing to USB-C, but if you are still living in an old USB world, then you won't have to buy any extra adaptors to make it work.

What's In (and Not In) the Box

AirPods come like every other Apple device—in a very minimalist box. The section covers the AirPods Pro. What's inside the AirPods box is similar with two important details: the charging is not USB-C, and the Pros have tips.

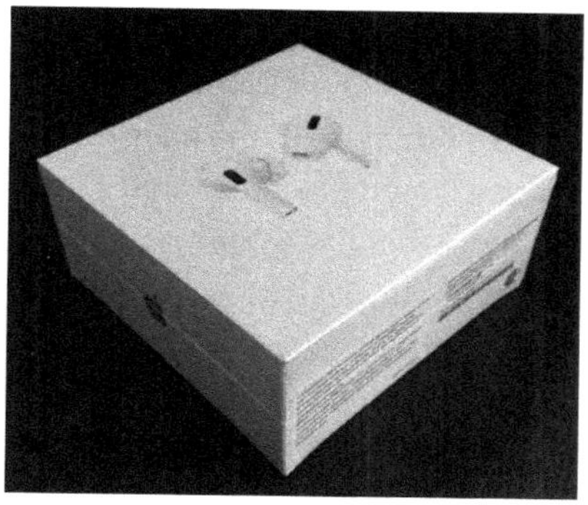

The first thing you see when you open the box is a very short guide that tells you how to use the device. It doesn't tell you everything—it's a high-level overview.

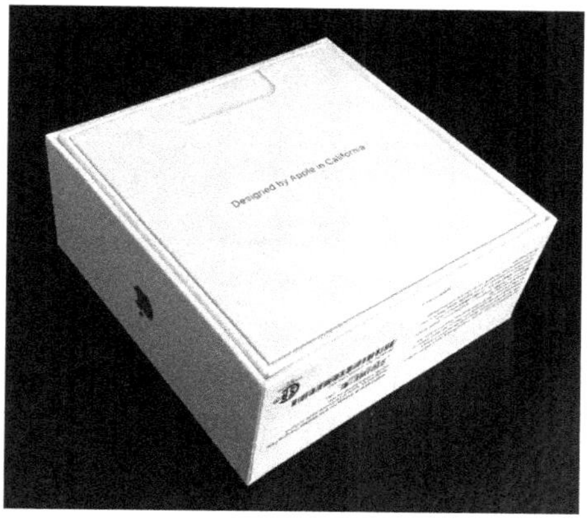

Below the instructions is the AirPods case (which also contains the pods).

Be careful as you lift out the case or you might miss the ear tips that are underneath it. The medium tip is already on the AirPods; if you want a smaller or larger tip, you'll find them here. Replacing them is as easy as pulling them off, then pushing the new ones on. The AirPods will automatically configure the sound based on the size you are using.

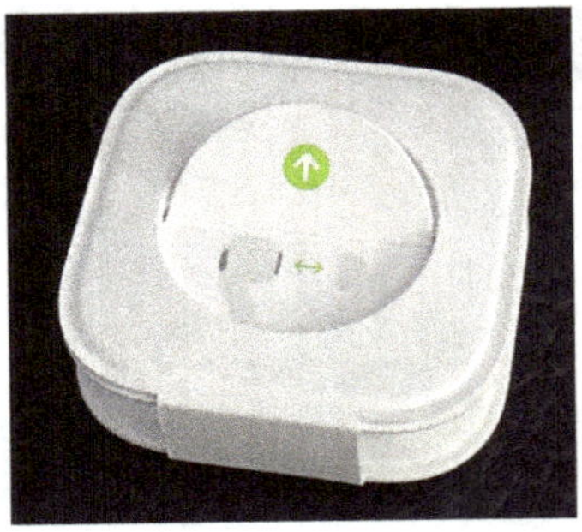

Finally, underneath the tips is the charging cable. Note the word "cable" here. There's nothing to plug it into. You'll have to supply your own. There's also something else very important here—it's lightning to USB-C. What does that mean? If you have a regular old-fashioned iPhone, then this won't plug into your charger. You need to get a USB-C adaptor to plug into. They aren't that much, fortunately, but it's still an inconvenience.

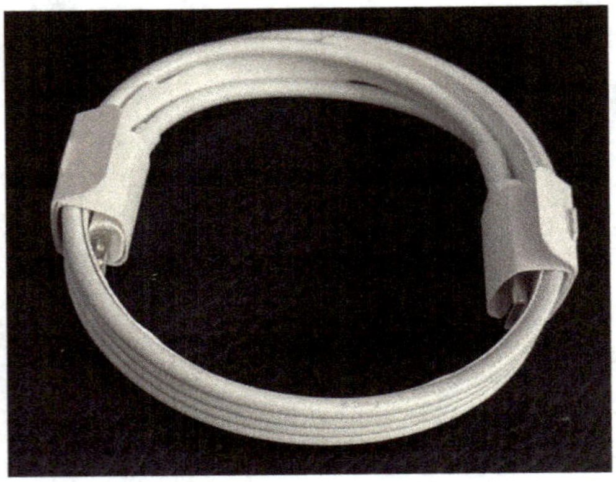

Setting Up AirPod Pro

Setting up your AirPods is a unique experience. It's ridiculously simple! Are you ready?

Unlock your iPhone. Put the case next to your iPhone. Open the case. That's it! This will launch a welcome screen on your iPhone automatically that will self-guide you to pairing them.

If you haven't updated your phone recently, then you'll get a message about limited functionality. If you want all the features to work, then update your phone to iOS 13.2.

You can see what version you have (and update it to the latest version) by going to Settings > General > Software Update. Software updates are usually quite large, so expect this to take at least an hour.

Assuming your phone is updated, you'll see some info about how your AirPods work. There is no skip here. You can either read it or ignore your phone a few seconds until it is gone.

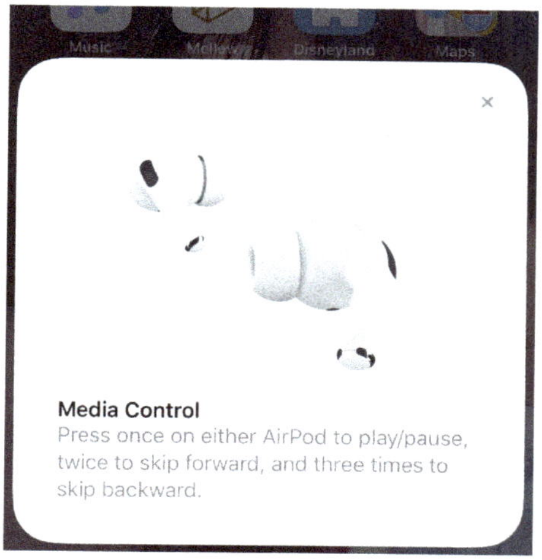

Near the end of the setup, you'll see a message about Announce Messages. You can turn this on or leave it off (you can turn it on later). Basically, this gives Siri permission to read messages to you without you having to unlock your phone. It's helpful if you are working out and don't want to take out your phone to read a message.

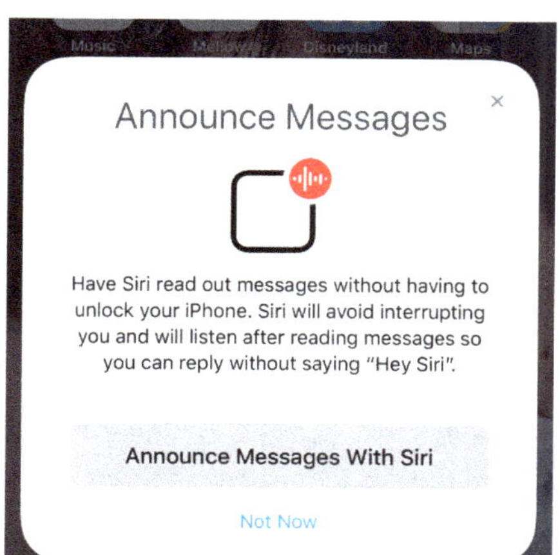

Once you connect your AirPods, you will see how much power is left in them; you can see this any time by opening the AirPods case next to your phone.

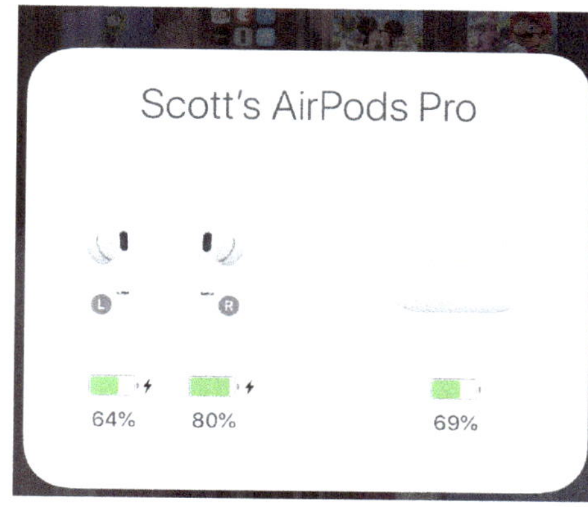

Once you add your AirPods to your phone, it adds them to iCloud. That means you can now connect them to any other Apple device (iPad, Mac, Apple Watch, etc.).

On any Apple device, go to how you would normally connect to Bluetooth (see the below illustration for connecting on a Mac), and select connect. If you are listening to something on your iPhone and tap this, it will unpair the iPhone and pair the new device.

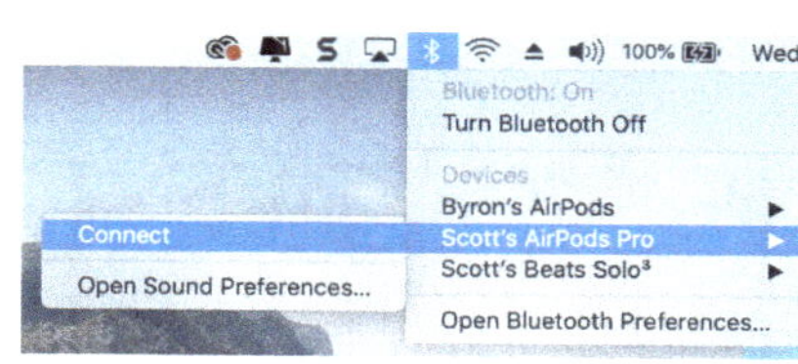

Setting Up AirPods

Setting up standard AirPods starts the exact same way. Make sure your Bluetooth is on, put the AirPods next to the iPhone, and open the case.

The biggest difference in the experience is after you tap connect, you're basically done. There's no message if you haven't updated your device, there's no tutorial, there's nothing about Siri. There's a message about how charged your device is and a done button. That's it. Tap done and you are connected. Anytime you put them in your ear from here on out, it will automatically connect.

Manually Pairing

You can use AirPods on non-Apple devices (such as Android phones or games); you can also manually pair them to other Apple devices that aren't your own.

It's actually a similar process to pairing any other Bluetooth device.

The first step is to open up the AirPods case; when it's open, press the round button on the back of the case and don't let go. When the LED light inside the case begins to flash, you are in pairing mode.

Now go into your Bluetooth settings (on an iPhone it's Settings > Bluetooth). It will show the device. Tap on it, and it will pair. To unpair it, just tap on it again, and tap Forget This Device.

Factory Reset

To factory reset your AirPods, make sure both of the AirPods are in the case, then open the lid. Next, press and hold the round button on the back of the case for at least 15 seconds. You can stop when you see it flashing an amber color.

AirPods Pro Gestures

Controlling your AirPods Pro is all about gestures. To activate any of these gestures, push the long stem of the AirPods Pro. These are the main ones that you should know:

Play / Pause – Press once. This also works to answer incoming calls.

Skip track – Press twice.

Go back track – Press three times.

Active Noise Cancellation / Transparency mode – To toggle between these modes, press and hold until you hear a noise.

Hey Siri – Siri is activated the same way it is on any other Apple device—by saying "Hey Siri."

AirPods Gestures

AirPods are a lot more simplistic then AirPods Pro. Where the Pros have several gestures, AirPods have one: double tap.

Double tap by default activates Siri by default. In the Changing Settings section, I'll cover how to change this to Play/Pause, Next Track, Previous Track—or turn it off entirely.

Control Center

When connected to your AirPods, you can also control your device from the Control Center (swipe down from the upper right corner). Press and hold on the sound control for your AirPods; this brings up an option to toggle Noise Cancellation / Transparency mode.

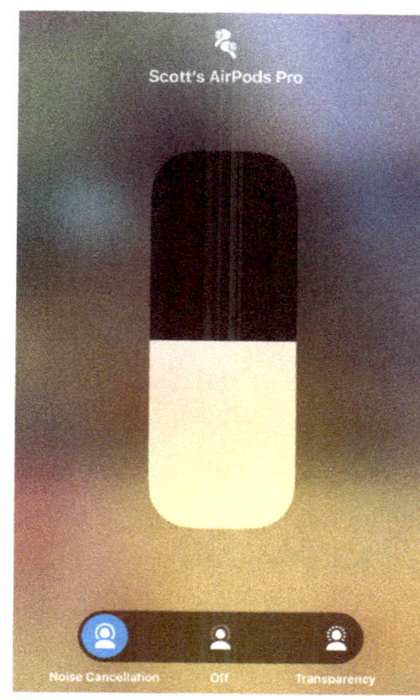

When music is playing, you can click on it from control panel and bring up an option to share audio. This lets you connect multiple Bluetooth devices to your device—so you could have two AirPods connected.

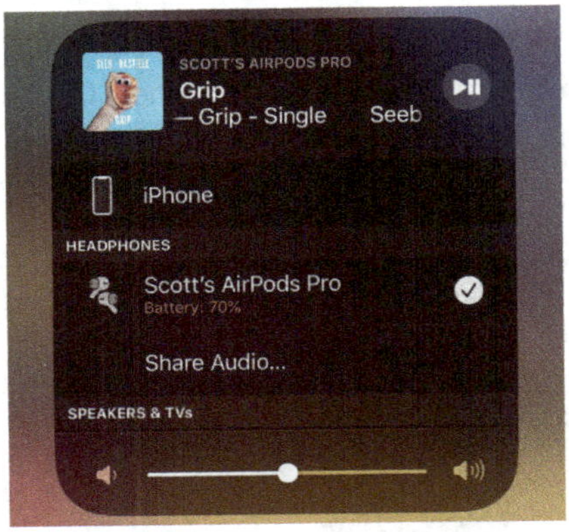

Changing AirPods Pro Settings

There are a number of things you can configure on the AirPods Pros, but you need to have them connected to your phone. If your AirPods is setup with your phone, but not currently connected to your phone, then you will not see the next steps on your device.

To get started, go to Settings > Bluetooth. Under My Devices, tap on the (i) next to Connected.

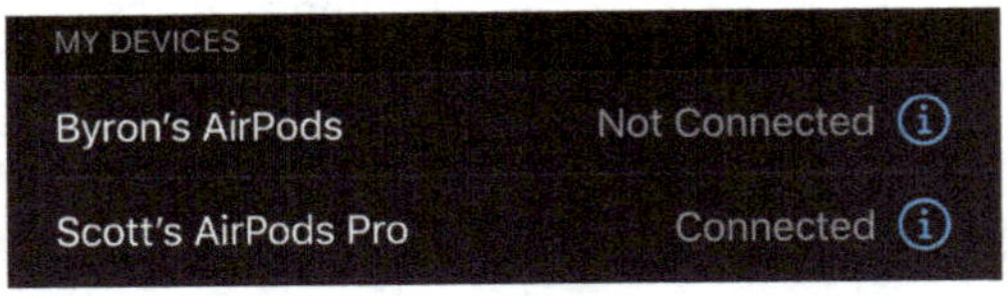

This brings up several options. If you want to unpair the device, for example, select Forget This Device. If you want to rename it, tap on the name in grey, then rename it.

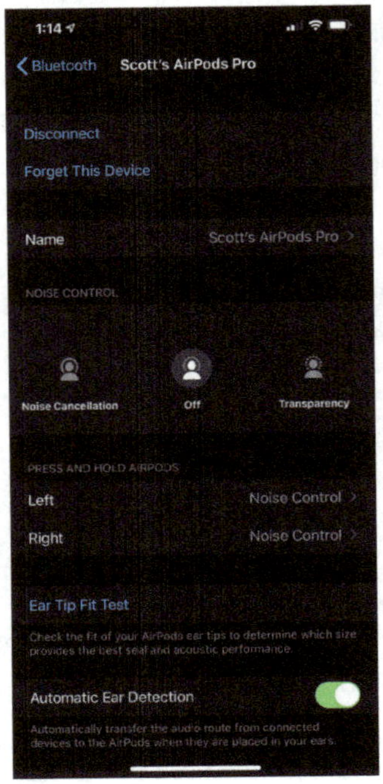

What I suggest starting with—before even using your device—is Ear Tip Fit Test. The AirPods are pretty smart, and they can make sure you pick the tips that fit you best. When I first used them, for example, they felt fine; I didn't even bother trying another tip until I ran the test.

To get started, tap the blue Ear Tip Fit Test.

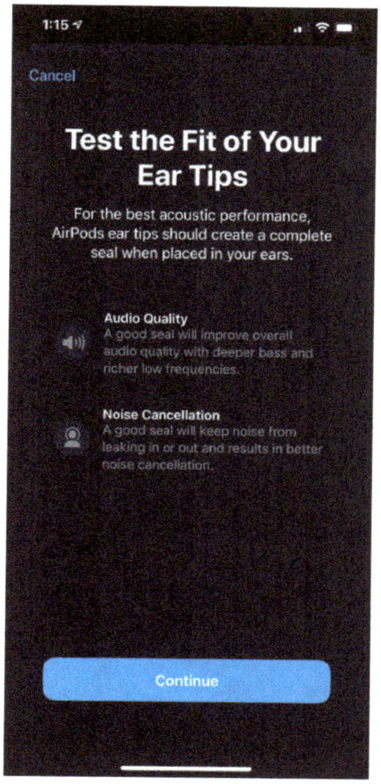

Once you hit continue, it will tell you to put each AirPods in your ear, and then press the play button.

You'll hear a song playing. After a couple of seconds, you'll see a screen with the results. My results say something went wrong. I either have the wrong tip size, I didn't push the AirPods in enough, or they're in the wrong ear.

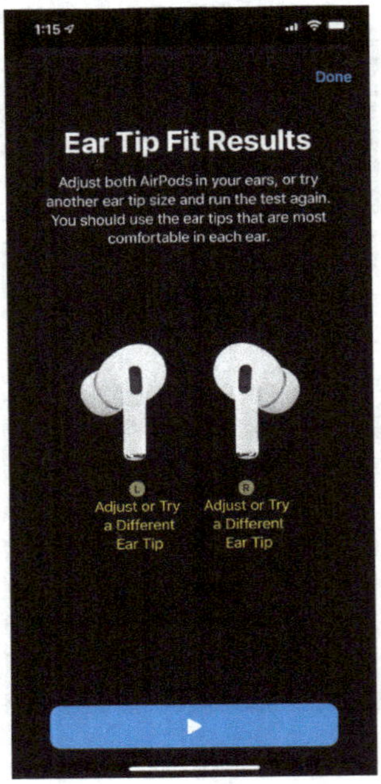

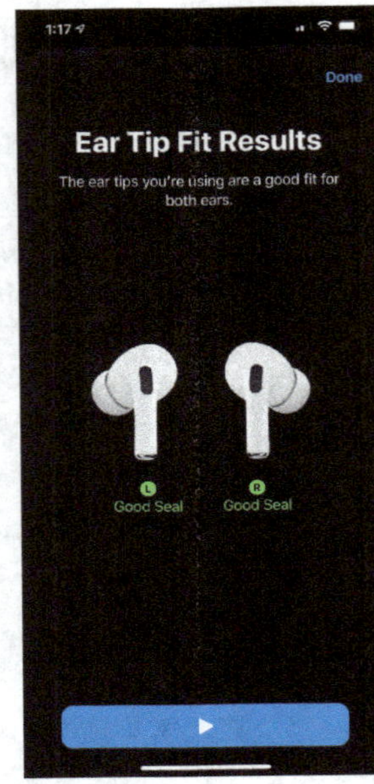

In my case, I knew they were put in right and they were in the right ear. So I put on a larger tip. Once you do that, push the play button again to run the test. With the bigger tips (medium in my case) the results said it was a good seal.

Changing AirPods Settings

There aren't as many things you can change on the AirPods, but there are a few.

To get started, go to Settings > Bluetooth. Under My Devices, tap on the (i) next to Connected.

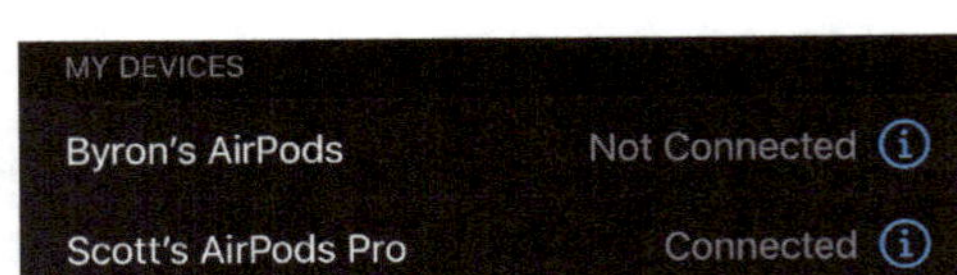

This brings up several options. If you want to unpair the device, for example, select Forget This Device. If you want to rename it, tap on the name in grey, then rename it.

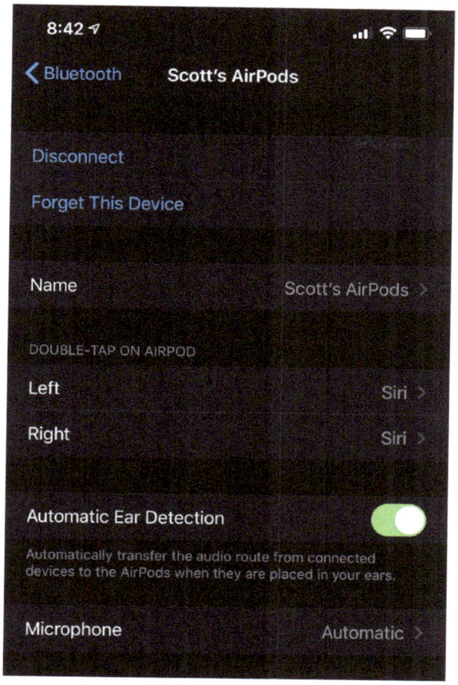

The setting you should pay most attention to is the Double-Tap on AirPod. This lets you change the tap gesture from Siri to something else—you can do one per AirPod, so technically, you get two gestures.

Once you make your selection, just tap the back button. It saves automatically.

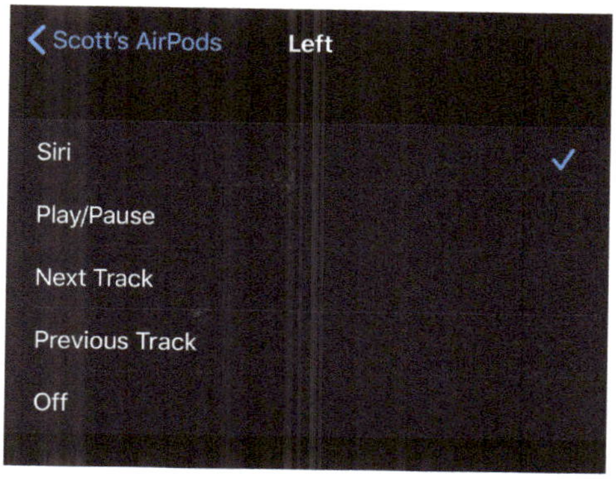

One other setting you may want to change is the microphone; by default, the AirPod will automatically detect the best AirPod to use when you are talking to someone on the phone. If you prefer to select this, then this is where you would do so.

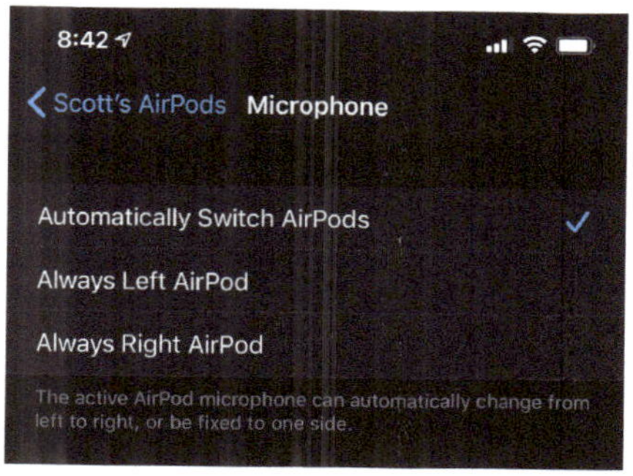

Accessibility

Unlike normal AirPods settings, you can control accessibility settings without connecting to your AirPods.

To get started, go to Settings > Accessibility.

Next, tap AirPods.

From here, you can adjust the Press speed, the Press and hold duration, and use Noise Cancellation even if only one AirPods is in.

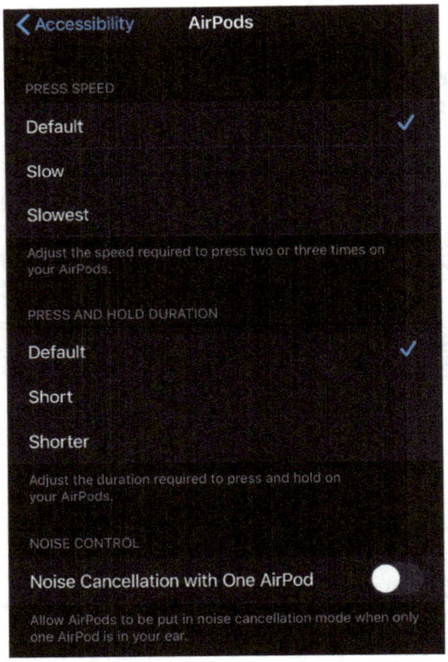

Hearing Aid Apps

AirPods are great for music, but they can also double as a hearing aid.

While the intent of the AirPods is certainly not to replace a traditional hearing aid, that hasn't stopped a number of developers from creating apps that help you use them as such.

Hearing aid apps actually work with any Bluetooth connected headset. That could be the expensive AirPods Pro, or the cheap headset you got at a garage sale. As long as you can connect it to your iPhone, then it should work.

The apps will basically help you amplify certain sounds to make hearing easier.

One popular example is TruLink Hearing Control. There are dozens of others. I would recommend trying several and seeing which one that you like the best.

INDEX

R

S

T

U

V

W

About the Author

Scott La Counte is a librarian and writer. His first book, Quiet, Please: Dispatches from a Public Librarian (Da Capo 2008) was the editor's choice for the Chicago Tribune and a Discovery title for the Los Angeles Times; in 2011, he published the YA book The N00b Warriors, which became a #1 Amazon bestseller; his most recent book is #OrganicJesus: Finding Your Way to an Unprocessed, GMO-Free Christianity (Kregel 2016).

He has written dozens of best-selling how-to guides on tech products.

He teaches writing for the Gotham Writers Workshops in New York and UX Design for UC Berkeley.

You can connect with him at ScottDouglas.org.

CPSIA information can be obtained
at www.ICGtesting.com
Printed in the USA
LVHW050523011222
734192LV00007B/177

9 781629 175768